Your Dreams What They Really Mean

by

Dr Elizabeth Scott

Copyright notice

Conditions of sale

Typeset in 12 pt Times by Letterpart Ltd., Reigate, Surrey.

Printed and bound in Great Britain by Cox & Wyman Ltd., Reading, Berkshire.

Clarion: published from behind no. 80 Brighton Road, Tadworth, Surrey, England. For information about our company and the other books we publish, visit our website at www.clarion-books.co.uk

Contents

(for details of Contents see page 4)

1

How to Use This Book

How to use this book to find out what your dreams mean

After the introduction, which explains what dreams really are, I have grouped dreams into five main categories and devoted a chapter to each.

There is also a chapter on children's dreams and a final overview with a word about some of the foods and medicines that affect dreaming.

- **Physical Feelings (or Sensations, page 26)**

Your dream may be triggered by internal body sensations such as a feeling of pain in your tummy, an itch, a need to go to the toilet, being too hot or too cold, being dry and thirsty or wet from water or sweat.

OR

Your dream incorporates sounds that penetrate your dreaming brain such as gales, heavy rain on the roof (you may dream of waterfalls), the alarm clock, your own wheezy breathing etc. Visual stimuli perceived through your closed eyelids may also create dreams (eg. lightning flashes).

• Sexy Dreams

A feeling of sexual desire or lust or just plain wanting to be kissed which may go on to full sexual intercourse, orgasm and ejaculation (wet dreams) with the most amazing people, page 77.

Sex is a strong emotion and if your brain is getting a message from you that you feel sexual deprivation it will give you some pretty exotic dreams.

• Scary Dreams

From a feeling of inadequacy and inability to cope, though mounting anxiety to fear or just plain terror and Nightmares, page 111.

You may not want to leave the safety of your bed for quite a time, especially after a nightmare. These are the most usual of all our dreams. It seems we are very sensitive to threat of all kinds and it destroys our peace of mind. So, by night, our dreams tell us to do something about it.

• "Downer" Dreams

A feeling of being cast down by dejection, despair, misery, page 196.

You wake wanting to cry or feeling desperately lonely, sad, frustrated, plain disgusted, jealous or cross.

• "Upper" Dreams

These leave you happy and content or striving to achieve your heart's desire, page 253.

The feeling you wake to is excitement and looking forward, happiness, contentment and a sense of well being.

There may be a mixture of feelings in your dreams such as frustration and sexual desire, or a need to go to the toilet and anxiety. You need to find all the things your dream is trying to get across. When you wake, list these feelings in order of importance in the dream, and then look them up in the correct chapter. In each chapter you will find other people's dreams that typify the feelings or emotions described in that chapter, and an interpretation from the dreamer.

In the end you are the best person to interpret your dreams. This is because only you know the reasons for your dream and only you can remember the things that happened to you the day before, or indeed many years ago, that resurface in your dream. Only you know your secret wishes and desires.

Then there is comment and advice on that sort of dream from me so that you can go back to your own dream and make sense of it.

Remember you may have to look up several chapters if there are several feelings in your dream.

• Children's Dreams

They do not differ from adult dreams but are often simpler to interpret and unlike grown up dreams a parent or caring person who knows the child well is often a great help to a child wondering what his or her dream was about. Page 270.

Children's dreams can also make parents aware of bullying and worries that a child won't naturally report unless encouraged.

LET US START
CHOOSE THE MAIN FEELINGS FROM
YOUR DREAM FROM THE LISTS BELOW

Feelings or emotions that you wake to:

Section 3 page 26
Dreams from physical feelings
You wake feeling:
- breathless/exhausted 26
- cold 29
- deprived from past addictions 30,
- discomfort/itch 37
- dry/thirsty 42
- hot 44
- hunger 45
- notice light 46,
- need to pass faeces (diarrhoea or constipation) 49
- need to urinate 51,
- noise from outside 55
- pain 60,
- perception of abnormality in your body or someone else's 65,
- touch 70
- wet 74

Section 4 page 77
Sexy Dreams
- Sexual arousal/lust 79
- just plain sex 84,
- sex with an other? 90
- sex with animals 92,
- sex with people you really oughtn't 95,
- dreams of perversion 101
- sex with close relations 102

4

Section 8 page 270
Children's Dreams

May help parents to realise if their child is stressed, bullied or just wants something badly. Children's dreams are often simple to interpret.

Section 9 page 286
Drugs and Dreams

Section 10 page 294
Interpretation Overview

Turn to the Appropriate Section

Now, if necessary, look up key words in that chapter. If for instance you are looking in the **SCARY DREAMS** chapter and your dream was about lions chasing you, you will move to the big animal dreams in the "scared" section to read about similar dreams and follow on to read the interpretations which will show you how to do the same sort of interpretation for your dream.

Things to look for in your dreams:

Dreams always have material from the day before. It is as if this is the background picture for a dream. It may also be the feeling in the dream. It usually is part of the material that makes up the dream story.

Look for it.

For instance, your dream may be set in a jungle if you have been watching a television show about the Amazon before bed. You may be in a desert if you had been reading about the Foreign Legion.

You may have been talking to someone and mentioned some person or place that comes into your dream. Material from the day before will certainly be there. It is significant in that it sets the scene for the feeling your dream is trying to get over and it points you in the right direction to find where your problem lies such as with your family or at your work.

There will also be memories from long ago, so long ago that you may not even be aware of when they were tucked into your brain's memory banks. They can be people you have known, places you have been to or read about, things you have seen, eaten, drunk, but all from way back. They may remind you of strong emotions you had then which are similar to the ones triggering your present dream.

Look for them too.

Very frequently there may be sexual material in your dream.
Sex is one of the strongest of your emotional needs and it is always inching into your dreams, however old you are and however well satisfied you are sexually.

It is fun to look for it. Don't be afraid of it. Don't feel guilty. You cannot control what you dream. Accept what your dreaming brain throws you and look for the underlying messages.

Look for the punch line. The dream always leaves you with a strong feeling, or someone in the dream says something absolutely clearly that is an instruction. This is what your dreaming brain wants you to do something about or pay attention to.

Repetitive dreams are always important. They tell you that you are really worked up about something and need to sort it out by day as soon as possible so that you reach peace of mind.

Now that you have got the main feelings from your

dream let me show you how to interpret it. Look at the chapter headings for the strongest feeling that is left with you after you wake and turn to that chapter to see how you interpret your dream.

Remember to look at each part of your dream. It may be a series of unrelated messages, but all of them important.

2

Where Dreams Come From

How do I remember my dreams?
Try keeping a dream diary for a week or two, jotting down the main story line of your dream when you wake. It makes fascinating reading if nothing else but I believe you'll see trends of thought and needs that will open your eyes to your real desires in life.

If you had a dream last night, your first problem is to remember it! Dreams melt like butter in the sun and ooze gently out of your memory – unless they were so powerful that you are still thinking about them days later. This is normal.

Most dreams are just mild reminders of unfinished thoughts and needs hanging over from the day before or even earlier.

The ones you remember without an effort are meant to give you a jolt. Don't ignore those ones.
They'll leave you with a strong feeling (emotion) or sensation of some kind such as fear, anxiety, loss, desire, happiness, resignation: sometimes a physical feeling such as pain or irritation affecting some part of your body. Take a good look at these dreams and do something about them.

This book can tell you what.

How are dreams made up?
Dreams are made up parcels of thoughts that your brain wishes you to look at closely.

There may be several emotions or feelings that your brain wants you to address, so look at each part of your dream carefully. For instance, you may dream that some huge creature is lumbering about the office destroying things in a crazy manner but eventually spies you cowering in the corner and bites your hand which begins to swell immediately. When you wake you may find that you have indeed got a midge bite on your hand which is a little itchy and in fact triggered that part of the dream, but most of the dream was your fear of an impending assessment at work which was announced the previous day and for which you do not feel prepared.

You may be too busy by day to pay attention to these feelings so at night your brain highlights them for you. Don't ignore them!

Where did that dream come from?
The first thing dreams show you is what your current feelings are. Your dream will leave you with a strong emotion. You may think you are only slightly anxious and have an ability to shut out your worries by day, but in your dream you may be pursued by werewolves. By contrast, serenity seldom forces its way into your dreams and your sleep is often apparently dreamless when you are content.

What is your dream trying to do?
Your dreaming brain is working for you to achieve peace of mind every night as you sleep. By day, events upset that contented equilibrium that allows your body to function at its best. By night, in dream sleep, it is make and mend time for the mind. It may

not manage to ameliorate all the strong emotions dammed up during the day and the previous days so it shows you, in your dreams, the problems you should resolve during the day. If the problem gets worse, so will the dream that night. If you solve the problem you will sleep apparently dream free.

Look at each episode in your dream.
Episodes come from material you have seen, heard, read or thought about the previous day. They also come from material you have absorbed over the years, and sometimes do not even know that you knew or remembered, because the memories come from so long ago.

Your dream may have an element of physical feeling too. For instance an asthmatic person might have a scary dream where he is running away and feels very breathless as he does so. When he wakes he finds that he is in reality breathless, and in need of his inhaler. That feeling has been incorporated in his dream story material. Look for any physical feelings in your dream. They may be significant pointers to how your condition is progressing if you have been unwell.

Lastly there is often an element of sexual desire. Sex is a strong emotion and creeps into most dreams even if in a peripheral way. So look up the chapter on sexual dreams as well as the one describing your main feelings.

Who is the best person to interpret your dream?
You are, without a doubt. You know what the symbols mean. You can get help by seeing what other people make of their dreams and so I have included a great many dreams about all sorts of subjects in this book. I have been through those

dreams with the dreamer to get the interpretation they are convinced by, as well as offering advice on how you should set about your similar dream. Let me give you an illustration.

A teacher told me she had had a dream in which she had applied for and been accepted for a post in a good school in her area. She had been happy in that dream until the staff had given her a Siamese kitten with only one eye and three legs that she was to look after as well.

She had wanted to get rid of it as soon as possible but knew that it was too valuable because it was Siamese and also because she couldn't help being fond of it. She had been brought up in a house with Siamese cats that she loved dearly all her childhood. She woke with this promise of a super job but weighed down by this time-consuming little creature that she loved too much to get rid of. Nevertheless she knew it would hold her back from her work which she also adored.

She told me that she had a much loved son who had eye problems and who was a problem in school and took a huge amount of extra attention at home. She had been considering boarding school for him. This would have left her able to apply for promotion, and full time work, and she wanted that very much.

Her dream had highlighted all these problems and also shown her her heart's desire. The bottom line was that she could not send her son away and get on with her life. She knew she was the best person to care for him. She would have to put her own career on hold. What had seemed a dilemma by day had been resolved by her dreaming brain.

She knew it. She was reluctant but she accepted it. Who else, told that dream could have given the various factors their true weight, would have been convinced by the result, except herself? I could only help and suggest. She knew what her dream meant. So though you may have to learn how to dissect your dreams, you are the only person who can truly know what they mean to you.

When do you dream?
Scientists have shown that you dream in all parts of your sleep but not all are memorable dreams. The ones you remember come in Rapid Eye Movement sleep when the blood circulation to your brain is greatly increased and your brain seems to be caring for itself.

What happens when you go to sleep?
When you shut your eyes, the electrical activity in your brain changes. The electroencephalograph shows a low irregular pattern. You are said to be entering Stage 1 non-Rapid Eye Movement (non-REM) sleep, and you feel the dropping off sensation that boring lectures, or watching a late night television movie, also engender. This is close to the brain activity stage that those who practise Transcendental Meditation reach.

As your sleep deepens, small spindles of mounting waves and K complexes (where there is a sudden wave surge) creep into the wave pattern. When these are established you are said to be in Stage 2, non-REM sleep. You can still wake easily from this stage if, for instance, someone calls your name or there is an unexpected sound. In fact sounds in this stage are magnified to your sleeping ears. A cough sounds like gunfire, a knock on the door like a drum beat.

As you fall more deeply asleep and become less easily aroused, your brain waves become large and slow and you are said to be passing through Stage 3 into Stage 4 non-REM sleep.

At this stage you are fast asleep and not easily roused. It is in these deep stages of non-REM sleep that growth hormone is released into your bloodstream. This hormone furthers the growth of children and masterminds the repair of damaged tissue in the fully grown adult. It is in this deep non-REM sleep stage that night terrors and sleep talking and sleep walking occur.

As the night progresses you tend to move back into the lighter stages of sleep and then into Rapid Eye Movement (REM) sleep, also called paradoxical sleep, where the brain waves become irregular, low, and spiky. The circulation to your brain is greatly increased in REM sleep, a sign of enhanced activity. Your brain is looking after itself in this stage and preparing for the day ahead.

It is mostly in REM sleep that you experience the dreams that you wake to and that your brain wants you to pay attention to.
In REM sleep your brain is sorting memories, ameliorating strong feelings, and generally trying to get you to reach peace of mind to tackle the next day. If it finds this is impossible, it ties the whole question up in a vivid dream and lets you have it and wake to it and remember it. You can sort the whole question out in your mind by day and try to have moved yourself a little nearer serenity before the next night. If you have not managed this, you are likely to wake to another dream about the same problem.

If the problem is one giving you increasing anxiety you may even experience a nightmare.

Towards morning REM sleep stages alternate with

gradually lightening stages of non-REM sleep until you wake.

These sleep stages seem to be just a continuation of the normal body's daily habit of preferring to do something different every two hours, more or less. If you wake after a good night's sleep you will have been through all of them without being aware of it.

Do I move about in Dream (REM) Sleep?

No you do not.

In Rapid Eye Movement (REM) sleep, nervous command of your muscles is switched off. Nearly all the muscles of your body lie flaccid and unmoving. Only that great muscle, the diaphragm, which continues to supply your power to breathe, and the small muscles around the eyes (which contract in an uncontrolled way causing your eyes to move behind closed lids) are working normally. Look at a young baby sleeping and you will see that eye movement that in fact gives the name to that part of sleep.

The muscle paralysis is a safety feature. You cannot carry out the wild happenings in your dreams. You lie pinioned to your bed, although you may be dreaming that you are walking out of the window and flying through the air.

I sometimes wake feeling unable to move. Why?

This is a bit of a scary feeling. It happens, usually, following a noise or disturbance that wakes you suddenly right out of Rapid Eye Movement sleep. In fact it wakes you so suddenly that the normal recovery of movement, which occurs when you pass on into the lighter stages of non-REM sleep before waking, has not quite occurred. You feel imprisoned in a dream, helpless and unprotected, as you strive to move. Suddenly you are free. It is as if your body is hit by movement.

People used to think that when they were asleep their soul left their bodies and wandered round the world. These wanderings, they said, were half-remembered in dreams. The returning soul could be felt as a jolt as it re-entered your body, enlivening it again. This is not so. It is merely the switch back to normal enervation of your muscles that you are feeling. If you know that, you have no need to panic when you wake suddenly from REM sleep and find your arms and legs won't move. Don't fight it. Relax. In a second, or less, movement returns to your limbs without a struggle.

What are Night Terrors?
Night terrors occur in deep non-REM sleep.

Night terrors are not nightmares. They happen in deep Stage 3 and Stage 4 non-REM sleep, whereas nightmares are serious anxiety dreams and come in REM sleep.

Night terrors mostly occur in children. They are a frightening experience for any parent. If you happen to be watching, you will see your child sit up in bed suddenly, often with his eyes wide open. He then starts to scream and throw himself about. Gathering him to you and comforting him has no effect. You cannot reach his senses. He is, in fact, deeply asleep, locked in with whatever horror is motivating his reaction. He sweats. His heart rate leaps to a fantastic rate and just when you, his parents, are at your wit's end your child lies back and continues to sleep as if nothing has happened. Even if you manage to waken him, he will just turn over and go back into quiet sleep. Usually children have no recollection of the episode next morning and do not report any extraordinary dreams.

Children usually grow out of night terrors, just as they outgrow sleep walking which occurs in the same deep sleep stages of non-REM sleep. They are rare and there is often a familial tendency. Boys are more usually affected than girls.

Night terrors occur within the first three hours of going to sleep, when most deep sleep occurs. They are extremely rare in adult life, a good thing because the sight of a full grown man screaming and throwing himself about in the middle of the night is a frightening experience. An adult with night terrors certainly needs urgent professional help because adults are too big to control easily and so may hurt themselves or others in the throes of a terror.

With children you should make sure your child is all right and does not hurt himself during the time of throwing himself about. You should offer reassurance and if you feel it appropriate, gentle encouragement to waken. See that he does not hurt himself and wait. Your child will either wake and just go back to sleep again as if nothing had happened or he will return to quiet sleep without waking. In the morning you, his parents, may be shattered but he will not remember anything about it. There is usually little doubt when a child is having a night terror but you should consult your doctor about them. He will be able to refer you to a sleep specialist, who can investigate and treat any cause for the night terrors such as pent up feelings of aggression or distress. It is also important to exclude other night time problems such as fits, which may give a somewhat similar picture. Night terrors are very frightening episodes for parents to cope with and should be reported to your doctor.

People with night terrors in sleep laboratories are wakened fully and some report sudden and terrible feelings of being choked or shut in small places. Susceptible people may trigger a night terror by hearing a certain sound, or have it triggered by some physical stimulus. Unexpressed aggression and bottled up fear may also be the basis of night terrors. If your child has night terrors, try to find out during waking hours if he has any secret fears or resentments. Is he being bullied at school? Is he being made to perform better than he is able? Is he anxious about the stability of his home life? It is amazing what makes children anxious, and so often they keep their fears to themselves. As your child does not remember his night terror, he is not going to volunteer the memory of a bad dream. It is up to you, his parents, to elicit any hidden anxieties and lay them to rest.

There are medicines that can suppress Stage 4 non-REM sleep and so halt the occurrence of night terrors in the short term. When these are stopped the terrors just seem to recur unless the cause has been found and the feeling of aggression allayed. Children need Stage 4 non-REM sleep because that is the time when growth hormone is secreted to help them grow. But adults also need this hormone to facilitate healing and tissue regrowth, so long term treatment that prevents Stage 4 non-REM sleep is not an option.

Why do I Sleepwalk?
Sleepwalking also occurs during the deep stages of non-REM sleep and this too tends to run in families and be confined to childhood. There is no definitive causation known for sleepwalking. Some doctors

18

suggest that in children the cause may be physiological because it tends to occur in early childhood and be banished by the body changes that puberty brings. They suggest that sleep walking occurring in adulthood is less likely to disappear by itself and that psychological causes (as well as alcohol overuse and other substance abuse) may be causative factors.

Sleepwalkers do not give the picture of confused wandering that demented patients show. Their movements are purposeful. Children often get up from bed, go to the bathroom, urinate and go back to bed while still deeply asleep. They may only be found to be asleep if their parents try to talk to them or if they miss their way and choose the wrong room. They may move their toys about or appear to play with them and then go back to bed. They may just sit up in bed for a few minutes and then lie down again. If wakened gently, or just encouraged, they will return to bed and sleep and have no recollection of the whole episode next morning. Stress, tiredness or fever are all said to encourage sleepwalking. If your children do it, make sure they are not worried about anything, and that they are not overtired or unwell. There is a strong family tendency. If your family has a history of sleepwalking it is sensible to be aware that your children might also sleepwalk and take precautions so they won't hurt themselves.

In some rare adult cases, obstructive sleep apnoea (heavy snorers whose oxygen supply is reduced in sleep), and some medicines may be the cause. Treatment of the condition or stopping the medication may then be curative but should be done with the co-operation of your doctor.

If you sleepwalk, or have sleepwalkers in your family, it is important to make sure that you and they remain safe during the episodes. Unguarded stairs, open doors and widely opening windows should not be accessible. Passageways should be kept clear. If the walker has a definite pattern, he or she should have a lighted path so that gentle wakening into familiar surroundings may be encouraged. This may be especially important if a sleepwalker is away from home in unfamiliar surroundings, for instance in a hotel. It is a myth that sleepwalkers never come to harm. Again this is a condition that should be discussed with your doctor.

Do sleeptalkers tell all?

Sleeptalking is not associated with night terrors, or sleepwalking, and is much more common. It occurs in all stages of sleep, and may be clear and decisive or just mumbles. It is possible to have conversations with sleeptalkers where they do seem to be answering your questions, although you get the feeling that it is merely the sound of your voice stimulating speech in the sleeper, and not an accurate answer.

Sleeptalkers do not give away secrets for the asking. It is unlikely that the speaker and the sleeper are both on the same subject. It appears to be caused by stimulation of the speech centre in the brain and may be associated with dreaming.

Like sleepwalking and sleep terrors, stress may encourage sleeptalking. To that extent it may be a sign to you that you need to unwind more, relax in mind and body, and look for peace of mind.

Can any other Sleep Stages be useful?

The lighter stages of sleep as we drift off have their uses. Sleep onset dreams from Stage 1 and Stage 2 non-REM sleep are unlike REM dreams, in that they come from day dreams which are under the daytime control of your mind. They arise from your daytime thoughts and considerations. REM dreams do not. REM dreams are thought to be associated with unconscious wishes and fears within your mind, as well as being influenced by external and internal stimuli. You are unlikely to begin a REM dream from an extension of your daytime thoughts, though material from day time occurrences may well find a place in your REM dream. *REM dreams are usually associated with physical signs of sexual arousal*, while sleep onset dreams are not. In fact, if a man complains that he is unable to achieve an erection, it is possible to check whether his problem stems from physical or psychological causes by allowing him to sleep in a sleep laboratory and when the sleeping trace from his brain shows that he is in REM stage sleep, check to see whether he has an erection or not. Repeated lack of erection during REM sleep would tend to support a diagnosis of a physical cause, whereas finding an erection in REM sleep allows the doctor to reassure his patient and treat the condition as an emotional problem.

Sleep onset dreamers have their own personality. Their dreams reflect their ability to let go. Their daydreams may lead them into sleep comfortably though in some cases it may take them longer to "get over" than it does the more uptight personality who simply crashes out.

Sleep onset dreaming may not be useful for interpretation, but may be used for self assessment. If you have never been able to daydream and realise you have become a highly strung rigid personality, you may want to try to become more relaxed and easy going by using mental and physical relaxation techniques such as the Alexander Method, Yoga exercises or meditation.

However if you put your head on the pillow and

crash out, this is just as good a way into sleep. There is no special benefit in having sleep onset dreams. They merely appear to be associated with laid back socially confident types who are not ruled by conventions.

Can I make use of Sleep Onset Dreams?
It does sometimes happen that your waking dreams allow leaps of conjecture that can provide the answers to problems that you have been mulling over. There is a story about Friedrich August Kekulé, the renowned German chemist. He was sitting half asleep by his fireside wondering for the umpteenth time how to explain the chemical formula of benzene when there appeared to be too few carbon atoms to make up the usual straight chain model of a molecule. As he dozed off, his thoughts became fantastic in the way they do in sleep onset dreams and he saw the lines of atoms wriggling about like snakes. Suddenly one of them caught hold of its own tail and started to whirl around. Kekulé woke to this picture and realised that he had just seen in this ring the rationalisation of the benzene molecule. So, faced with an insoluble problem, if struggling with it and tearing your mind to pieces does not bring a solution, it might be a good idea for you to relax and let your mind run free. See if sleep onset dreaming can bring lateral thinking and alternative resolutions to your mind.

Lateral thinking is very much a product of sleep onset dreaming. Use it to enhance your imagination. If you have an amazing idea as you nod off, you usually wake with it so you need not fear having it washed away by the advancing tide of sleep. It is wise, however, to write it down before you venture into sleep again.

Why do I suddenly wake feeling I am falling?

A sudden feeling of falling that brings you awake is quite common in the early stages of sleep. It is probably instigated by a sudden noise or internal stimulus, such as a muscle twitch which shocks you out of stage one or two non-REM sleep. All your muscles contract in the same way that a baby's do in the Moro reflex (a primitive reflex causing an infant to appear to grab forward as if on to a parental figure as baby monkeys do when afraid). You may remember a short dream leading up to it, like pushing a wheelbarrow over a cliff or tripping on a step, or you may not remember a dream at all. Although common, it has no apparent significance. If it happens often it is sensible to check that your bedroom is quiet enough for sound sleep to develop. It may also occur if you are in an excitable state about something, when your gentle passage into sleep may be disturbed by sudden distress or excitement.

What are Lucid Dreams?

Just occasionally in a dream you are aware that you are dreaming. Usually you are close to waking when this happens. You are in some unusual place doing something odd and you say to yourself, "This is just a dream and I will waken soon." This sort of dreaming is called "Lucid Dreaming"

Some people think it is a gift that should be encouraged. Many analysts feel that dreams are a path into your unconscious store of memories and if you could train yourself to enter that store knowingly, you would be able to browse around like you do at a library. You could pick up a memory here and there, and use your cerebral store more effectively. This has not proved possible. Encouraging yourself to be able to reach a state where you are aware that you are dreaming, so that you can influence what happens in that dream, is counterproductive.

Dreams tell you what your unconscious is struggling with. To change that changes the message your dreaming brain is trying to give you. It defeats the purpose of the dream, which is to point you to the problems that prevent your peace of mind. You are meant to remember the dream and act on it. Change the dream and you lose that message.

What you are likely to be doing in Lucid Dreaming is rising into a sort of mixture of REM and light non-REM sleep stages, where you have partial control over your thoughts. This sort of dreaming can be used to nullify nightmares, and is close to one of my techniques for doing so, although I don't think you need to re-enter REM sleep to find a pleasant finish to a nightmare (see pages 178-195 for Nightmares and Their Treatment).

You know that a nightmare stems from overwhelming anxiety. Ameliorating its ending is beneficial. You can use Lucid Dreaming to achieve this. Few people manage it to any degree. I feel that struggling to develop Lucid Dreaming is counterproductive to full relaxed sleep. You are shortening the length of time your brain has to sort your memory functions. You may miss those messages with strong feelings attached that your brain is trying to get across to you.

When you first start looking at your dreams they appear a hotch-potch of different stories and feelings. This is because you have done nothing to sort out the various thoughts that have disturbed your peace of mind for a long time. You won't be able to sort all the dream messages at once. Take the main ones and get peace of mind from them by, for instance, making decisions about anxieties by day. You will find that, as you do this, your dreams will become much more simplistic, offering you just a single message that is easily interpreted and can then be dealt with. You almost develop a dialogue with your dreaming brain where it picks up the main things that have worried you the day before, so that you can deal with them when you wake. That way you maintain your peace of mind, and function at your best.

3

Dreams From Physical Feelings

You wake feeling:
breathless/exhausted 26, cold 29, deprived from past
addictions 30, discomfort/itch 37, dry/thirsty 42,
hot 44, hunger 45, notice light 46, need to pass
faeces (diarrhoea or constipation) 49,
need to urinate 51, noise from outside 55, pain 60,
perception of abnormality in your body or someone
else's 65, touch 70, wet 74

● **Breathlessness / exhaustion**
A woman who had altitude sickness on a holiday trip to Tibet told me this dream:

"Night after night I dreamed I was walking across the yellow stony waste rising into foothills that I could see from my hotel room. The sun blazed down from a clear blue sky. I was tired, so tired, and my legs were like rubber, but I had to go on or die. In my dream I knew that. There was a weight on my back. I must have been carrying something but I did not know what. I could not get rid of it. I just plodded on and on, apparently all night. I was thankful to wake from that dream. By contrast the day seemed a better time. I had more freewill to help myself. I was brought oxygen in funny rubber pillows and told to suck it in through a valve. It all helped and eventually the pills I was given worked and I felt better, less breathless, and the dreams stopped."

Interpretation:
There was some anxiety in that dream. The feeling that I had to go on or die was a bit worrying but most of it was just giving me a picture of the breathless feeling I had by day only worse. I was thankful when I started to feel better and the dreams stopped. I knew it was a good sign.

Comment and advice:
Her breathlessness came from her mild heart failure caused by the altitude sickness. I have visited patients with heart failure who had similar dreams and a good way of telling when treatment is beginning to work is to ask what my patients were dreaming about. The repetitive dream shows that it is one to take seriously.

Any condition that affects your lungs, and therefore interferes with the oxygen supply to your brain, has an effect on your dreaming. In Rapid Eye Movement sleep (the stage of sleep when you usually dream), the blood circulation to your brain is greatly increased. Your brain is obviously searching for and requiring an increased supply of blood-borne nutrients to do the job it needs to do before morning, to set your brain ready for the strains you will put on it all day.

You have to remember that in Rapid Eye Movement sleep (REM sleep) your muscles lie flaccid, all except your diaphragm which continues to keep your breathing going. However in REM sleep the ancillary muscles of your chest and shoulders are not working so people who routinely use these muscles to assist their breathing process are not getting the help they are used to by day.

Asthmatics and those people who suffer from chronic bronchitis are used to this and take extra medication to assist their lung function by night. However the first sign that they may have a chest infection starting, with its effect of worsening the lung function, or indeed any worsening of function, is often highlighted by a change in normal dreaming to dreams of running races or hurrying for trains; in fact always being late and breathless. These dreams may also have touches of anxiety in that the dreamer may sometimes be pursued. But the main feeling is one of breathlessness. I believe it is a significant finding and one that, if repeated, should be further investigated as soon as possible, even if by day there is no obvious reason for it.

Serious snorers sometimes go on to that condition called Obstructive Sleep Apnoea where, because your soft palate falls back to block your throat periodically, your inspiration is limited and you begin to suffer chronic lack of oxygen in the brain as well as in other organs. Your brain in dream (REM) sleep demands extra oxygen and gets it with the extra blood circulation that occurs. If that doesn't happen you tend to suffer anxiety type dreams. You find yourself running away from a Tyrannosaurus Rex through a tangle of jungle plants or some such. You feel breathless and frightened and may, in fact, go on to suffer repetitive nightmares. Your brain does not put up with oxygen shortage. It lets you know about it in your dreams. So, if you are over-weight and know that you snore loudly, and then your dreams suddenly change for the worse, it is worth checking with your doctor that you don't need treatment for the condition. There are sleep laboratories in most big towns these days and Obstructive Sleep Apnoea can be diagnosed very easily and treated efficiently. You don't need to suffer bad dreams if you listen to what they are telling you.

- **Cold**

This dream came from a young music student.

"I was in a sledge going somewhere. It was pulled by huskies and I could see them barking ahead of me. It seemed quite dark all around and there wasn't much room on the sledge because it was narrow. There was a man in a hood up ahead driving the dogs. When I asked about the sledge he said all racing sledges were narrow. My leg on one side kept falling out and catching in snowdrifts.

"Don't do that," said the man driving. "Your leg will drop off."

I was beginning to wonder how I would play the cello with only one leg, when I woke. My leg was outside the duvet and it was cold. There wasn't anything else wrong with it. It was still well attached. I was most relieved!"

Interpretation:

I had no particular feelings from that dream except a mild relief when I woke to find my leg undamaged. I tucked it under the duvet and slept fine for the rest of the night. I had read about a sledge race in the newspapers some weeks previously. I have a quartet concert coming up in the conservatoire which we were rehearsing the evening before my dream, so may be I was a bit anxious about that.

Comment and advice:

A mostly physical dream. Her dreaming brain sensed her cold leg and conjured up a dramatic dream that she woke to. The dream picture was almost certainly from the newspaper article which had resurfaced to provide the background. Most music students seeking to improve their playing have insecurities about their progress. That is normal. So her waking worry about how she would play might have had a small input from the impending concert, making her feel a sense of slight anxiety rushing along on a sledge at night and the threat of her leg falling off. But she clearly has it all in hand, and her mind is really at peace, so she is doing well.

- **Deprivation (see page 93 for sexual deprivation dreams)**

Deprivation Dream 1 (Tobacco smoking)
From a lady patient who had given up cigarettes four years earlier, after smoking about forty a day for years.

"I was walking over George IV Bridge in Edinburgh towards the National Museum. I was going to meet someone there and have a coffee in the restaurant. I like that museum. Its hall is large and airy and no one smokes there. I was looking forward to it. As I walked along I suddenly realised that I was smoking a cigarette. I was enjoying it hugely and watched the smoke dribble out of my mouth with delight. I knew people were looking at me and thinking that I should not be smoking but I told them, "I only smoke five a day so I am outside the statistics for lung cancer." Then I woke and my first feeling was of utter thankfulness that I hadn't smoked for four years and didn't have to go through all that business of cutting down and quitting. I even lay and smelled my own smoke free bedroom air with delight, before falling asleep again."

Interpretation:
This is a plain dream of deprivation. I have heard that I may get them even though it has been so long since I smoked. The dream did not make me want to restart. It made me thankful I had stopped.

I went on a bus tour once and we got to talking about how difficult it had been to stop smoking and most of the other ex-smokers said that they had had dreams of smoking after they had in fact stopped.

Comment and advice:
Sixty per cent of ex-smokers get dreams of smoking, sometimes quite frequently. In a way this helps them continue to kick their addiction, as, when they wake, they are usually thankful to find that they haven't smoked for years. Certainly they are not going to increase their chances of lung cancer by smoking in their dreams so it may be the best way to smoke if you have to!

She had stopped smoking by cutting down, five cigarettes at a time so when she talked about only smoking five a day in her dream she was in the last stage of quitting. Clearly it was the hardest for her and she must have often wondered if she could remain at that stage, only smoking five a day, and so minimising her chances of being in the lung cancer statistics. I was glad when she told me she had stopped entirely. I told her that if the dream became repetitive she should come back to me and we might try medication to block it but she said that she didn't often smoke in her dreams. She said she always felt happy to have stopped when she woke after dreaming about smoking, she felt the dream merely offered her a treat, not a temptation.

These dreams usually get less frequent the longer

you are from smoking cessation. They may be prevented by occasional use of nicotine gum or patches, but are seldom such a serious problem that you need to resort to these steps once you have stopped completely, and need no day time aids to keep you abstinent.

I did once attempt to smoke a cigarette. It gave me no pleasure and I have never done so since and I have never smoked in a dream. Non-smokers seem not to. This is a pure dream of deprivation where your body still misses in dreams what you have decided against by day.

Deprivation Dream 2 (After Alcohol withdrawal)
This was told me by a middle aged man, who had overused alcohol for years, but had eventually given up drinking alcohol altogether as the only way forward.

"I occasionally dream that I am walking down a road and I see a pub. Sometimes it is a country pub and sometimes it is a town road and a glass fronted modern job. Which ever it is I go into it and that familiar smell of beer and old cigarette smoke that seems to hang in the air grabs me.

I ask for a pint and the man or woman behind the bar draws it and I take the glass and feel that amazing feeling of cool beer sliding over my throat. I push the glass back for another and I know I'll want another after that and already things are going blurry and then I wake. I am stone cold sober and I am in bed and it is just as well there is no alcohol in the house so I could not have a drink if I want one. I go over all the reasons why I stopped drinking and they are good ones, from keeping my job, which I enjoy, to having spare money for holidays and most of all still having my wife with me. Not taking any alcohol is difficult but for me it was the only way to give up drinking too much."

Interpretation:
I see that dream as my mind trying to get me back to drinking. It must be the bit of it that was ensnared by the alcohol in the first place. My Grannie drank too much and we used to find her on the floor. The doctor thinks that addictiveness runs in families and that there is a genetic tendency that is handed down and makes you want to drink too much or smoke or take drugs or gamble. It comes from the same genetic tendency.

When I first stopped drinking I had the most dreadful nightmares and dreams. For the first three months the nights were horrendous. Then it started to ease off, and after six months the bad dreams stopped but I still get this dream of going into a pub and having a drink and feeling that buzz as the beer goes down. I have learned to count my blessings next morning and have something sweet for breakfast, like pancakes and syrup or cereal or toast and honey. That helps me to forget the urge. I don't get so fat these days so I can indulge myself at breakfast occasionally.

Comment and advice:
If these dreams become oppressive his doctor can give him a short course of medication to suppress dreaming and give him a break. As time goes on they will become much less frequent. Continuing scary dreams and nightmares would point to an underlying problem that he should talk to his doctor about. It may have been the reason why he started drinking in the first place.

This chap seems to have stopped drinking to excess before the alcohol has thoroughly poisoned his liver. I say this because he talks as if alcohol made him fat, which it does if all your organs are working, because it carries so many calories.

Later in the alcoholic story your liver becomes cirrhosed and works less well so you do not absorb the calories and you become thin and suffer from oesophageal varices which may give gastric bleeding and your memory begins to lapse. At this point your dreams reflect your mental state and are flat and depressed with occasional nightmares.

Counting his blessings or reinforcing the positive benefits of abstaining is a very important part of staying alcohol free. The same technique is used to maintain freedom from any addiction.

I had a couple as patients who told me that after they stopped smoking they would exclaim "It is marvellous to be able to smell the flowers again. We couldn't do that when we smoked. It helped to still any lingering craving for a fag."

Deprivation Dream 3 (After Opiate withdrawal)
From a recovered heroin and methadone addict.

"When I decided to come off I was on methadone but using anything else I could afford. Anything that gave me a buzz was just fine. It was not so much a case of getting high as getting back to normal when I could function. I used the methadone to try to stop my withdrawal symptoms but when I eventually stopped everything I had copious diarrhoea and night sweats and nightmares. I did not want to go to sleep, it wasn't easy anyway and there was always the fear of the dreams in wait for me. That left me exhausted by day. My doctor gave me something to stop the dreams and just a week of getting some sleep really helped. After that the dreams came back but not so often and I could cope. It took six months before I was anything like normal. Since, though, I get some nightmares and occasionally I get a dream where I am shooting up with some of my mates and slipping into blissful relief. I hate those. I get up and do something that takes my mind off it, like work at a crossword or write a letter to someone. Reading is not enough. Sometimes I repot a plant or clean a room. Luckily I live alone. It makes me tired the next day but then I sleep better the night after. I am not going back.

I have been getting fit by swimming and jogging so I am sleepy by night. That was part of the problem to begin with. I wasn't tired. My mind seemed to be racing and the sweating and aches and pains were dreadful. The diarrhoea was difficult to manage too."

Interpretation:
I expected to feel bad and I did. However I got sucked into taking heroin by my mates at school and it became hard to come off. Then I went on the methadone program and really got sick of being treated like a second class being. My heroin mates have drifted away and my other school friends all have jobs and a decent salary. I began to think I might like that too so I stopped doing drugs.

I am on a hairdressers course and enjoy it. One day I'll have my own salon.

Comment and advice:
After stopping all opiates you experience dreadful dreams and nightmares, diarrhoea and sweats and myriad aches and pains. Restless legs, where your

legs twitch uncontrollably in sleep are also usual. The first three months are the worst, and symptoms may persist for six months or more but diminish as time goes on. To some extent it depends on how long you have been addicted.

Interestingly there are not a lot of old opiate addicts about. At least they don't attend surgery. They may all be well settled on methadone but I do not think so. I believe opiate addiction is a young person's problem and is encouraged by groupy-ism and the drug pushing that goes on around pop music and youth culture. Eventually addicts either die or think it is no longer worth it. Stealing from shops may have an aura of excitement for a teenager, but becomes positively embarrassing for someone in his twenties. It leads to jail too and that is not a pleasant experience. So for one reason or another it does seem that opiate addicts become abstainers. They will be likely to get the odd dream where they are shooting up, which someone who has never done it is very unlikely to. In the end the wish to not be dependent on drugs has to be stronger than the temptation.

Amphetamine (uppers) addiction, if continued, tends to lead to disordered mental states. Dreaming while under the influence of excitatory drugs may be pretty wild and very frightening if you manage to get to sleep at all. After stopping, your dreams are likely to be flat and depressed, or the type that are associated with the underlying mental state that precipitated the need for these excitatory drugs.

Withdrawal from psychedelic drugs like LSD leave few problems with dreaming after you are stabilised. Unfortunately, years after stopping, you may experience flashbacks mimicking the LSD experience, which occur in times of acute anxiety. If the anxiety is during the night, these experiences may be similar to dreaming and be pretty frightening. Worth having a word with your doctor if they happen. He can offer techniques to allay anxiety even if he can't stop the flashbacks.

- ### Discomfort / Itch

Discomfort Dream 1 (pins and needles)
This is one of mine.

"I am walking along the road with a friend and we see a swarm of bees on a tree branch. "If you pick up the queen who is in the middle of that swarm the bees won't sting you" she says.

I seem to put my hand up though I am very dubious because I cannot see a queen bee to pick up and suddenly they are all round my hand like a buzzing boxing glove.

I think, "This is a bit of a dangerous position. They might sting me at any moment." I am not very frightened though, just have a feeling that things could get worse. Then I wake. I find I have been lying on my arm and my hand must have gone to sleep. Then I must have rolled over because I woke to the pins and needles of my hand coming back to life and it was very like the tickle of thousands of bee feet."

Interpretation:
I know the saying, pick up the queen bee and the others won't sting you. I have always thought it pretty dubious because you can't see the queen to pick her up until you have disturbed the other bees from around her. However I am not afraid of bees. I value their products and think they do a good job.

My feeling that things could get worse was entirely accurate. This was a dream caused by returning sensation to my hand. It was not serious but I suppose it could have been some other rash starting. Until I woke and dismissed it as trivial I didn't know. The dream tickle of the bees on my hand was a very good simulation of my sensation, though a bit OTT and a bit scary.

Comment and advice:
The dream shows how the dreaming brain exaggerates the feelings it thinks you should be taking notice of.

I remember a young man who came in to my surgery for some trivial problem. However I spotted a rodent ulcer, a pre-cancerous lesion, which often starts at the prenatal skin joins of the face. His was at the inner corner of his eyebrow.

"When did that start?" I asked

"I've had it some time," he confessed. "I kept hoping it would go away but it hasn't. It seems to be getting bigger and the funny thing is that I have started dreaming about it. First I had a bird on my head pecking me there and then I had a huge blister that seemed to bulge out before me and though no one seemed to notice as I walked along but I felt like a freak."

"You should have come to see me about it and especially when you started dreaming about it." I told him. "But you are in plenty of time now. It is still a very early ulcer and I will have it treated in no time." He never did have a recurrence but his story certainly suggests that our bodies do use dreams as an early warning system.

Discomfort Dream 2 (a rasping sensation!)
From a young man who likes cats.

"I was driving a sports car down one of those sunk

lanes with high hedges on either side, the kind of country lane that you see in Cornwall and sometimes in the West of Scotland where the brambles and wild flowers are pushed up and supported by hedges of hawthorn or deciduous saplings.

It must have been summer because the hedges were in full leaf, the white cow parsley was flowering, and the air was warm as it rushed past. I was sitting with both hands on the wheel but one arm was resting comfortably on the side of the car. Suddenly as I raced along my arm became entangled in the bushes alongside and was drawn up behind my head and torn off at the shoulder.

I woke at that point, not in pain but in considerable shock and alarm. I felt a bit of a wally because I found my right arm curled comfortably behind my head and still well attached.

However my new little golden Burmese kitten which I had allowed on to my bed, because he was still settling in to the house and wanted to be with me, had crept up, I suppose looking for warmth, and was curled up in my armpit licking it with his rough little tongue and purring like a little motor. I removed him back to his box and explained this wasn't on, but he wasn't impressed."

Interpretation:
The sound of the car was just like my kitten's loud purr. That is where the car came from. My duvet was down round my waist so I could feel air circulating round my upper body but it was summer so it was not unpleasant. My kitten's tongue with its raspy feel must have made me dream my arm was torn off. I felt no alarm, no emotional stress. Just a physical dream. I think.

Comment and advice:

His interpretation says it all. This dream needs no action except perhaps the removal of the kitten to its own sleeping place. But notice the huge exagerated picture of an arm being torn off when the reason for the dream was just the lick from a little kitten's tongue.

Early man was very much at risk when he slept. Caves were scarcely safe houses. At that time it was essential that, even when asleep, he should be alert to any change in surroundings. Touch and sound and light can and do percolate into the sleeping brain and are interpreted as wildly exaggerated dreams that wake the sleeper. This facility stays with modern man and woman! There may be material in these dreams that you want to look at.

I asked the chap whether he felt he wanted a sports car? Whether he had a problem with the car he drove? Whether he felt anxious in his dream? The answer to all of these was "Not really". In fact he mentioned his surprise that he had felt so little pain or distress at having his arm wrenched off. He said that in the dream he had been merely interested to feel it go just before he woke. This dream may be treated as purely from an external physical stimulus. Even his mild distress at losing his arm left him with no pain and the distress disappeared at once when he woke and saw the cause.

Discomfort Dream 3

This one came from a friend who is a great gardener.

"I dreamed that my leg became covered in black scabs. I was horrified and asked a passer-by what it could be. "Plague," he said. "It happens all the time in summer. It comes from the gardens, you know!"

As I mulled over the idea that I was starting a pandemic or was part of one, I woke to feel an itchy area on the back of my leg which, on investigation, was obviously a bite from some insect that lurks in the grass. I had been gardening the evening before and after cutting the grass and doing a bit of weeding I had sat down on the lawn to enjoy the flowers. It was really warm and dry but I expect the berry bugs were in full cry.

Plague it was not. Nor was it serious. Application of a suitable salve removed the itch and any recurrence of that dream."

Interpretation:

A berry bug bite whose itch invaded my dreams. Having plague didn't seem to worry me a bit so I don't think there were any feelings involved in the dream. I had seen a television programme on the Black Death a few weeks previously and it impressed me. I think I was thinking over all the things that those sufferers had to do to prevent spread of the disease when I woke. I wouldn't otherwise have known to think about protective measures.

Comment and advice:

The dream picture is always more intense than the actual triggering mechanism. His dream background was certainly the television programme. It is interesting that dreams use material from the night before and then again after a week or so. Material from just a day or two ago seldom seems to be used. It appears as if it is on its way to being laid down in memory and is not yet ready for retrieval by your dreaming brain.

This chap sounds slightly worried about himself

and I suggest that if he is anxious about the chemicals he is using on the garden that he wear protective clothing when using strong sprays.

- **Dryness / thirst**
One of my dreams.

"I was walking over some foothills in Scotland somewhere. There was a chunky sort of man with me. I didn't know him but he was a real climber with a rope and boots and a knitted hat. He was leading and I was toiling along behind. I had a backpack but I was in a summer dress and sandals. It was hot and the sun beat down on us. I wanted a drink but I knew my backpack only had clothes. Eventually we came to a little mountain stream bubbling from a spring down the hill side. I sank gratefully down and drank huge gulps of bright clear water. But suddenly it dried up and my companion said, "See what you have done. You've stopped the flow." I woke, embarrassed but very very thirsty and got up immediately for a drink of water."

Interpretation:
We had been out to supper with friends and they always use far more salt in their food than I do or than I am used to. They gave us wine too and no water so I was thirsty even by the time I got home. I did take a drink of water but I was so tired that I just fell asleep and woke, really, really thirsty. That was the main bit of the dream I suspect. The rest came from an episode in surgery the previous day. I ran out of small injection needles and went along the corridor to my Partner's surgery because he has the store cupboard with our spare equipment. I did

knock and when he said, "yes!" went in. He was taking blood from a patient so I stopped in my tracks but he removed the needle and sighed and said "You've stopped the flow. Just as well it was the last tube. I've got enough blood I think." I felt embarrassed and irritated with both myself and him. But at the time I naturally apologised though in fact it was not my fault. It was the same feeling of "It wasn't my fault the spring dried up and there is no use trying to put the blame on me" that I got in my dream and my companion used the same words as my partner so I guess that I had gone to sleep harbouring a little residual frustration and resentment from the day before. But the main problem was that I was dry and thirsty, and the body does not tolerate thirst well, so my dreaming brain was telling me I needed a drink of water. In the morning I went into surgery and organised a spare supply of equipment to be stored in my room, so that sort of episode should not happen again.

Comment and advice:
You should have asked for water at your friend's dinner and you should have eaten as little as possible of her very salty soup or made an excuse to duck it entirely. Then you would not have woken thirsty.

However if you can't eat your friend's salty soup and look as if you like it, what is friendship coming to!

Though it was thirst that woke you because it is a commanding feeling, your loss of peace of mind came from your irritation with yourself and your partner.

Thirst is a powerful body sensation. Asleep or awake, we tolerate it poorly.

●   **Hot**

This one came from a female university student who was doing a degree in French before becoming a teacher.

"I was in a bed somewhere foreign, I think it was Africa or South America, certainly tropical and jungly. The room had simple white walls with one window and I could see heavy tree branches outside with large dark leaves. I was wearing a new white broderie anglaise nightie and had a sheet up to my chin. There was a mosquito net all round me and the hum of mosquitoes outside. I was very hot and I tossed and turned and then Stephanie (a friend of mine in my French class) came in.

I said "It's really really hot isn't it?" and she replied, "Yes, I guess so, but the house is on fire so I came upstairs."

Neither of us seemed at all worried by the place being on fire and I just woke up feeling my duvet much too hot. I was sweating under it, and decided I needed a lighter tog now that summer had come."

Interpretation:
I had been watching a film about the kinds of plants that grow up the Amazon before I went to bed. That was just the sort of place my dream pictured me in. The broderie anglaise nightie was one I had seen while I was pottering round the shops with Stephanie two weeks ago. I had fancied it rotten but hadn't enough money left over to indulge. It has been in my mind ever since and I mean to have it even if I have to cut down on everything to raise the cash.

The mosquitos puzzled me for a bit. They were so

very loud but several nights later I heard a motor bike zooming past and realised it was the same sound so that was where that came from. As for the rest, it was a dream about being too hot. I was sweating when I woke. Summer had come with a rush and my tog 9 duvet really had to subside to tog 4. I resolved to take mine home and change it. Mum had told me to take both but I couldn't be bothered and it was cold at the beginning of term.

Comment and advice:
This was a mixed dream, but mainly her body telling her she was uncomfortably hot. Into the dream wriggled a wish for a new nightie and the sound of a motor bike. The dream material of a tropical jungle was conjured from the television programme of the evening before. This is a very common source of the background to your dreams. She certainly needs to sort out the temperature in her bed. Then that dream will not recur. The wish for that nightie was also quite a strong emotion. Time to start saving towards it, or the wish for it might creep into other dreams.

• Hunger
This is one of mine. I was on a strict diet which allowed no sweet things and only half portions of any main course when I dreamed it.

"I was walking down the road between shops and I came eventually to a bread shop. In the window were the most marvellous looking cakes in slices, sponges, strawberry tarts covered in shiny syrup. It was truly mouth watering. I went inside and chose a pastry sandwich filled with cream and covered in white icing. The lady serving behind the counter passed it over on a small square of white greaseproof paper.

"Do you want to eat it now?" she said.

I took it. I nodded and I opened my mouth and took one delicious bite. As I did I woke to find my mouth full of duvet which I had clearly taken a mouthful of."

Interpretation:
There were no other feelings in this dream, just a desire for a huge sticky cake and that came straight from my hunger and sweet deprivation. I might be strong by day but my dreaming brain was telling me how hard it was. I thought, "Poor old body. It will just have to put up with feeling hungry. I want to be thinner and this is the only way."

Comment and advice:
When you deprive your body of anything it will tell you about it in your dreams. In the case of hunger the dreaming is usually quite specific, as it is with thirst. Hunger can colour other dreams, such as anxiety dreams, but in this case there was no other emotional input except a wish for delicious food.

● **Light**

Light Dream 1
This is one of mine.

"I seemed to be outside in a country place, perhaps by a river and there were big old trees full of leaf. I saw a single dark swallow high in the air against a blue sky. It was dipping and weaving as they do, and I said, "Oh good! It is going to be a fine day." Then I woke wondering what the rest of the dream had been about. My very act of concentration on that part had allowed the rest to slip out of my memory and, though I tried to go after it like a man trying to lift a fish from a stream with his hand, it escaped me.

I was left looking at an extra light morning sky through my bedroom curtains and had a feeling of looking forward to a good day."

Interpretation:

This was an instance of what Freud called extrinsic stimulation causing dream pictures. The effect of light on my retina, even through closed lids, told my brain something. It was certainly not a memory of the previous night's weather forecast which had been for showers and blustery winds.

It wasn't an important dream which was, perhaps why the rest of the dream got lost. It was just another fine day which might mean a round of golf but also watering the garden while wet weather would have let me off the latter but wrecked the golf.

For me swallows flying high betoken good weather in the offing.

Comment and advice:

Something in the quality of light coming through the bedroom window curtains and your closed lids must have triggered your retinae and through them your brain to recognise a good day in the making. The tail end of your dream picked up the stimulation from the light, offering you a picture you would understand.

If you had consulted a dream dictionary, swallows would have meant travelling. Psychologists might have suggested you were seeking escape. None of these had any relevance and that is why it is so important that you learn to interpret your own dreams. Only you can assess the significance of your dream pictures.

This dream was just caused by the light from your bedroom window. It left you with a feeling of contentment, so could also be classed as an "Upper" Dream because it left you with peace of mind to start your day.

Light Dream 2
This one came from a middle aged lady, a patient of mine who was lucky enough to be able to holiday in France every year.

"I was walking along the top of rolling hills. I was on holiday in France at the time but these hills did not look like anywhere in France. We usually stay by the sea somewhere but these hills were more like the Pentland hills that I can see from my house back home in Edinburgh.

The grass was short and springy and I had a companion with me who was a bit shadowy. I did not recognise her but I was happy to have her with me. As we went along, tulip shaped explosions burst out here and there, on the horizon, in the valley, over a little village that I could see in the distance.

"Don't worry about those," I said to my companion, who seemed a bit alarmed. "They are just spontaneous combustions. "

We wandered along with these yellow explosions going off here and there in the distance until I began to hear the sound of cartwheels on a cobbled road and looked round for the sound and as I peered about I woke to the growl of thunder. I was in the middle of one of those spectacular sheet lightning storms that grumble away down the west coast of France in August.

Interpretation:
The spontaneous combustions were the lightning flashes. I had closed the shutters but they had a tulip shaped hole in each of them that were the same shape as my explosions and my retinae had definitely reproduced that shape of light in flashes. The sound of cartwheels on cobbles was the thunder, of course. I wondered for a long while who my companion was and in the end I decided that she was my more cowardly self because, though I put a brave front on it, I am very afraid of lightning. I certainly retreated under the bedcovers which is my usual response to these storms.

Comment and advice:
I think you got that interpretation right. You did not wake to any strong emotion so your rather alarmed companion might well have been a representation of your inner nervousness but only for the lightning. Where there are no strong feelings left after you wake, look for a physical or external cause to the dream.

- **Need to pass faeces**
(usually caused by diarrhoea or constipation pains.)
   Related to me by a man of about fifty who had been happily married for years and had a fifteen year old daughter.

"It was our wedding day and I was getting ready for the ceremony in a large hotel. I wanted to defecate and thought that as the groom I shouldn't have something like that on my mind on this special occasion. I went into a toilet, though I was aware that time was moving on and I should be in the church before my bride arrived. The lavatory itself was a thing like a small electronic weighing scale in the middle of the floor. I was disconcerted to find that there were large and completely transparent windows and the bathroom was overlooked by several other windows in the same building. I moved back against the wall for greater privacy, but this seemed to make things worse. Somehow the bathroom was now in the open air; also I knew that if I didn't hurry I was going to be late for my wedding. I moved again, this time to a trench on the other side of a small ridge; however this was overlooked by student quarters. The students didn't seem to take much interest, but unfortunately I now discovered that the trench was also occupied by several English people, some of them actually eating sandwiches. I was just wondering what I was going to do when I woke needing to go to the toilet urgently with diahorroea."

Interpretation:
I was coming up to my twenty fifth wedding anniversary and my wife had been talking about having a party. Naturally we had been going back down memory lane together but our wedding was a happy one that went off without any problems such as I was having in my dream. This one was not a bit like it. For one thing we were married in church. However, the night before, I do remember saying to my daughter that I hoped that if she ever came to tie the knot she wouldn't choose the top of Everest now that it was possible to get married almost anywhere. So maybe it was a wish of mine to attend a wedding in a hotel in comfort. I don't know. What was absolutely central to that dream was a need to go to the bathroom and when I woke the need was urgent.

Comment and advice:
You are right. This is another dream caused mainly by intrinsic body functions. It is interesting to see that despite your urgent need to defecate you do not soil the bed and you wake when your urgency is overwhelming. It is as if your dream is telling you that you need to find a bathroom with increasing rapidity. The need to hurry is your only emotion and that is related to your bowel function.

Your family discussion produced the story of the dream, as material from the evening before so often does.

- **Need to urinate**

Need to urinate dream 1
Told me by a man in his mid thirties who travelled a fair amount in his work and had to stay overnight at a great number of hotels.

"I was in a hotel, in the corridors and needed the toilet. There were apparently no "ensuite" facilities. It was the sort of hotel where guests have to compete for the communal bathrooms. The nearest one was occupied and there was a nasty looking middle-aged blonde woman hovering around waiting to get into it. I walked along a bit, through a labyrinthine 3-dimensional maze which had corners, dog-legs and short flights of up and down stairs every few yards. To my surprise there was a little toilet, its door open, right ahead of me. As I was heading towards it in delight and relief I woke, needing in fact to urinate."

Interpretation:
The hotel reminded me of some of the Victorian bed and breakfast places that I have stayed in. It had

that combination of long uneven corridors and stairs all lit by forty watt lights. I have stayed in ones like that when I travel but this one was more like the places my mother and father used to take me to when they went to the Scottish Highlands to have a golfing holiday. Things have changed a lot. So this picture came from my childhood but except for a mild urgency it was really only about needing the toilet.

Comment and advice:
Interesting that you should recognise that the dream material came from really long ago. Perhaps you had felt the need to urinate then and this was a remembered mild anxiety to find the toilet that came from your childhood and your brain had thrown it up to give the correct picture of need.

Need to urinate dream 2
From the same man as dream 1.

"I was staying in a sort of small hotel or large guest house. I wanted a pee and left our bedroom, stark naked in the dead of night, to look for a bathroom. There was a right turn into a room-shaped corridor at the end of which I heard the heavy breathing of someone fast asleep. To the right, opposite the other door was the bathroom which I found with infallible intuition. I switched on the light from the outside and entered the fussily laid out bathroom and peed into the bowl which was set at the extreme end of the long narrow room. At that point I woke."

Interpretation:
Mainly about needing a pee. I get a great number of these dreams and always wake needing to urinate.

However I don't get several in a night so I do not think I am going to the toilet too often. Just when I do get the urge and am asleep I seem to dream about it. This one was interesting in that I did actually urinate in the dream but when I woke I had not wet the bed. I still needed a pee.

Comment and advice:
The body's control mechanism is very strong. Once you have stopped wetting the bed you seldom do it again. A few people have a weaker control and this sort of dream might lead to damp sheets but most do not. I believe that a full bladder tends to contract and relax in a rythmic way, and in your dream, if it is contracting, your dreaming brain will suggest you are actually voiding urine. However because of your innate control you don't. Then when relaxed the bladder seems easier and so you dream it empty. But you wake just the same to the need to go to toilet. There is a slight feeling of insecurity in this dream suggested by you getting up naked to go to toilet in a hotel. As your work lies in travelling I think this puts the unease squarely in a work context. You might be dealing with a new product whose properties you are not yet completely sure about or something like that. The cure is to get well prepared and the insecurity will not resurface. The sound of someone breathing is interesting and might be you snoring or your wife sleeping beside you. The dreaming brain does incorporate ambient sound into its dream adventures.

Need to urinate dream 3
From a man who had been house hunting with his wife and had been seeing round all sorts of houses in the previous month or so.

"I was in a gent's toilet but a very ornamental one. The urinal was done in extremely ornate Victorian ironwork, painted in two shades of blue and looking like a sort of window seat with swags and tassels hanging round it.

In order to stop people from accidentally sitting down on it instead of peeing in it there was a fence round it which still allowed it to be used for its primary purpose. I was just lining up to pee in it from a distance, hoping not to wet the floor when I woke."

Interpretation:
I needed a pee when I woke and the dream was mostly about that. However I have seen every sort of bathroom from fancy to revolting in the last few months so perhaps some of those crept into my dream. I do get dreams of needing to urinate but seldom in such beautiful surroundings.

Comment and advice:
Certainly precipitated by the need to urinate, but is there a deep seated wish in that dream? I think there may be. It sounds as if you would really like a large and luxurious bathroom. If you are still looking for houses you should keep that in mind.

Need to urinate dream 4
From a nurse who worked in the outpatient department of a big hospital.

"I was doing an outpatient clinic, taking the patient's names, weighing them and telling them where they could get changed but it all seemed suddenly to be in my own flat. It was a larger and more elaborate place than my flat really is with nooks and crannies and twists and turns. There seemed no separation between the domestic and clinical areas either. I was late, very late but somehow I didn't seem to be able to summon up energy to start on the first of my patients. One of the patients started following me around trying to tell me about all the mishaps that had befallen her, and I was trying to get to the toilet. Going upstairs and entering the bathroom, I looked back to see a stranger apparently also looking for the toilet, trying a door on the half landing which had somehow materialised in my flat. I woke needing to urinate."

Interpretation:
I am always running to catch up! The clinics always run late and there is something waiting to be done so the dream gave not a bad picture of my mental state most days. However it was mostly about wanting to go to the toilet. What the inability to start was I do not know. I am mostly rushing about like a maniac.

Comment and advice:
So far so good. I think the inability to move was your brain's appreciation that in dream sleep your limb muscles lie paralysed and sometimes that feeling creeps into the dream. It certainly does into nightmares!

Your dream is also telling you that you are beginning to be pushed beyond what your body can take. Is there some way you can share or delegate so that you are not always running and always late?

- **Noise**

Noise Dream 1
From a woman who works as a temp in an office. She was at the time helping out in a dentist's surgery

and was working at filing records on the computer.

"I was doing something with a computer keyboard in which the keystroke <CTRL G> carried out some fancy global action. I had inadvertently put something heavy down on the keyboard and the machine started warning me that all was not well by emitting a loud beep beep beep, which then started repeating regularly. I woke to find that the repeated tone was in fact my alarm clock."

Interpretation:
I am used to fitting in with different types of office. That is part of being a temp. I enjoy the variety and when I find an office I really like I'll look for a permanent job in a similar place. This way I get paid to try round and it is good experience. I didn't feel any real anxiety or worry about the beep. It was just annoying and intrusive. I think the dream was trying to let me continue sleeping but my alarm clock wasn't having any of that and continued till I woke. I had been out partying the night before.

Comment and advice:
An honest interpretation and I think you got it right. This was just a dream to incorporate a noise that your brain did not find frightening but it was unwanted!

If you sleep on a noisy street you get used to the rattle of traffic and your dreams are usually unaffected by it but a friend from the countryside, coming to stay, might dream of armies marching or tanks sweeping across the desert and would eventually waken to the noise. Your brain will accept the normal noise of your night-time environment and will not turn it into a wakening experience unless it changes its character.

Noise Dream 2
From a young mother who takes her seven year old girl to swimming lessons.

"I am in a swimming pool at the deep end and I am fairly nervous of water because I don't swim well. I don't recognise the pool. It seems very big and has a high glass roof. I am hanging on to the side which is covered in pale coloured tiles. Then I see my daughter running towards me down the side of the pool and I call to her to be careful and not to run in case she slips and falls. I am nervous that she will come jumping into the deep end and I know she cannot swim and I am not much use either so it might be difficult to help her. At that moment a man dives in beside me, "Bang" he goes right down to the bottom, cracks his head and is dead. I know he is dead. I don't know how. Just one moment he is diving in and then this "Bang" and he is dead. I wake and I think "Now where on earth did that dream come from?" "

Interpretation:
I think this set out to be an anxiety dream. I have dreamed that sort of dream before where my daughter is going into water or is near it and I am worried and then it all gets worse. I work in my own business so I am often a bit anxious about making ends meet and I am certainly anxious about swimming and water as I am such a poor swimmer. That is why I am making sure that my daughter is well taught so she won't have the same worries. However the dream went pear shaped and stopped suddenly with a

"Bang" and the shock of seeing that completely unknown man upside down in the pool and dead. I didn't feel anything about him just the shock of the noise. I was still wondering about it at breakfast but something my daughter said gave me a clue. "Those people upstairs were making great big bangs on the floor last night weren't they, Mummy?"

Well, I am tired and I sleep very soundly. She is, and always has been, a light sleeper. I think this was just a loud bang from upstairs that broke up a dream that had started and woke me.

Comment and advice:
Almost certainly right. However you were in the middle of a stress anxiety dream so something is making you anxious. Because it concerns your daughter it is probably an anxiety from home not your work. You should think about what is disturbing your peace of mind in your home situation and sort that out.

Noise Dream 3
This is one of mine.

"I seemed to wake to the door bell ringing and I leapt up and went downstairs to find the postman at the door with a huge parcel wrapped in brown paper. He said it was not for me, but I could see that it had my name on it. We stood arguing until I suddenly realised I was just wearing my see-through nightie and standing in full view of both the post-man and any passers-by. I then woke. It was quite muddling at first. I lay absolutely still and tried to come to my senses. As I did I heard the tink, tink, tink, of a blackbird, annoyed by something just outside my window and the sound exactly mimicked the door bell sound in my dream.

With a sigh I sadly abandoned the thought of a huge parcel. I thankfully realised that I had not been exposing myself and became aware that it was becoming Spring again with the attendant escalation in bird song."

Interpretation:

A dream instigated by the noise of the birdsong which was extremely loud and intrusive. Blackbirds have big voices when they are upset. Mixed into it was a mild insecurity whose origin had to be at home. I suspect it had to do with my see-through nightie which was an impulse buy and, although my husband appreciates it, it is not really the thing to wear in a family situation where I am likely to meet the children on the way to the bathroom. It necessitates always using a dressing gown or nipping quickly along and back if I am sure they are all asleep.

Comment and advice:

Throw a brick at the bird and bin the nightie! However if you like blackbirds just accept that this one is welcome to wake you any time he wants. Put the nightie back in its drawer to wait for a slinky weekend à deux.

Noise Dream 4

This dream came from a chemistry student who plays guitar with a group of other students.

"I was in a lab and it was more like Frankenstein's parlour than the Uni. I drifted round and there was this highly coloured stuff in a glass jar, and I lifted it, but the bottom fell out and the stuff splashed all over and started to eat away the bench. I backed off, wondering if any had got on me but it didn't seem to. Then I was in a sort of auditorium, with a stage, and it was absolutely full of people. I couldn't get a seat so I went forwards until I found myself on the stage. I had my guitar and there was a group playing and everyone was going bananas so I joined in. I got some very odd looks from the rest of the group who clearly didn't think I should be there. But they were playing a piece I'm very fond of and know well, so I was giving it everything when I woke and it was my mobile, which I had recorded that piece on to as the alerting tone."

Interpretation:
What a sell. I was so disappointed. I had been Top of the Pops and probably the nearest I'd ever get to the stars. My mobile had produced that end of the dream. The rest was probably warming up to be one of those dreadful dreams where everything goes wrong and you wake feeling thoroughly wrong footed. I get them when exams are approaching and I have too much on my plate.

Comment and advice:
A nice ending to what was going to be a dream of anxiety. You should pay attention to the first bit and think what it is that is making you anxious. It is clearly to do with your work. Have you got all your projects written and ready? Are you revising steadily?

- **Pain**

Pain Dream 1
An old lady who is also my patient told me this one when she came to see me on quite another matter.

"I recently cracked a rib. It was very foolish as I know my ribs fracture easily, but I was putting a sleeping granddaughter into her cot and my arms were not quite long enough to ground her gently. As I leaned further over, she turned and I held her safe but my weight on the cot side did the business. I felt the rib go and knew I was in for three weeks of pain until the first spicules of bone healed across and held the broken ends together.

That night I dreamed I was at an Olympic Snooker Tournament. All at once the judges came to me and asked if I could adjudicate a match. "But I don't know the rules!" I excused myself. They paid no attention, merely pointing to a table and suggesting I learned how to play. I found myself bent over the table, the rim digging into my chest and all the while asking pathetically if someone would teach me the rules of the game so I would know how much to score for each shot. When I woke I realised that the place where the table was digging in to my ribs was exactly where the fracture was."

Interpretation:
I recognised the digging in from the snooker table was from my cracked rib. It wasn't too bad while I lay still, a sort of dull pressure, exactly like the feeling in the dream. The agony comes when I try to get up! As far as the snooker match was concerned it was a mixture of frustration that no one would help me and a feeling of incapacity to cope with being a snooker judge. These feelings were very much what I felt at that time because I live alone as you know. I really need to be able to lift things and tidy and so forth and the pain when I tried was commanding. So I felt frustrated at my own weakness and a bit helpless all round. As for the snooker, there was

nothing else on the television the evening before and I find snooker watching very restful before bed. I've never learned the rules, though.

Comment and advice:
Your dreams may highlight pain from other quarters. For instance, you may dream that you are on a battlefield and someone has stuck a bayonet into your abdomen. You may not feel frightful agony but you know in your dream that it is serious and you are going to die. Waking, you find you are experiencing a mild colicky pain or perhaps an early bladder infection. I believe these sorts of dreams are worth paying attention to, especially if they recur or you have a similar dream on following nights. Repetitive dreams are always significant and if they point to some bodily discomfort for which you have no firm diagnosis, you should talk them over with your doctor. Your body tells you things in your dreams that your waking mind may dismiss by day or prefer not to notice. Pay attention!

Footnote:
I was delighted to hear about this dream. I did some tests and decided that she needed treatment for those slightly osteoporotic bones. If she lives alone she needs to be strong. In this case the dream alerted her and me to a significant pain.

Pain Dream 2
From a young single mother of two primary school children.

"I have my own house now and it is quite hard work trying to keep a job even though the kids are both at school. My mother lives along the road and helps out but I'll tell you that the last thing I want is another baby so as you said dreams were important, Doctor, I wondered what on earth this dream meant. I was in some sort of hospital on a trolley. There were lights all round but no one was particularly interested in me. I realised suddenly that I was having early labour pains and was going to have a baby. I expected someone to come along but they all just walked by as if I wasn't there and I thought "Well, I'll have to get on with it myself," and I woke and was really pretty thankful to realise I had just started a menstrual period. I get fairly severe pain with my periods. I'm used to it and take a couple of aspirin which usually fixes the pain. For a while after having the children I had no pain and it was marvellous but the pain has returned in the last year, just like it used to be when I was younger."

Interpretation:
Mostly I know that it was just a dream brought on by my menstrual period. The pain I get is very similar to my early labour pains. I was appalled at the thought that I might be wishing for another child. Nothing could be further from my daytime thoughts. I had been watching Casualty the night before so I guess the hospital scene came from that. Was the thought that no one was helping so I would have to get on with it myself significant?

Comment and advice:
The feeling that you woke to was certainly significant. Most single mothers must feel that the world hangs on their shoulders at some time or other. Getting up and getting on with life is the only way to survival and happiness.

But the dream was probably set off by your period

pain and because you had not had such pain for some years your body found it unusual and brought it into a dream. Very often dreams around the beginning of menstruation are sexual ones due to the engorgement of the vaginal and clitoral area (see Sexy Dreams). In this case the pain you felt was your problem.

Of course you need to check that all is well, cervical smear normal and all the rest so a visit to your doctor is a sensible precaution, but in the end you know you can control the pain with a mild analgesic.

You need to find some help in your home situation. It is easy to become ghettoised with children. You need to make the effort to get more help. The social work department and your health visitor may offer outlets. Friends may share outings. Have you any willing relations? Sometimes grannies are just waiting to be asked.

Pain Dream 3

From an overweight middle aged man who came to surgery to tell me about it.

"Last night I dreamed I was in the office, well it was some sort of office because I was sitting behind a desk and this young chap came in with a polystyrene cup of something he said was tea. I don't drink tea in the office, just coffee. I expect I drink too much of that too but my dream wasn't about that. He put the tea down and started fiddling with the papers I seemed to have piled up on one side of the desk and they all fell down. I got furious and got up and shouted at him. He didn't seem to hear, just went on making a worse mess and I shouted louder and woke with a headache from my fury and shouting. I've had several dreams like that and they are not at all like me."

Interpretation:
I don't know whether my fury is causing the headache or my headache is causing the dream of fury.

Comment and advice:
The second is the correct interpretation. Dreams when you are ranting about in a dreadful temper, shouting and stamping and wake to a headache are usually caused by the headache. If repetitive they are worth talking to your doctor about.

Footnote:
In this case my patient had high blood pressure which caused his morning headache. His morning headache was a warning symptom. I was glad he brought that dream to me. Once treated, and his high blood pressure controlled, that sort of dream did not recur.

- **Perception of abnormality in or on your body or someone else's**

Perception of abnormality Dream 1
This is one of mine.

" I had been a doctor on an obstetric ward and at that time had determined to make my career in obstetrics so I was reading books and examining patients very closely and had built up a pretty fair expertise. When I conceived, shortly after getting married I was delighted and expected a normal pregnancy as I could see no genetic or other problems. Gradually I became uneasy about my baby's progress. It was not one single thing, just a coming together of so many little targets not quite met. Remember this was before the era of ultrasound pictures so I was dependent on examination. My consultant was happy. My general practitioner was confident. I was not. I felt my swelling abdomen for the baby's contours and I did not like what I felt. I spoke to the specialists and they laughed at me. Typical nervous doctor, I guess they thought. However I began dreaming that I was delivering an anencephalic baby, where the head is not completely formed and the baby is born dead. It was not a nice dream. I ignored it the first time. The second time I spoke to my general practitioner but she told me firmly that the specialists were happy and I should relax. In pregnancy one thinks silly things, she said and of course she was right. By day I accepted her assumptions. By night I continued occasionally to dream that I had an anencephalic baby."

Interpretation:
Of course I was right. I wished I had not been. It took months before the specialists also became unhappy about my progress. At the time I was a specialist and I knew what I was feeling in my abdomen. My dreams told me the truth when my daytime self was able to shrug off my findings and believe the doctors.

Comment and advice:
Later, much later, I realised that I had probably had German measles at the time when I conceived. Again, at that time doctors did not know of the foetal dangers inherent with that disease. I never thought about it at the time. Nowadays I would have been a great deal more careful. You get over these things and once you have your own big lovely family the grieving does not hurt you any more. It is the luck of the draw and has made me perhaps, a more

caring doctor. I hope so. My dreams of that baby did not recur after I had a definite diagnosis, nor thereafter. This was not a casual dream. It was an interpretation of what was going on in my body as assessed by a specialist in the field. If I ever met a similar case I would make very sure that the dreams had no substance before I dismissed such a vivid recurring dream as a nervous reaction to an unknown situation.

Perception of abnormality Dream 2
From a patient of mine who is middle aged and has an elderly mother who lives by herself.

"It is silly, doctor, but I keep dreaming about my mother. I don't see her so often because she lives in Glasgow but I ring her and she seems fine but I was over a month ago and since then I keep dreaming that she is getting lost. I seem to be going out with her and then we go into a shop or out for a walk and she is not there any more and I start hunting for her. I used to have dreams like that about the children when they first started coming home from school by bus by themselves. But my Mum hasn't changed anything. Perhaps she was a bit forgetful but then you get that way when you are older, don't you? I really hate those dreams."

Interpretation:
I guess I am worried about her living alone. She doesn't seem as able to keep her house any more. She said she had a bit of a cold and had just left things be the past week but would be up and about in no time. I sorted the place myself before I came home. Some of the dishes looked as if they had been there for some time and there were things in funny places.

Perhaps I am worried about her dying?

Comment and advice:
Maybe a little of both these things but why are you suddenly dreaming about your mother getting lost. You don't wake grieving. You wake after trying to find her. Losing your mother when she has not become ill or apparently changed in any way and searching for her, especially as it has been in more than one dream, must be significant. I believe you noticed something when you were last visiting. What you said about finding things in odd places strikes a worrying chord. Could your mother be becoming forgetful? Dementia starts in just this sort of way, things put in unfamiliar places. Normal chores not done. To begin with, the old person covers up her problems by offering excuses. "I wasn't well". "I have been too busy". "I'll do it once you have gone." When you are there they brighten up and return to normal but left alone their mental processes become muddled again. I should make another unheralded visit soon and take it from there. Her doctor may need to be involved. Early dementia is now treatable to delay its progress. If there is any suggestion that it is beginning her doctor should be allowed to assess her.

Perception of abnormality Dream 3
From a patient of mine who has asthma.

"I was in a long distance race of some kind, some sort of marathon. I was wearing shorts and a T-shirt with a number on it and there was a whole bunch of us running up this grassy hill. It wasn't very high but it went on and on and I was really toiling and breathless and the others were passing me and I was being left behind. Then I woke and needed my inhaler."

Interpretation:
I was breathless when I woke up, more so than usual. I used my inhaler and got up and walked about the room a bit before trying to get back to sleep. However I think I am getting a chest infection. Everyone in the office has a rotten cold just now and I have been waiting for it to get to me. It is such a nuisance. Everyone else just gets a cold and gets better and I have to go to the doctor and get a course of steroids and antibiotics and such like and it takes ages to settle. I would never have gone in for a marathon. I could not run that far but I had been out watching my young brother in a fun run a week or two ago and it was very like that experience in my dream.

Comment and advice:
The dream picture almost certainly came from watching the fun run. There may be a bit of wish fulfilment in your dream about that. You probably wanted to join those contestants you watched in the fun run. However the main cause of your dream was your feeling of increasing breathlessness.

Asthmatics often put up with discomfort to an amazing degree by day. But at night your dreaming brain is very sensitive to oxygen shortage and lets you know when you are toiling in a very accurate way. It is time to have a word with your doctor and get back to your normal breathing levels.

● **Taste**
One of mine

"I used to be a chocoholic but gave it up to please

one of my children who found it made him unwell. To begin with I found it quite hard. At that time I had the occasional dream of having a big bar of Cadbury's fruit and nut chocolate in my hand and opening it up and savouring the taste. Though, in fact, in my dream the taste was more the sensation at the back of my tongue and closer to aroma."

Interpretation:
Mostly a dream of deprivation. (See deprivation dreams)

Comment and advice:
Taste seldom plays much part in dreams. This may well be because you clean your teeth before bed so go to bed with the taste of toothpaste which you are very used to, and therefore it does not stimulate dreaming. Deprivation (slimming or stopping some much eaten food) is the only stimulus that might produce taste dreams and even in these it is not strong.

● **Touch**

Touch Dream 1
This dream was told me by an older lady who is a friend of mine.

"I find myself walking near a building site with a lot of rubble, at the edge of town, and I am looking for a way through to get back to the centre. I turn right towards some broken, low walls which look like they are marking a fairly narrow pathway. A lorry comes up behind me and suddenly I find its bumpers pushing me from behind. There is no way to step aside. The walls won't let me through. I realise I am in some danger, and then I wake up finding that my small pillow is pressing uncomfortably against my neck just where the bumpers of the lorry were pushing me."

Interpretation:
There is a mild anxiety about the dream. I don't know where that comes from. I think that because I live alone I am often a little anxious towards night time. But I felt that most of that dream was conjured up by my little pillow which was really very uncomfortable and I shifted it back where it should have been.

Comment and advice:
Minor anxieties like this are scarcely worth pursuing unless they become repetitive. Any small problem through the day such as having to go to an occasion and being a little unsure of the way, could have caused it. This was a dream caused mainly by your pillow causing discomfort. It is a "touch" dream but it is worth looking at "discomfort" dreams (page 37) for similar dreams.

Touch Dream 2
This famous dream was reported by the psychologist Maury and was also written up by Freud in his book "The Interpretation of Dreams".

"Maury describes being ill and lying in his bed at home with his mother sitting beside him. He dreamed that it was the time of the French Revolution and he witnessed a number of frightful scenes of murder. Then he himself was hauled before the revolutionary tribunal. He knew who they were, so he must have been reading about that period in history or be knowledgeable about it. He saw

71

Robespierre, Marat, Fouquier-Tinville and many other important revolutionaries. He was questioned by them and found himself condemned to death. Next he found himself on the scaffold surrounded by a huge crowd and was tied to a piece of wood and fed into the guillotine which chopped off his head. He woke in great alarm to find that part of the bed head had fallen off to strike him on the neck at exactly the same place as he had felt the guillotine hit."

Interpretation:
For years following this dream, psychoanalysts disputed whether dreams were such fleeting fancies that, in the space between feeling the bed head strike him and waking up, Maury had dreamed the whole complicated dream. Later it became obvious that this is not so. Maury had a miserable frightening dream of being the victim of the revolution, probably because he wasn't feeling well. Illness often precipitates wild dreaming but when the bed head fell the dream stopped. The stimulus of the touch on his neck brought the dream to a halt with a guillotine stroke and woke him. (See Noise Dream 2 page 57 for a similar dream finish.)

Comment and advice:
Dreams are now known to last much longer than a few seconds. We may spend over an hour at a time in Rapid Eye Movement sleep where most dreams come from. Most of this dreaming is not remembered. It seems to be the way the brain files memory and throws old unwanted memories into the background. The dreams you wake to are the ones you remember.

Touch Dream 3

Told me by a teacher who knew I was collecting dreams.

"I teach home economics which is cooking to you, doctor, and it means I am on my feet all morning. I get an hour and a half in the staff room at lunch time on a Tuesday and very often I snatch forty winks in an easy chair if no one else is talking to me. I must have drifted off because I was in some other kitchen, all shiny surfaces and there was a terrible clutter of pots and pans and an awful noise of people working around me. I didn't seem to be doing very much. There didn't appear to be anything for me to do. Cooks were rushing back and forwards behind me. I didn't know any of them and they looked pretty useless. Then this quite small man with dark hair under a chef's hat came up. He was carrying a vibrating saw like an electric carving knife, though actually it looked more like the electric saw I gave my husband for his birthday. He is always chopping things down in the garden and it is really tiring with a hand saw. He said very politely, "If you stand quite still I'll cut your leg off." I started to protest, "But I'll need it at the weekend", because in my dream I wasn't frightened but I thought it was a bit unnecessary. However he just went ahead and I woke with my mobile, which was in vibration mode as I always leave it when I am in class, vibrating like anything at just the place that my dream man was cutting.

It took me quite a few seconds to realise what had happened."

Interpretation:
I don't know how long the phone had been going but that was what gave me the cutting off my leg bit

of the dream. As for the rest it was a bit like a replay of the chaos during a lesson and may be it was just that. I was not anxious, even at the end of the dream. The man looked a bit like a French teacher in the school whom I had been talking to about gardens at lunch.

Comment and advice:
Your interpretation sounds about right. Interesting that dreams follow daily living and your brain can produce pictures to suit modern inventions. Freud's friends could not have dreamed that dream. Mobiles weren't invented then!

• Wet

Water Dream 1
From an adolescent boy who I saw for a routine travel inoculation.

"I remember when I was younger, about eight or nine, I got the flu. I must have had a high temperature, at least Mum said I had. She said she put a hand on my forehead when I was asleep and it was burning up so she got a bowl of cool water and sponged me down with it. I woke while she was doing it but I'd had the most amazing dream. I was in this forest and it began to go on fire. Soon it was all around me and getting hotter and hotter. I knew it would reach me soon and that would be the end but I wasn't worried for some reason. Then this helicopter appeared overhead and a man looked out with a bucket in his hand and said "Stay still and I'll empty this over you". Then he did and I felt the coolness all the way down and then I woke."

Interpretation:
Mum said I had been looking at the forest fires in Australia on the TV and I remembered that I had seen helicopters emptying buckets of water and wondered what it would have been like to be hit by a dollop of water like that.

Comment and advice:
A purely physical dream. Your high temperature conjured up the forest fire pictures in your brain to explain your feelings, and being sponged down was beautifully depicted. When you woke I expect your mother gave you a cool drink and medication to lower your temperature so the dream would not recur.

Water Dream 2
This is one of mine.

"I had been gardening and eventually, because it remained really sunny, got out a rug, put it in the shade and started reading. It was a book about the life of Kathleen Ferrier, a truly glorious contralto who died very young in her career.

I must have gone to sleep because I found myself on stage in the opening of Carmen which I know well. I was in the lead role and giving it my all when it started to rain. "Don't worry about the rain," said one of the cast. "In these old theatres it often happens. They didn't use roofs a hundred years ago." This seemed entirely reasonable at the time and I turned to sing again but woke instead to feel a sprinkling of water on my face.

"It's raining!" I shouted, getting to my feet in a dopey way. Then I realised the sun was still shining and I looked round to see grandson number three sloping off towards the back door with a watering can in his hand."

Interpretation:
I was not amused but he explained that I had told him about the student experiments with water precipitating dreams and it was too good a chance to miss. He said it was only a tiny spatter of water. I had to forgive him because it had been so successful.

Comment and advice:
The dream pictures came from the book I was reading. I have the voice of a crow with tonsillitis and have no pretensions to professional singing. Just as well because no one will let me open my mouth in song unless there are enough others to drown anything I produce. I suppose there might have been a suppressed wish to be able to sing like Ferrier but I guess most people have that.

Being sprinkled with water created the downpour, an exaggerated dream picture because my face when I woke was scarcely wet.

Never go to sleep when experimental grandchildren are about.

4

Sexy Dreams

What makes you dream of having sex? Not getting enough!
When I talked about writing a book on dreams the first reaction I got was, "How interesting. You know if I haven't had sex for a while I dream of it."

In fact in Rapid Eye Movement sleep it is common for men to get a penile erection. This can be a useful diagnostic sign when a patient complains of difficulty in getting or maintaining an erection.

If he spends a night in a sleep laboratory the doctor can wait until the electroencephalograph shows that his patient is in REM sleep and can then look to see if his patient has an erection. If he has an erection the problem is more likely to be psychological and if there is no erection the doctor will be more likely to suspect a neurological cause.

- **Everyone has dreams of having sex. No one speaks about it.**

Usually no one likes to speak about dreams of intercourse. Many people don't even want to think of them in case it shows that they have abnormal mental activity. But dreams of sex are very normal and are usually dreams of deprivation. Psychologists suggest that your sexual urge is one of the strongest in your makeup. Unsatisfied, it surfaces in your dreams at night, though by day you are too taken up with your job or family to have time to settle down and desire sex.

By day your adrenaline is running and sex is put on the back burner. By night, when you are relaxed, your brain reminds you of the natural urges that are normal to humans and if you have not had intercourse for some time your dreams may be pretty wild ones.

- **Adolescent Sexual Dreams**

For those who have never had intercourse, dreams of sexual deprivation are often those of yearning. I believe some dreams of flying, where you are swooping about in marvellous attire, showing off in front of an admiring audience or cuddling comfortable objects may be early sexual dreams.

Boys learn about masturbation and intercourse at an early age. My male colleagues assure me that by adolescence, boys are perambulating penises; their waking moments full of fantasy or hope of sexual encounter and in their night time dreams wild encounters lead to intercourse and orgasm. " Wet" dreams are very much a normal part of male adolescence.

- **Men's Sexual Dreams**

Men normally have an erection in REM sleep. It is clear that sexual desire is a strong male motivator and if a man does not satisfy his sexual urges by the time he goes to sleep, he may well wake to a remembered erotic dream.

- **Women's Sexual Dreams**

Women's sexual dreams may be just as erotic as their male counterpart's but do often have a considerable input of cuddling and warm, loving caring. Perhaps this reflects their greater desire towards achieving security in a sexual relationship. This naturally varies both from woman to woman and indeed from man to man, as well as changing as sexual status changes. There is no blueprint for sexual dreams through life.

- **Sexual Arousal / Lust**

Sexual Arousal Dream 1
From a forty year old man.

"I was walking down a path by a small river with a female friend of mine who works in the same organisation. She was asking me how my daughter was progressing with swimming lessons. To demonstrate, my friend plunged naked into the water, informing me as she did, that there was a certain race in which the participants were allowed to do a combination of three strokes, two front and one back. To demonstrate the back stroke, she reared up in the water, stark naked, and did a somersault on to her back. To my credit, I actually looked away discreetly when I saw what she was about to do."

Interpretation:
I woke with a hard on and I think that I was simply getting an urge to have sex. However my dream woman was clearly not the one for me. No lust for her though she is a very fit woman. I say that to my wife and she sniffs but is clearly not worried. She has no need to be. However my daughter was taking swimming lessons and the evening before, she and I had been talking about all the strokes she needs to learn if she wants to go in for the races at the end of the training session. My fit friend has much the look of my daughter's swimming teacher so my dreaming brain might have got them muddled up.

Comment and advice:
An innocent dream. From nine to ninety sex will creep in to most men's dreams unless they are exhausted from it. Your interpretation is true I think. Take it bit by bit. You had gone to bed still thinking about how much more your daughter needed to learn to be secure in the water. The chat about the three strokes probably came from the swimming teacher at some time. She always organised the swimming gala for her pupils at the end of the training course and you took your daughter to her swimming class so you knew her well. You have a sound satisfying relationship at home if, even in your dreams, you turn away from all that nubile flesh!

Sexual arousal Dream 2
From a forty five year old man who works as a representative for a large brewing firm and travels a great deal. Attending receptions is part of his job requirement.

"I was at some sort of reception, perhaps at a large hotel. I was showing off that I could remember all of the "Minute Waltz", by which I apparently meant the "Beautiful Blue Danube", and to prove it I began somehow to play it (I'm not sure how. May be I was humming it) while whirling a little dark haired woman on to the floor. As we waltzed from room to room she began giving me provocative little kisses on the lips. Then I woke and, yes! I had an erection."

Interpretation:
My wife wasn't with me so this was work. I often attend these receptions alone as I am there to glad hand the hosts and get to know their needs that my firm can supply. My wife used to come but it was a bit boring for her as she seldom saw anyone that she met there again. The receptions can be miles and miles away. I often think I live in my car. The little dark haired lady was a cracker. I did not lust after her when I woke. My wife was in my bed and enthusiastic. I asked her if she had woken me and she said she had put her finger on my lips two or three times to see if I was asleep or awake because I had been muttering.

Comment and advice:
A sexy dream. You wanted sex I suspect before you went to bed but fell asleep before you could get around to it. However the physical feeling of touch also comes in. Lips are sensitive erotic areas and your wife's touch both woke you and was translated into kisses in your dream. I just hope your wife is a small dark lady with lots of get up and go.

Sexual Arousal Dream 3
From the same man as told me dream 2.

"It was quite muddling because I dreamed I was in
bed with my wife and in the half dark of the room I
saw my wife's best friend come in to our bedroom.
She walked up to the bed, smiling and ran her finger
nails playfully across my hip under the covers and I
woke in shock."

Interpretation:
My wife's friend has the longest most highly
coloured nails of anyone I have ever met. I do not
know how she manages to keep them like that while
holding down a job as a secretary and managing a
home. I don't like to mention them to my wife but
they do amaze me. I don't mention either that she
gives me a look occasionally that I can't help feeling
is less than platonic. She hasn't a hope but it is quite
pleasing to know or think you know that you can
still pull a bird at my age.

Comment and advice:
Watch out. Your dreaming brain may have sussed
out the situation quite accurately. Best friends on the
loose are well known time bombs in a family situation. Keep your cool and let your wife help her on
with her coat next time she comes to dinner.

Sexual Arousal Dream 4
This one was from a rugby groupie (female) of
about twenty two.

"I was in a bar and I seemed to have come with a
team but I didn't know anyone there. This great
rugged square looking player came up to me and

said something like he was a prop and wanted to get an arm round a hooker. I seemed to want to hug him dreadfully and just fitted myself to him, even though he was a total stranger but he was so powerful and comforting and it felt good. Then I woke and I had my pillow tight in my arms and it was warm against my front."

Interpretation:
Sad really. It was just the warmth of the pillow that conjured up the dream. I'd heard the joke about the prop and hooker a thousand times. The men keep thinking it's new, especially after a couple of pints. I am between guys just now. I am getting a bit old to be following the team without a steady boyfriend I guess. Last Saturday I thought that I would have rather gone for a walk instead of watching the boys batter themselves to pulp. They lost of course which is never a big hit and they all seemed to have someone of their own and I was shovelling out the burgers and getting greasy and hot and when it came to loading the dishwasher there was no one at home but me!

Comment and advice:
There is a big dollop of need for cuddling as well as need for sexual satisfaction in this dream. Most women's sexy dreams have this overtone of also needing a caring presence. It seems that lust is not enough. There is also a requirement for security.

Your dream is definitely highlighting your time off. You do not say what you work at for the rest of the week but it would seem sensible to suggest that you look there for a steady companion. You appear to have outgrown the scrum.

• Just plain sex

Sexy Dream 1
This one came from a happily married woman of about thirty five with two children, whose husband was posted South to his London Office for three months while she remained in their house with the children who were at school.

"I had a series of three dreams on the three consecutive nights running up to my period in the second month of my husband's three month Sabbatical. The first night I was out walking in Glasgow, not a town I know well, but I know George Square close to the railway station and I was there, I think. These two men in suits caught up with me and we walked together. It was dark and we walked close and then one of them started to kiss me and he did it so well that I had to melt into his arms and we were in a small flat like I used to live in when I was a student and we were making love. I couldn't really see him. He was tall and dark but he was loving and he excited me and I responded and the sex was wonderful.

He came again the next night. This time we were already in the flat, and the night after, and I climaxed that night, I don't always but I did then and woke and my period had started. Strangely the thought in my mind when I woke and realised what was happening was that it was just as well my period had arrived because a dream child would not have been very explainable."

Interpretation:
I realised when I woke on the third night that this was me working up to a period and the engorgement

84

of my sexual area was the cause of those dreams. I felt slightly guilty about them. I did enjoy my dream man. I comforted myself in that he was very like my husband who is also slim tall and dark. Much of his touching and stroking was very familiar. But it was not explicit in the dream and my dream man and I went further than John and I usually do and I enjoyed it. I thought I could bring some new techniques into our familial sex pattern. I wondered how I would explain them.

Where did they come from? Some at least came from an old student boyfriend I had almost forgotten until that night. He had been a pretty fleeting experience at best but educational while he lasted. Then there was a film I had seen that suggested extensions to our regular sex and I had forgotten that until the dream.

I don't use a vibrator to masturbate with while John is away. I don't need it. I sleep sound because I am tired after looking after the kids and working part time while they are at school. But those three nights were different. It was like a holiday for me, especially. They made me feel sexy, and in a way got me looking forward to John coming back as my bed partner. I decided to keep them to myself."

Comment and advice:
Wow! A three night affair with a dream man. Who could ask for more? You have pinpointed your sources and they are probably accurate. No one but you yourself could know about them or what they actually meant to you and what your memories of those times were.

You go to films and get different things out of them. You seldom share the things that affect you most. You store them and your dreaming brain can make use of those memories, just as it can dredge up the sweetness of a fleeting student encounter that gets shouldered aside for real life.

Had you used a vibrator or masturbated to orgasm you might not have had those dreams. But what a pity to miss them. Clearly your love life is confident and satisfactory. Your dream has no frustrations, no suspicion, no guilt. Because you are premenstrual your sexual organs are engorged and your dreaming brain merely interprets that as a series of passionate affairs.

Enjoy the memory and don't share it. No one else would understand.

Waking to the thought of explaining away a dream child is interesting. It sounds as if this might be a suppressed wish. It is always difficult to know when to call a halt in the reproduction stakes. Nowadays you can plan your families and decisions may be made on economic grounds. These may be sensible but throughout reproductive life and even beyond (look at the newspaper articles on those fifty plus women who are being fertilised and brought to parturition) women hanker to conceive and give birth. This is definitely something to discuss after your husband comes home unless you already know his answer.

Sexy Dream 2
This one was told me by a male disc jockey of about twenty eight.

"I was in a sort of disco hall. It must have been early in the evening because the room wasn't full. Most of the dancers were down one end and I was swanning about the middle, looking at the equipment that was at the other end of the room. It was very fine and I longed to get my hands on it. Then the music started and suddenly this well known woman disc jock appeared and moved towards the equipment ahead of me. She was about to climb the steps into position when she turned round and saw me and smiled.

Well now! I moved in close and then she bent over and raised her already short leather skirt above one thigh, almost to the hip. It was an astounding view and one I was just about to explore further when I woke. I was sweating and enthusiastic. It was quite sad really. There was no one there and I was up and ready for it!"

Interpretation:
I am between women just now and find it kind of hard. My best scenario is when I have a tender lover ensconced in my pad and can add a bit of flummery on tour. That way I get clean clothes without having to stick them through the wash myself and I'm never without clean T-shirts or sex. It comes and goes.

That disc jock was quite something. When I saw all that shiny bronzed thigh appearing in front of me I really needed her. I wanted her job too. "

Comment and advice:
In dreams the truth creeps out.

You are every woman's nightmare. Forget the Jane bit. Tarzan is off playing in the woods and may or may not come home.

Your dream highlights your singleminded, go getting personality and brings out the only person you have any interest in which is yourself. Go getters often succeed and you can see why. Our world is made up of all sorts and no one is better or worse than another. We all have goods and bads. Just don't confuse the go getter with a family man or you will find you are petting a piranha.

This dream comes from your work ambitions. You want to be top jock. So this is also an "Upper" Dream of ambition and pursuit. You feel confident in your occupation. In this dream, you look at that really modern equipment with longing not awe.

Then enter the seductive lady. You want to have sex. But there is also a feeling of wanting to get on top of her, put her down and clamber into her job.

I would suggest that you are an ambitious, single-minded man with enormous self confidence and a strong sex drive who is still too young to have learned about the milk of human kindness. You should follow your dream. Who knows where you will end up! It is the old who lose their blood lust and cultivate gardens. You need to watch your back, however. The climber is always out on a limb.

Talking of watching your back reminds me to mention avoiding infection.

The need for sex can override sensible precautions. Don't let it. Better to say no to yourself and partner and accept a sexy dream or masturbate than catch the HIV virus. AIDS infected people wear no label. The golden years of flower power when the worst could happen to you and be cured with a pill are over.

Sexy Dream 3
From a secretary in an estate agent's office.

" I am in a car beside my boss and we are going to look at a house that someone wants us to sell. I have the address and a pad on my lap and as we drive I can feel my boss looking at me again and again and I am getting quite excited.

Then we are in this room which has a four poster bed and looks really comfortable and my boss is right behind me and we tumble on to it and he is kissing me and fondling my body and I am responding and then he is inside me and I am completely his and I am wondering what will happen next when I wake on the thought, "But he is quite old".

Interpretation:
I was completely embarrassed when I woke. My boss is a man in a suit and years older. The man in my dreams was in the same sort of suit and though it was my boss in the dream he was younger. In fact when I think about it he was more like the chap who came in looking for a house the other day. I thought he looked really sexy and fancied him quite a bit but he didn't really seem to notice me. I scarcely dared look at my boss all the morning after my dream in case he could know what he had been doing with me the day before!

It was stupid. He was just the same as usual. He chats us all up equally and doesn't get close at all. He probably couldn't. His children must be my age.

I have a boyfriend of my own besides. He is very different. I have known him since school and we've been together for two years now.

I'd like to try some of the things we were doing in that four poster with him but how can I introduce the idea?

Comment and advice:
Your dark suited stranger got tangled with your dark suited boss in your dream. This was just a remembered sexual urge, felt while you were speaking to a sexy client, that surfaced later in your dream.

But why did it surface?

Your own sex life must be missing something.

You should indeed encourage your boyfriend to try other positions, more foreplay, get yourselves really steamed up before you couple. There are books. Buy some and leave them around. Pretend they are just a giggle but let him read them. There are films. You can always copy.

If you are sexier than your partner, don't despair. If he is the man you like living with and want as the father of your children he is worth keeping and looking after and loving. You will get old like your boss, and have a bad back and be thankful you have your childhood sweetheart to massage it. Sex is only part of a good relationship. Anyone can learn a few bed tricks and he will probably enjoy doing so. Who knows he may be holding back because he thinks you are square.

• Sex With An Other?

Even if sexually satisfied, men have dreams of arousal. I have heard dream reports from happily married men of exotic women from the previous night's television viewing, or particularly attractive friends from work or their wife's social round appearing in their bedrooms, pressing up beside them in bed or dancing with them so close that they can feel their bodies all the way up.

Women get them too, depending on their temperament, though often there is more cuddle than sex if they are well happy in their home relationship.

Don't feel guilty. Enjoy!

There is no need to feel anxious or guilty about these dreams. They are merely coloured pictures to illustrate your feelings. You may find yourself having sex with animals, sons, daughters, casual acquaintances, or even the Wife of Bath if you were reading Chaucer's Canterbury tales the night before.

Whom you have sex with is of no significance so long as when you wake you are aware that your dream was merely illustrating a feeling, that you have no desire to actually repeat the occasion for real and that in some of the cases, the idea is completely unacceptable and would disgust you very much.

What about really perverted sex dreams?
I have no expert knowledge of the dreams of sexual perverts. My guess is that if they dream of their perversion they wake to want it or at least they have no strong feelings of conscience that provide the normal feeling of being offended in their mind for having produced such an unwanted dream.

You cannot control what your dream shows you.
You can look at it in the light of day and find it unacceptable but use the feeling from it to tell you that perhaps you are seeking more natural loving or sex and searching for that instead. I do not believe that your dreams are trying to turn you into a pervert. I believe that when your dreaming brain is searching after material to colour a picture of sexual deprivation it looks for strong feelings of desire and picks them up from a filing system that we would not naturally use. It may be that your short term memories of a recent dinner with an exotic friend of your wife's have been laid down beside your current sexual need and so, when the one feeling is triggered, the brain uses the nearest available material to colour its feeling with a picture. It does not mean that

you love your wife less or that you lust after someone else's to any degree. Though of course it might
do. Only you can tell the real meaning and interpret
the essential feeling that has been shown you.

• **Sex with animals**
The Ancients were not against it!

Old Egyptian writings from thousands of years
ago discuss the meanings of dreams of having sex
with animals.

"If a woman dreams she is having sex with a goat
she is likely to die; with a dog, she will be delivered
of a boy; with a cat she will have many children."

It doesn't make much sense now but it did then. A
goat was the common sacrifice in the temples. So
dream of being with a goat and you were living
dangerously.

Dogs were considered macho. Many people still
think so and, as for cats, they do still have impressive
reproductive power if not prevented.

Sex with an animal Dream 1
From one of my patients who admittedly has three
children at the present count.

"I was in bed hugging my cat.

Of course it was ridiculous. My cat must have
increased in size considerably to make it possible. I
felt his warm cuddly black fur all round me and it
was very pleasant. Then he turned round and we
were side to side and I felt him entering me and I
was encouraging him and going for it. Then I woke
and of course I felt very guilty and pretty stupid
because it was such a ridiculous dream."

Interpretation:

I knew where the dream came from. My cat was in my bed curled round in the middle of the bed doing its best to push me out. I was probably touching him in my sleep so the feel of warm fur would enter my dream. As for the rest I had not had sex with my husband for some nights and miss it if that happens.

So what did I do about it?

I didn't stay to worry about my crazy dream. I just vacated, got into my husband's bed and he was delighted to find me all excited and we had excellent sex. I then put the cat back in his own bed where he should have been put last thing that evening, tucked up in my own bed and finished the night satisfied and dreamlessly."

Comment and advice:

Your husband is a large dark haired man so your dream may have had some of its origin in that fact. Your dream filing system is not similar to your waking office system. It sounds as if the outcome of your dream was pretty good.

Footnote:

Suffice it to say that any dream of having sex is usually a dream that follows sexual deprivation. Some people need sex more frequently than others to maintain their peace of mind so they are likely to have dreams of intercourse more frequently unless they can keep up a satisfying hit rate!

If your dream is about sex that you find abnormal you will wake to an immense sense of guilt and revulsion as you review your dream material. That shows that you are completely normal and need have no fears that you are a pervert. But it is also very understandable that you don't want to tell that dream to your nearest and dearest.

Sex with an Animal Dream 2
This was told me by a stable girl working in a race horse training stable.

"I had been helping with the mating all afternoon. We have a lovely mare and the Boss had brought a stallion over from Ireland. The expense was enormous apparently so they were very keen that it should all go well. I muck out Roxy's stable and she likes me so they suggested I stay with her and keep her calm. The mare gets put into a sort of pen that holds her and then the stallion is brought up and he mounts her. In this case there did not seem to be any translation difficulties between the animals. Roxy got a bit restive but she was certainly not unkeen and as for the stallion, he appeared to have read the manual.

That night I dreamed I was tied on a sort of table bed with my legs apart and this great stallion came into the room and he sort of inspected me and then went up on his hind legs and was about to give me the works when I woke having an orgasm. I was a bit shaken."

Interpretation:
I asked the senior stable girl about it and she said it is not unusual to dream about sex with horses. She said I had been standing watching it too long. That was the trouble. I have not had it off with any one for months. My boyfriend is in the Merchant Navy so he is away for great chunks of time and I miss him. I miss him to come home to and talk to, I miss him just not being there, and I miss him in

bed. However that is the way life is going to be till he retires, I guess.

What the head stable girl said made me feel better. I had really felt that I might be getting quite peculiar. It was such a dream and I felt so strongly in it. My top half was saying "No, no, no!" and my bottom half was quite looking forward to it.

Comment and advice:
It is very emotive to stand and watch sexual intercourse, be it between huge animals or hamsters. That is what pornographic pictures are produced for. They raise your libido and make you ready for sex. I am not surprised that you dreamed of sex with a horse.

I don't think being tied down should make you worried about being into bondage unless of course you want to try it. It might suggest that you prefer the passive role in intercourse. Only you will know that.

The head stable girl was perfectly right and her sensible advice should make you feel a great deal better about what was just a feeling of missing sex with your boyfriend and a dose of pornographic material on the hoof, so to speak, and as such a great deal more potent than dirty movies or suggestive pictures.

• Sex with people you really oughtn't!
Telling the boys and girls at work that you dreamed you had it off with some sex symbol or other is an act of bravado that provokes catcalls and half envious teasing.

Boasting that you had sex with your mother, your father, your sister or brother, your grannie or your Auntie Jane, to say nothing about your own children, is simply not drawing room conversation.

Yet people do dream these things and positively enjoy them too.

Your guilt is brought on by knowing that in your dream you have broken a rule that you have been educated to respect.

If you had no such training and indoctrination you would not feel guilt about any of your acts. Society would be mayhem. Even animals have inbuilt rules of conduct. In humans these have been laid down in sophisticated legal and religious systems where punishments or social ostracism threaten those who break the regimen of the accepted code of behaviour.

So if you wake, having had warm and loving intercourse with a near relation, your first morning thought is, "What a disgusting thing to have done, let alone think of doing." That is perfectly understandable.

I do not believe that your brain is trying to show you the joys of an incestuous relationship. It is merely that your body is missing the delights of sexual intercourse and in giving you that message it may use any body that you love or any body that you have seen and admired. It is seeking to show you the type of sexual involvement you are looking for, perhaps something more exciting, more caring, more exotic. The hints are there so look for them. Turn away from the dream with revulsion by all means but look for the hints it is trying to give you.

Say to yourself, "Now that was completely out of line. I am revolted by the whole idea of, say, having sex with my mother, but is it that I am looking for someone with her welcoming warm love that would be for me only?

Is my dream using my mother but meaning someone who gives me those feelings? Someone who I haven't seen for some time so is not immediately available to my dream material file, whereas I saw my mother yesterday and I felt I could really talk to her, just as I did Miss X, now that I remember her. Perhaps I am beginning to want to settle down and have a more lasting relationship with someone I can really talk to."

Again only you will know what the dream really means. What you can be pretty clear on is that the feeling is not as simple as the dream. Unlike Freud, I believe you are unlikely to be actually wanting to have sex with your mother. If you are, the dream is perhaps a warning that it is time you matured and looked for the same qualities in someone your own age.

Your REM brain is not matchmaking; it is simply trying to create a picture of deprivation.

After you have got over the shock and horror of having intercourse with someone or something that is totally unacceptable, look further into the dream, ignoring the actual love object but concentrating on the feelings you felt with them. Because the sex urge is a strong one it attracts other strong desires to it. Look, therefore, past the act of intercourse to what you felt at the time.

Did you have a desire to be held and comforted?

Did you wish to show off and be admired?

You may accept the simple message that your body is missing sex. That may or may not be easily remedied. Having sex with your partner will stop dreams of sexual intercourse repeating, but remembering the feelings your dream engendered may allow you to improve your relationship or encourage variety in your love making.

It is more important to understand the desires that went with your dream. Did you feel young, strong and beautiful and want to be noticed? Does that mean that you feel unappreciated at home or in the office? You can do something about that. Relationships may be improved by understanding. Talking things out may help.

Did you dream of having sex with your boss? You don't need to, to improve his opinion of your work. Your dream was probably telling you that on the one hand you were missing sex and on the other that you felt your boss did not appreciate you sufficiently. There are two separate feelings amalgamated here in one dream. Of course your dream might be telling you that you fancied your boss rotten. You are the best person to know which is the true meaning.

Did you feel safe and warmly loved in your dream?

Did you enjoy long dalliance before hand?

Could you make these things better with your real life partner?

Your dream may be suggesting you would be more content if you do.

Mediaeval herbals are full of recipes to prevent "dreams of lechery." Herbalists of that time were well aware that the sexual urge was one of the strongest in our physical make up, and tended to surface in dreams when physical satisfaction of it was denied.

Having said that, they did not go on to suggest that the feelings included in your dream deprivation package are likely to be just as important and possibly easier to do something about.

Interestingly, you seldom seem to have intercourse with your own partner in dreams if he or she is readily available. That would be wholly acceptable and very agreeable. I believe that this is because if you do have intercourse before your sleep you are not deprived, so you don't dream about having sex. If you have not had intercourse for a while your brain in REM sleep gives you pictures of sexual deprivation but adds in any other strong feelings it can't mitigate and file in memory. So the dream picture material is never simple.

For instance, if you lack assurance, your dream might be of being cuddled by something big and strong and comforting, as likely to be a bear as a person. On the other hand if you are simply sex deprived, you may dream of intercourse with a television character viewed the night before and have little added feeling, just the satisfaction of the act itself.

It may be that if you have recently lost a partner you will find yourself having sex with him or her. Your dream may be comforting or bizarre. The two motivation forces acting in your dream are your own sexual deprivation coupled with your feelings of perhaps, loss, anxiety, anger at being abandoned or need of comfort. Accept that sort of dream as part of a grieving and healing process.

Husbands and wives in the hurly-burly of family life have dreams of sexual deprivation. Again the feelings that come with the dream may show where unsatisfied needs have built up.

Are you looking for more interest in yourself, more loving attention? These things communicated by day can enrich a relationship that has become humdrum.

Did you feel warm, loved and cared for?

Is this something you miss in your daytime life?

Can you do something about it? If you are lonely can you join a group of people with like interests. If your sex is not satisfying, can you encourage your partner to enjoy it more in a way that gives you that loved and cared for feeling? If you are young and entering a relationship, is the dream highlighting a lack of loving that you are unwilling to acknowledge or hope will improve with time? Make sure it does before you finalise the relationship for life.

Because it is embarrassing to talk to anyone about these sexual dreams it is sensible to be able to interpret them yourself. They are usually very obvious once you have got over the guilt and shock following the event.

If there is no guilt, because yours was an unattached person's dream of sex with a beautiful partner, look carefully at the subjects of your dreams. Notice the parts about them that you like best, their manner, their build and colouring, the feelings they engender in you. It may tell you a great deal about the sort of ideal mate you are looking for.

This may or may not be the person you later form a loving relationship with, once you realise that body form is not the first requisite for long term happiness. It is, however, a type, be it tall and dark or short and red haired, that you have a natural preference for, and may keep as your pin up for life. If your lasting relationship is a good one, there will almost certainly be something of that man or woman of your dreams in your partner.

If you are celibate through religious decision or from lack of an available partner you will be prone to dreams of intercourse. Women are more likely to have them towards and during menstruation when their vaginal area is engorged and more sensitive, also at mid cycle when they are ovulating.

Men have no such cyclical increase in dream libido

100

but thoughts of sex the previous day or explicit or erotic pictures seen on television often precipitate sexual dreams. Both men and women may wake to orgasm, even if the woman seldom gets an orgasm at intercourse.

Menopausal and post menopausal women do not stop having sexual dreams. Young partners are often dreamed of and there is usually a strong need to be cosseted and loved shown in the dream material as well as active sexual action. If you are disturbed by this sort of dream repeatedly, masturbation to orgasm or increased intercourse with your partner will almost certainly reduce their frequency. Otherwise accept them as occasional comfort to your sexual nature. If you need to seek pardon for it, do so, but we are all human and though human urges may be well sublimated by day, dreams are not under the control of our waking mind.

Dreams of Perversion
One word of warning: if you are not affected by guilt or shame following a violent, abnormal or seriously antisocial dream involving sex and in the day time you begin to fancy repetition of that act, knowing it to be illegal or seriously against normal social or religious views, you should seek help and advice from a doctor. Perversion may show itself first in your dreams and is more readily cured before it becomes an actuality.

In the main, a dream of intercourse that you have enjoyed should be accepted as a loving experience, whose feelings could be transferred into your own more socially appropriate day time relationships, to make your sex act more satisfying and your relationship more fulfilling.

• Sex with Close Relations

"No. No!" Dream 1

Julius Caesar dreamed that he had sex with his mother and told everyone.

What is more, they all congratulated him on a very auspicious dream as they felt he was getting one over Mother Earth and so would conquer the world. They were almost right too.

He almost did.

"No. No!" Dream 2

Told me by a menopausal woman who was worried by it.

"I was in some big city with lit shop fronts and rather sleazy sort of hotels and my grown up son was with me. I was pleased he was there. It wasn't the sort of place I like and I was nervous.

Then we were in a hotel room, a cheap and nasty one and we were having sex. It didn't seem strange. I enjoyed his young excitement and suddenly he was a baby and I was helping him from between my legs and I could feel blood flowing and then I woke. I was having an unexpected period."

Interpretation:

I did not know what to make of it at first. I felt revolted by the whole idea. I did not want to see my son. I did not like it at all. Then after I talked to you, doctor, I began to realise that he was really not the son I know. He was much closer to the husband I used to have sex with when we were young, and George hadn't got arthritis which does slow him down a mite though he is very willing. The baby bit, I know, is me looking back to my own younger days and wishing I had them again.

In one way I am delighted to be losing my periods. They were getting awfully heavy and I felt drained. On the other it means I can have no more children, not that I want more. A boy and a girl were enough. So I realise I am inconsistent.

The sleazy hotel in down town somewhere came straight out of the television film George and I were watching before bed. Then I had been worried about my son. George says he needs to grow up, that's all. He says, leave him alone. He'll do fine. I am worried that he makes the wrong decisions about his work and about his girlfriends. He doesn't seem to think about his future. So I suppose he was much in my mind as well.

As for the sex. With George's bad back we are not as frequent as we used to be and I miss it, especially just now when it makes me feel younger and still desirable. I always used to enjoy sex best just before a period.

I certainly am not going to tell any one about that dream, not even now when I understand that it was not me into abnormal sex.

Comment and advice:
You are absolutely right. The scene was from the late night movie you watched. The main person in the dream was the son that you were worrying about and the sex was simple deprivation triggered by the engorgement of your vagina and sexual area due to a period coming on.

The one thing it was not was perversion.

You can be reassured. You love your son, so your dreaming brain found no trouble fitting him up as a sex object. It might be that you are getting too exercised about him. Your husband's advice to let him grow up and make his own mistakes is probably good. If you have given him a sound upbringing he will do no worse than you and your husband did.

"No. No!" Sex Dream 3

Told me by a female university student studying for a Social Work degree.

"I am walking along with a boyfriend in a park somewhere. It is summer because the trees are green and we are on the grass by a stream. He turns to me and takes me in his arms and starts kissing me and I am loving it and feel really keen and then his tummy seems to get fatter and I am in my father's arms and I wake up and I am disgusted at the thought that I should have been kissing him like that."

Interpretation:

The boy was the man who sits next to me in class. I've not got to know him well yet and I've certainly never kissed him. But I do fancy him rotten. I like his smell. It is sort of expensive deodorant and tweed from his jacket. I know because I had to lean over him once to pass something to another girl.

He has hair much the same as Dad's used to be I guess. Dad's hair has gone for a Burton and slid right off the top of his head but it used to be red too.

I still give Dad a hug and a kiss when I go home but not like I was doing in the dream. I would never tell him that dream. It is disgusting. I never thought of Dad like that anyway. I've seen Mum kiss him like that on the lips. They are good together.

I'd like someone of my own too. I realise now that because I am so like my Mum I might see me in her position. But that dream is about Darren, my class mate. It makes me want to get to know him better and see if we kiss as well as in my dream. I am going to ask him if he'd like a coffee after class tomorrow. I don't think I'll tell him he is the man of my dreams – not yet anyway."

Comment and advice:
Yes you are right. Darren is the man of your dreams. He may not be your final partner or he may. Only time will tell. But it is clear that his pheromones are doing something to you, that or his deodorant. You have not kissed him yet so the only object that you are fond of that you could put in his place was your Dad.

However he was not meant to usurp your dream man's place and you woke as soon as he did because the whole idea was repugnant to you, even in a dream. You are well orientated within your family. You love both parents but you are now searching for your own mate. Good luck to you.

"Yes. Yes!" Sexy Dream 1
Told me by a young male asthmatic.

"I am jigging up and down at this disco. The lights are flashing and the sound is all around and I am opposite this busty sweating gorgeous girl with dark hair in a huge frizzy halo round her head and it is going up and down not quite in time with her. I am mesmerised and get closer and closer and then we are on the floor somewhere and I am giving her one. She is shouting and I am breathless and I wake and I am certainly on my front in bed and I am wheezy. The useless oaf next door has got a party in full swing, with what sounds like the whole of his office in attendance."

Interpretation:

Good dream. I enjoyed that one. The disco came from next door as did the shouts from my woman. The exhaustion came from my wheeze and where my dark haired beauty came from I am not sure. I do know a fit looking woman at the sandwich bar where I get lunch. It might be her. I'll look at her closer tomorrow. I won't tell her what was going on in my bed though.

Comment and advice:

Yes a simple dream of sex. Young men have a fantastic sex drive so they are very often going to get sexy dreams about almost anyone they encounter and fancy, unless their sex life is very full. It is safer to dream than to have casual sex.

"Yes. Yes!" Sexy Dream 2

This one from an eighteen year old girl who is a music student.

"I am in an evening dress with a v-neck that comes almost down to my waist and it is some silky stuff that clings and billows. I am in a huge park and there are other groups of people sitting around. We are all dressed up. I seem to be looking for someone so I wander on and I come round some bushes and this man is there and I walk into his arms and he lifts me and carries me to a sort of grassy hollow. He lays me down and kisses me and then we are having intercourse and I am sort of anxious because I am wondering what his name is and how we will see each other again. And I am worried that other people will come and see us too and he is simply getting on with it and it is pretty good really and then I wake.

I don't know whether to be glad or sorry. It's not the sort of thing I would contemplate normally."

Interpretation:
Who was the man? I know that. He was the ticket collector on the train that I took yesterday. Did I fancy him? Not that way. I thought he looked like a film star but I did not try to chat him up. I don't think he even noticed me. He is however the tall dark type I like.

I have had intercourse with my boyfriend for almost a year now. We don't get together that often as we both live with our parents still. He is tall and dark too. The place was from a magazine I was reading on the train all about a music festival in America where people come and picnic and small groups play in the gardens. It looked fantastic. Pity the weather here is so uncertain or we could do it here too.

Comment and advice:
The dreaming brain often seems to bring out memories from the same time and place. So the gardens in the magazine on the train and the ticket collector all came in to her sex deprivation dream. This is a young woman's dream. She is fairly new to sex and her wish for more has triggered the dream.

Her boyfriend is tall and dark but he was not the chosen man of her dreams simply because the scene was from her train home the evening before the dream.

I expect that she and her boyfriend have sex in some interesting places where she may often feel nervous that someone will burst in on them. That feeling came into her dream from her own experience. Dreams often superimpose other figures on the man they actually mean to portray. She has no interest in the ticket collector. But possibly she felt, when she looked at him, that he was able to sweep her off her feet and her dreaming brain tells her she might fancy this. She might see if her boyfriend could oblige.

It may be that she is now looking for more emancipation, a home of her own and a man of her own too. She should think about this and discuss it with her boyfriend if she thinks he might be the partner to share her life with.

An Odd Sexy Dream

From a man of about twenty five who wanted to discuss its meaning. He is a violinist in an orchestra from the South.

"I am in this green room waiting to go on stage and the manager says please will all the violins go on two by two. So I pick up my instrument and they are going on ahead of me with a man one side and a woman the other. The manager says, "You'll be going to bed together afterwards," and that seems fine by everyone except when it comes to me I am going on with a man who I don't know.

He is a bit like a boy I used to have as my best friend at school. We went everywhere together and used to tell each other everything. He went down to London and I haven't seen him for nearly a year but I don't think we would change.

Anyway I say to him. "I'm happy."

I feel we could get on just fine and he agrees so we go on stage together and then suddenly we are in bed together and I have no clothes on and nor has he. I think he looks clean and lovely and I would like to stroke him but I don't want to be too forward. It is awkward. He should have been a woman. I am thinking about this when I wake."

Interpretation:
Does this dream mean that I am homosexual?

I like to go out with both men and women. I've had sex with a girl who I knew at school. She was very keen and it was OK. I live at home so I don't get much chance to bring in anyone other than for meals.

When the orchestra go on tour I usually go to the bar with the men. Half of them are having it off with the women, even the married ones with wives at home. I'm not tempted. What do you do with the woman afterwards? She is always there. I don't want to have it off with any of the men either.

Comment and advice:
I don't think this dream means much more than that you need a good friend. You clearly miss your friend from school days and have not managed to replace him with either a man or a woman.

This is a "one off" dream. It is a dream of loneliness and a need for companionship, together with an increasing desire for sex which is very normal at your age.

If you continue to have dreams of sex with men you might want to think about your sexual orientation. If you have sex with women as frequently in your dreams, your dreaming brain is giving you no real pointers in the sexual field. You are better to think by day what it is that you really enjoy on the sexual front.

Orchestral life is very exciting but it may not bring friendship. You might want to join a club or organisation outwith the hothouse that is your working life, so that you can do simple things like chess or rambling where simple friendships may grow.

School provides lots of friends to choose from. It is not so easy afterwards. You have to help yourself.

5

Scary Dreams and Nightmares

Inadequacy anxiety 111, stress anxiety 124,
threatened and terrified 137, automobiles 138, big
animals 143, birds and other flying creatures 147,
fish 148, nastycreaturecrawlyuppers 149, small
animals 153, people and 'sort of' people 154, snakes
157, werewolves and vampires 170, nightmares 178.

Scary dreams are the most common dreams to wake
to. So this is the largest section of the book. I have
divided it by degree of scariness!

● **Inadequacy Anxiety**
This is anxiety from a cause inside you. You are not
prepared enough. You have a sense of not being up for
it. You are in a crowd with no clothes on. You are
sitting an exam you haven't prepared for. Your teeth
start to fall out suddenly.

Inadequacy Anxiety Dream 1
This one came from a friend of mine who is a
medical student.

"I dreamed that a neurologist was doing an extremely

complicated set of tests on me which seemed like an intelligence test but with the added feature that you always seemed to have a choice of writing your answers on a space provided on the exam papers or in spaces on the test material itself, and the two did not always match.

I started off well but as time went on the crowd of about a dozen people in the same room, who were chattering and pottering around, tried harder and harder to distract me.

I said I hoped the test wasn't timed because I was slowing down a lot and having difficulty filling in a list of similes linking the words disillusioned and disappointed. Then one of the people commented, "Professor when I was helping you set this up, did you tell me that it is timed so that there is only three minutes left?"

The Professor agreed!

I thought, "My reaction to this unexpected stress is probably part of the test!" Then I woke."

Interpretation:

We had just started clinical work and I was getting used to being in a side room with others doing other experiments. I had to check case sheets and write up case histories and get the results on the pink pages and the history on the white sheets and the name and number and details of the patient on all of them. It is quite complicated when there isn't room to spread out and the other people working in the room are chatting and walking to and fro on their own work. The examination room reminded me of that.

It also reminded me of learning to drive when the instructor seemed to expect me to look in my three mirrors, watch the road ahead, change gear and use the clutch, all at the same time. I thought I would never manage but it has become automatic now.

Likewise in the hospital, I feel very useless at the moment. But I know inside myself that I have to continue and it will all come right. I think the dream told me that. It certainly made me feel pretty useless.

Comment and advice:
This is a variation of the "examination" dream where you are sitting an examination and nothing goes quite right, making you feel more and more inadequate and anxious about the outcome, until you wake. The two words, (disillusioned and disappointed), that you have to find similes for are interesting. I suspect that having chosen medicine as a profession you have suddenly realised that it is not all simple book learning or life saving operations, or even small surgical operations and clinical examination. It entails a great deal of meticulous clerking that has to be done right. There are always days in a student's life when you go home disillusioned and disappointed. Instead of saving the world, you appear to be a glorified bookkeeper. However the next day will bring interest of some kind. If you really want to be a doctor, the boring bits of the training are worth enduring and doing well. They will stand you in good stead sometime.

Inadequacy Anxiety Dream 2
This one came from a young executive who had fairly recently joined a new firm.

"I was in a new office in one of those tall buildings looking out over the Firth of Forth. Nothing was connected up. Although I would have liked my computer and desk set up at the window, the special plug socket and IT outlet were away from the light at the other end of the room.

This was a pity because the view from the window was especially fine, including an artificial pond or perhaps a flooded garden and beyond that the sweep of the water. As time went on I found I had no shoes on. Then, as my secretary started talking about the trials of living with an alcoholic husband and other people started taking part in the conversation, I found myself in a bed which had somehow appeared in the room and I had no clothes on. I knew I was expected to set up my computer but I wondered how on earth to do so from this embarrassing position."

Interpretation:
I had newly moved house and started a new job. I was settling in to both of these when I dreamed this dream. It appears to be work related because my wife and child and cat do not feature at all. The people in that office are strangers. My new office is not at all like that. It is a traditional room in an office block but I remember that we had been talking about how they were building a new Government building in Leith and what fantastic views of the Forth it must have.

At the time I felt a bit inadequate. All the others seemed to know what they were doing. It was hard to see where my expertise would fit in and there did not seem much work coming my way. Of course it all changed and work became routine in a week or two but that dream sticks with me. I must have felt pretty inadequate most days to begin with.

Comment and advice:
You are right to say your dream comes from your work insecurities. You feel at sea and so in your dream you find yourself with no clothes on in an unfamiliar room with unready and badly positioned equipment.

Did you have a passing thought for your old familiar job? I am sure so. However these dreams don't show severe unease. As you get used to the job you will stop having this sort of dream.

Talking to your supervisor and to your new colleagues will put you in the picture and give you a role. You will almost certainly find that the expertise that you can bring to the job is both welcome and looked for. You will then feel part of the team.

All dreams of finding yourself dressed inappropriately (dressed like a chicken at a formal party; wearing no trousers at a cricket match; naked in a crowd at a fun fair) have the same shape. You are nervous that others will notice your deficiency but they very seldom do, or if they do, it is without real emotion. These dreams are about your feeling of unpreparedness or inadequacy.

No one turns to point. You just fear that they might. That is the reason for the dream, your feeling that you might prove unable to deliver.

But in behind this dream must be the security that in fact you are up for the challenge. The others never notice your problem, only you are nervous. If you were truly anxious that they would think you were not up to the job your dreams would be very different (see stress anxiety dreams, page 124).

Inadequacy Anxiety Dream 3
This one was told me by a young actress who is trying to make her mark in television.

"I am on the beach lying on a beach towel that is sort of yellow stripes. Suddenly someone says that I am late for an audition and I jump up and rush to the car. I know where to go and I am suddenly driving in thick traffic all going the same way. I look down and see that I have no shoes on and I am still in my bikini with a shirt on top. I wake mortified and thankful it is a dream"

Interpretation:
The beach towel was curtains in one of those house make over programmes. I was watching it the night before the dream and really liked them. I remembered the colour when I woke.

As for the rest. I have just received an acceptance for a new part on a soap, so I suppose I am nervous about going in to rehearsals. They start next week. Though I think I know my part, I am never sure of myself until I have worked with the others, and gained the confidence I get from the director and other actors.

Comment and advice:
You are right about your dream. To minimise the risk of having more dreams like that you should work away at your part, even if you think you are secure. The more familiar the lines, the less chance of your feeling inadequate.

Inadequacy Anxiety Dream 4
This is one of my dreams.

"I was sitting in a big bare hall at a school desk. There seemed to be only me. I was expecting to have an examination on General Medicine but when the paper was put before me I could see that it was a specialist examination about eye surgery.

"I can't do this. It is not for me," I protested. The rather grave figure who had given it to me said. "You must sit it first." "It will take me years to revise for this," I complained. "Turn your papers over and

116

begin," he said and went away and left me.

I started writing but without much hope and I felt inadequate and resentful."

Interpretation:
I had just been asked to write a book on dreams and was delighted at first. However it became obvious that I needed to do a great deal of reading before I started writing and with a deadline closing in on me I felt both incapable and in a way resentful about my own inadequacy. Maybe the examiner was my publisher. I don't know. I had been talking about one of my sons the previous day. He is an eye surgeon and I remember I had said that I would not like to sit any of his exams as he was now so specialised that a simple family doctor was not in the same league. My dreaming brain had remembered my thought and reproduced it to confound me.

Comment and advice:
"I can't do this. It is not for me!" is the punch line from this dream. You know you are not ready to write the book. Get started on learning enough to do so. Even beginning to do the research will prevent your dreaming brain repeating that sort of dream.

The exam dream where you have to answer questions you have not prepared for is always caused by unpreparedness. It may be a relationship that you are being expected to take further and do not feel ready for. It may be a work situation where you are nervous of starting. It may be that you know in your heart you are not working hard enough. Your dreaming brain is suggesting you do further work and thinking on the subject. This dream seldom comes when you are sitting exams because you are usually pretty well prepared or doing as much as you can. If you are not, then look out! Your nights as well as your days could be unlovely.

Inadequacy Anxiety Dream 5
Told me by an older man who had been in the Foreign Office in the days when they wore bowler hats and carried umbrellas almost as uniform. Who knows? Maybe they may still do?

"I dreamed this when I was in my first year at the Foreign Office and I was still very green.

I was walking down Whitehall in my shiny new black lacing Churches, which my mother had bought me, because she said that really good shoes were important, and I had my umbrella and bowler hat on. Otherwise I was stark naked. It was summer and the breeze was welcome playing around my nether half and I was enjoying the walk swinging along, nodding to my friends and they appeared unmoved by my lack of clothes. But as I went along and saw all the other men in dark pinstripe suits I began to wonder if I shouldn't be wearing one. Then ahead I saw the head of my Section, an old buffer who demanded meticulous reports that were keeping me in the office far longer than I expected because I had to look up so much. He was dressed in a dark grey suit and a white shirt and a navy blue tie with some sort of motif on it. I could see him in the distance and as he approached I got ready to doff my bowler as he had a lady that I took to be his wife on his arm.

As we approached, I began to think that perhaps I should have been wearing more. I began to feel very underdressed and unsure of myself, and I woke.

I remember that dream from so long ago. It was a cracker."

Interpretation:
I can see now that it was a dream of anxiety. I was new to the whole way of working. I had just come down from University. Nine to five (or more) was a very different deal from student hours. I scarcely remember if there was anything especially difficult that I was working on. I think it was the whole ambience of quiet competence and capability that the people working in my section seemed to exude. It made me feel inadequate and incapable. I suppose I looked competent after a couple of years and gave the next entrants bad dreams.

Comment and advice:
A dream to remember. What a splendid picture of feeling not quite on top of a new job. This is a new entrant's dream. The fact that you didn't have it again shows how quickly you adjusted.

Notice how you feel well and happy in your dream, swinging along the road with the objects you are proudest of, your shoes, your brolly and your bowler hat. That is significant. You are perfectly ready to do the correct social thing such as lift your hat to your boss's wife. It is only your boss who makes you feel insecure. So clearly this is a dream of inadequacy at work. In these dreams it is never the other people who point the finger. It is your feeling that you are improperly clad. Your feeling of inadequacy.

Inadequacy Anxiety Dream 6
From a University Lecturer who was long past sitting examinations!

"I had just come into the examination hall, where I expected to sit a written exam of some kind, and was waiting for the signal to start. Someone near me seemed to be writing already and I soon realised that the exam had started; how long before I could only guess. I looked at the paper and found that the subject was "English", something I had not known about beforehand. The questions were sparse and apparently all I had to do was write an essay – on the subject of "English"!

At first I was nonplussed but soon started filling some rough paper with notes for an essay, beginning with a definition of language and proceeding via a historical review of the development of English and its spread through colonisation to its place in the modern world.

The trouble was that I had no idea when the exam was due to end and the invigilator seemed to have gone into another room. In confusion as to whether I should quickly start the essay proper, getting all my points down in case I ran out of time, for some reason I decided to go to the toilet which I seemed to know was several class rooms away. As I returned I realised that I had no clothes on at all. It occurred to me that I ought to be fully dressed when the exam ended so I started putting on all my clothes, the exam room somehow doubling as my bedroom.

As I started to wake up and recall my dream I realised with a sort of shock horror that the blank front of the exam paper, on which I had assumed I was to write my essay might have been only the cover behind which there could be numerous questions which I had completely failed to notice and which it was too late to answer."

Interpretation:

My wife asked me what that dream meant when I related it to her and I answered "It probably means that I haven't got a clue what I am doing!"

In fact I had newly been appointed as lecturer in my own subject which I may say is not English!

However I am looking forward to the challenge and I hope I am better prepared than I was in the dream. It is always a bit nerve wracking when you move from research student to lecturer and I guess it showed in my dream. I did once miss the last page of a maths exam when I was at school, just didn't turn the paper over, so I knew the stomach sinking feeling it gives you and that I woke to.

Comment and advice:

You know it already. The answer to that dream is prepare, prepare, prepare! Don't leave anything to chance. If necessary write out your whole first lecture so you won't freeze when faced with a lecture room full of students.

Being naked in a crowd is very common in these dreams. It is surprising how no one except yourself notices it. It lets you feel a threatening embarrassment very accurately. Notice how the need to urinate came into the dream. I expect you went to the toilet as soon as you woke up. Dreams are often a mixture of feelings. Look at them and interpret them bit by bit.

Inadequacy Anxiety Dream 7
From a female university student.

"I am going along the road by the river and suddenly it sort of widens into a square with a red carpet and there are cars pulling up outside and glamorous men and women getting out. It seems to be the crowd round a film opening so I go nearer and the crowd opens. Soon I am on the carpet prancing up into this huge room which is full of people all talking and chatting and I seem to be able to talk to a crowd of them. They bring me a drink and I take it. As I am about to drink, I feel my front teeth loosen and fall into my mouth. I don't know what to do. I am worried because I know that without them to brace the others my back teeth are insecure. Sure enough, they start to fall out too.

I am spitting teeth into my hand and standing in this crowd and no one else seems to see my dilemma. I am sweating and petrified and thinking, "How on earth is my dentist going to get all these teeth back into place?" when I wake and I feel gingerly round my teeth with my tongue but they all seem secure. I am most relieved but still a bit shaken by the dream."

Interpretation:

I am in my first year at University and living away from home for the first time so I can't depend on my Mum saying, "You look fine," or whatever when she sees me dressed to go out to special occasions. I am going to the weekly bash at the student's union with a group of my friends this weekend and I am a bit nervous about how I will get on.

I don't have a boyfriend to go with. I wish I did. I would be confident then. I'm not much good in big parties. I tend to get lost and miss out. I think that feeling of being in with all those smart film stars in my dream and finding myself in an embarrassing position, unable to smile, and with a handful of teeth and a great need of help from a dentist, gives the picture of what I am feeling about this Union

Dance. I don't think it is much fun when my nights are made unlovely by my nervous feelings. It is bad enough by day. I had been watching the film opening of Harry Potter on television the evening before the dream.

Comment and advice:
This is a very common dream. Losing your teeth is a dream of insecurity and a feeling of inadequacy laced with a dollop of nervousness. Your smile is your passport to friendship with others. Take those teeth away and you are left without the persona you are used to and that you rely on.

Like being without clothes in a dream the crowd round you seldom seem to notice your dilemma. It is your feeling of shock, horror. You are locked into your own difficulties.

You need to escape from your nervousness. Try on the dress you are going out in. Ask your best friend if it looks all right. Look at her reaction. Is she also a bit nervous? Share your anxiety. You can laugh about it afterwards when you are a big hit, or even if you are not.

Enjoy yourself.

Going in to a new environment and meeting new people is stressful until you get used to it. Some people never do. Some thrive on it. The former may have other dreams of losing teeth, the latter are unlikely to.

The trick is to be interested in anyone you meet, not worried about what they are going to think of you.

Losing hair is a variant of this dream. Your top fuzz fades away and you feel it go. Again no one but you usually notices. You are usually thankful to wake in the morning with a full head of hair.

Men who are actually losing their hair, and know it runs in the family and are upset about it, are more likely to have dreams of a grieving nature, allowing them to wake to a sense of loss. They need to go through the stages of grief to equanimity and acceptance.

- **Stress is where the anxiety comes from outside situations. Everything is too much. You can't go on. You are walking down a road, afraid that a roof tile will fall off and hit you, for example.**

Stress Anxiety Dream 1
From a divorced working mother with school aged children:

"I'm a single mother with three sons living in a flat which always seems in need of tidying. In my dream I am standing in the middle of the drawing room with a mess of lego and newspapers all round my feet. The phone rings. I pick my way to it and it is my younger brother who has four children telling me he is about to have another and I think. "Oh the poor soul. I know what it is like to have too many and he is now going to be overwhelmed by kids." I say, "Do come and see me," and he accepts, so I realise I shall have to get the mess off my living room floor before he arrives or there won't be any room for him.

I start putting everything into cardboard boxes but the lids won't go down and if they do they spring back as soon as I let them go. My ex-husband drifts in, and I tell him to go away as he is just a waste of space, and he disappears again. I am struggling to get the house reasonably tidy with very little success. Then I wake, thankful to see the carpet in my bedroom clear of detritus and know that I cleaned the house the day before."

Interpretation:
I have a full time job as a teacher which sometimes keeps me late in getting home. I always seem to be late for the children and I feel guilty about that though they have a great carer who will stay until I arrive. However she has her own life too so I do try not to take advantage.

Then my eldest started a paper round. I did not want to dissuade him as he needs the money and it is good discipline for him to start a job. However, it was the wrong time to begin extra work. He has exams coming up and really needs to revise for them. So half the time I get home to find the paper round undone and I have to go out with the two younger children and complete it when it is the very last thing I want to do. We are all toiling and I feel really stressed out and anxious that we won't get the round completed before I have to feed the family. Then I feel anxious that I haven't given the younger children quality time or checked their homework. Then I feel insecure because what would happen if I took ill. My brother's wife phoned me yesterday to tell me they were going to get an architect to give them an estimate for another room added to her house. So she will be busy and I can't ask her to help. It leaves me vulnerable. I don't know why my ex-husband appeared. He never helped in the house so what he was doing in the dream I do not know. But I guess the paper round triggered that dream. I think if he can't complete it himself my son will have to give it up. It would make us all a great deal less stressed.

Comment and advice:

Life is all too much, there is something horrid waiting round the corner, you need to tiptoe between obstacles that might give you grief.

You are being asked to do more than you can achieve and it is all too much for you.

You are walking on thin ice with nowhere to go but onward.

In these dreams caused by stress anxiety you are usually following some normal everyday occupation and then it all goes pear shaped. You find yourself in a precarious position and you try to make it better, or you are unsure how to react in case something dreadful happens to you and it all gets worse.

The papers all over the floor are a straight give-away. They won't be got rid of. They may be stuck into boxes but they pour out again as the lids leap open. The house is being submerged in them. You are right about what triggered the dream. It was the new paper round.

What does it tell us about you?

You like a reasonably ordered life, love your job and your children and find the day just not long enough. There is a strong feeling of needing to get things in the house organised and comfortable to live in. There is a strong feeling of being overwhelmed by having too much to do. The tide of paper and mess is rising over your head and you feel you have no help, no way of keeping up and forging ahead. What is worse you feel you can expect no help from any one as in your dream your brother and sister-in-law are going to have a baby.

If you are a single Mum do you often feel like this?

It is not uncommon.

This is the sort of dream where the tide is coming

in and you can't stop it. You are being overtaken by events and becoming helpless to get on with life because there is just so much to do.

Any mother with too much to do can get this sort of dream. It sets the problem firmly in the home. This is not a work related dream. You can cope well with your job. The paper refusing to be subdued comes from the paper round your son took on.

That day your brother told you he was about to build on another room to his house? Interesting that in the dream you thought he was going to have another baby. You might just be right!

This is being the old woman who lived in a shoe with so many children you don't know what to do.

I've felt it. You've felt it. What do you do about it if you start to dream about it?

First of all you must think what triggered the dream.

This new paper round is one obvious cause. However the need to simplify your life is obviously very close to the top of your mind. You are overworked and need relief before this sort of dream will stop.

What should you do?

Minimise your chores.

You have to work full time, but you need to look at your work load and your commitments at home, and see if they are reasonably balanced.

Are you giving your home and your children enough time? Could you come home half an hour earlier every day by adjusting your hours? If you as a family are committed to the paper round and do not want to give it up could you ask your children to keep their rooms tidy by themselves and get them to tidy their bedrooms regularly so that you do not have to? Are your children old enough to do this and to use a vacuum cleaner? Could the oldest one vacuum all the rooms and the younger ones help him to tidy?

What about the appearance of your ex-husband? There are few lies spoken in dreams and if you told him to go away because he was a waste of space then that is what you feel about him. This, at least, means that you made the right decision when you left him. You don't want or need him. Far more troubling would have been if you had asked him to stay or looked after him with longing. It then might be worth getting together with him more often and seeing if old flames could be relit.

It could also be that you were not really thinking of your husband at all. His appearance might just have been a male figure. You have three boys so it could have been any or all of them rolled into one that you thought a waste of space. That is not an unusual motherly sensation when directed at growing boys! It makes it even more important that you involve them in helping you to feel more on top of your housekeeping. That way lies peace of mind and peace of mind brings quiet dreamless sleep.

Stress Anxiety Dream 2
This was told me by a teacher.

"In my dream I was meandering around a big store looking at the new fashions with delight, walking through the china department marvelling at the amazing colours and twisted designs, heading towards the computer department when I suddenly thought, "Oh my goodness. It is at least three in the afternoon and I should have been in school teaching classes since nine this morning!" I felt a huge sense of panic and pulled out my mobile which I found was switched off and had ten missed messages on it and I just knew who those came from!

I really did not know what to do and I woke, thankful that it was all a dream."

Interpretation:
I did once feel like that when I forgot I was due at my best mate's birthday bash and was visiting my Mum and she had just put the dinner on the table. So I do know the awful feeling of having committed a real bloomer. Really it is a realisation that I hadn't done something I ought to have and that was exactly right. I should have prepared a lesson that I was going to give later on that day and I was too tired and thought I would leave it to do in my lunch hour the next day. I've never left things so late before, because I guess I am a bit obsessive about being ready for class so this was a one off and I suppose my dreaming brain did not like the insecurity.

Comment and advice:
Yes you are right about your interpretation. This dream is very common in all its variations. We have all had a dream like this when we have left something undone that we should have finished the night before. The cure is not to let the situation arise. If you are a meticulous sort of person, your dreaming brain is likely to give you a reminder that makes you wake sweating.

You might dream you were having a bath when you remember you should be escorting the Queen round a race track.

You could dream that you are miles up a hill when you remember you had just started an operation on someone and left the theatre for a minute and just wandered off.

You are always missing a starring role that you

know others depend on you performing. The embarrassment is overwhelming. Sometimes the dream is pretty close to real life. That just makes you feel worse! Get the job finished before you sleep.

Stress Anxiety Dream 3
This one came from a young social worker whose workload was largely composed of visiting clients in their homes.

"Some gangsters were hijacking a plane, standing in the aisle and pointing their guns at the passengers who were also gangsters and who froze in the process of drawing their own guns from under their jackets. The plane was very wide with a central row of seats. This seemed to transform directly into the entrance hall to some flats in which there were two corridors with the doors of the flats every few feet. I was standing at the entrance and looking for Flat 1, where someone I knew had just moved in. I was there in some sort of professional capacity. I found Flat 2, and lots of ascending numbers, but I could not work out where Flat 1 was. Then some one showed me a side corridor on the right which I had not noticed before. There was even a notice indicating that this was the way to Flat 1. The corridor led to a flight of stairs going down one storey. At the bottom, was a large open lobby leading to the entrance to Flat 1. There were tables and chairs in the lobby. It was more like an open plan restaurant than someone's home. The flat itself was clearly visible because the lower and upper floors of the flat were fronted with huge plate glass panels which took the place of walls. From outside, the scale of the flat looked vast. This impression was confirmed when I got inside. The lower floor was a single huge open area. It was so vast that you couldn't really see from one end to the other. The people who had just moved in were something like my sister and brother-in-law, but also different from them. The ceiling was striking. It was a series of panels each of which was covered with loose silky cloth which hung in a sort of billow, so that the whole ceiling looked like an inverted rough sea. The room was sparsely furnished, but at the far end was a bed and some other furnishing which was surprising considering that there were other rooms off the main area and rooms upstairs too. To the left of the room, the ceiling hangings came down lower and making my way into this more obscure region I came upon some sort of extension of the silky cloth motif which formed itself into a shape much like a sleeping dragon. I noted that the character like my brother-in-law did not want to approach this apparition in case it "freaked him out"."

Interpretation:
The dream gave me the feeling of mild anxiety I get at the moment when I am searching for a client's house. I have a map. I have the address. But it is never as simple as it sounds. I know that when I get to know the area it will be a great deal easier. My colleagues know where to go and I don't like to seem stupid so I never ask exactly where to go. I use my map and get on with it. But that is where the dream material comes from and probably the anxiety. I have to get a certain number of visits done so I can't take too long hunting for the right house. As for the beginning, it came straight from the television news before we went to bed. There had been a hijacking and my wife remarked how dreadful it must be to be

131

caught up in one. It seemed to set the tone of the dream.

The billowing cloth I can't account for. It reminded me of my wife's new evening dress skirt that billows in the breeze. We were at an outside do last week and I thought it looked beautiful.

As for the huge house, I hate large echoing houses. I may have watched a house makeover programme. I find other people's houses a bit daunting anyway. It is always better if my supervisor comes with me, though he is a very canny man and won't do anything rash. I sometimes feel like being a bit more positive.

Comment and advice:
Clearly a work related dream this time. The feeling of looking for the right door and being mildly surprised by the inside of other people's houses is part and parcel of a young social worker's day to day life.

Break the dream down into bits.

The first part comes from material you have seen recently, probably off television news as a real hijacking or in a film about hijackers. It doesn't seem to worry you as much as expected so it is merely setting the scene of mild anxiety.

Then the dream becomes more specific, tying the anxiety to your work and your frequent unease about getting to the right house at the right time. It is being shown in the dream because it is a feeling that you must get quite often as you get to know your area.

Then the surprise about the way the flat is laid out and the furniture. Scottish houses often have a bed in the living room. Old ladies keep one room warm and live in it. You are merely learning the facts of life. The glass walls almost certainly come from some place you have seen or read about. Perhaps they derive from remembered windows of houses you have peered into in your search for the right place to visit.

Freud would undoubtedly suggest that the billowing cloth was a sex urge getting tangled in your dream. It may be so. You are married, so probably not sexually unsatisfied, but you are young, and your sex urge will be strong, so memories of your wife's curves may haunt your dreams. Your wife's new dress certainly comes to your mind when you describe the billowing cloth. Perhaps that is why you go on to think of close relatives. Your brother-in-law is slightly older and you clearly like him in the same way as you like your supervisor at work. You respect him, you like working with him or going out with him and you listen to his advice. The two men may have become mixed in your dream.

The last part of the dream is probably a previous memory of discussing a case with your supervisor where he was advising caution while you were all for getting more involved with a case. Let that sleeping dragon lie was probably your supervisor's advice and it stayed with you to reappear in your dream.

This is not a world shaking dream but a commentary on your state of mind in a new job in a new part of the town. This sort of dream is just a mild reminder that your daily work leaves you enervated and mildly stressed. The anxiety in it is mild. It is likely that as you get used to the job the work will seem much less anxious making and so the dream will not recur.

What can you do to gain peace of mind? Not a lot. Peace of mind will come with experience. You could spend more time getting about your area, take someone with you who knows the place well for a week if it is possible. Ask your colleagues or supervisor if they have any experience of your cases, until you feel as confident as they appear.

When you wake always consider if there is something you could do to give you peace of mind.

Stress Anxiety Dream 4
From a middle aged lady, now widowed, who has travelled a great deal.

"I am on a river bank, something like the Rhine, watching four ships or barges coming down past me. The first one is extremely long and self steering. A boy is with the others and seems to be in charge. I see one hitting a rock in the bend of the river and tumbling on its side. It has a yellow hull. The boy is thrown in the water. The next boat will run into it. I run and shout to the father to let him know and to help. A woman says she will go in her fast motor boat. I see a man has one ship already on the bank on its side and is bailing it out. How can one person upright a ship? How can it be done anyway? This is what I am thinking as I wake."

Interpretation:
I had been looking at old photographs the night before and some of them had been from a holiday in Bruges where we, my son and I, had watched long barges go down the waterway and been amazed that they did not ground on the bank. I remember he had said he would like to have sailed one. I suspect he was the boy in charge of the barge. They held huge containers that could take a whole house's furniture. I know that because when we moved to Scotland our

furniture was delivered like that. So when I look at piled cases I often wonder if it is the worldly effects of some family and where are they going. I have been thinking of moving to a smaller house but the effort of moving and doing it all by myself seems superhuman and I get very anxious at the thought. My friend Anna however had been talking to me about the benefits of a move and said she would help me. I wonder if this dream of possibly running into disaster and finding it too much was something to do with her visit yesterday.

Comment and advice:
I think you got the trigger for your dream right. "How could one person manage" is the theme of the dream and the thought you wake to. The transition from peaceful boats sailing down river to an emergency state with you rushing to help provides the feeling of anxiety that you went to bed with after your friend's visit. Your friend even appears as a single lady saying she will take her speed boat out to help.

You should make a decision, one way or another, and then not get anxious about that decision but set in place what you need to make it a success. If you are to stay you must arrange things so that your present house is ideal, perhaps get more help, or flat it so that you only live in a small part. If you are to move you need a house mover that gives you total confidence, you need to find the right place and you need a supportive lawyer. Then you will not wake feeling, "How can one person manage?" You may feel excited but that will not give you anxiety dreams because you will have peace of mind.

Stress Anxiety Dream 5
From a friend of mine who is a Community
Psychiatric Nurse

"I was working in a mental health centre but had a
small outpatient session arranged from about 3pm
to 4pm at a centre somewhere else in Glasgow. Time
was tight and I was forced to walk right out, quite
rudely ignoring several people who wanted to ask
me things.

I took the motorway, thinking that it was the
quickest, and that is where things started going
astray. Instead of a normal motorway it was much
more elaborate. First there were grassy sections with
road markings on them acting as one way valves.
Then the whole thing seemed to take on the appearance of an amusement arcade. I noticed that I had
passed some colourful information boards and after
some hesitation went back to look at them. However
the second time round they didn't look the same and
it was a futile exercise. Eventually I realised I was on
Govan Road and thought I spotted a notice for the
Clyde Tunnel, which would take me to Maryhill,
albeit by a rather roundabout route.

However Govan Road has those big bends and I
realised that in each bend there was an official
building which I could go in and I seemed to think
this might be a good idea as someone seemed to
think I was doing a clinic in another building. I
never did reach Maryhill and I gradually woke in a
thoroughly confused state."

Interpretation:
I had been working in Glasgow but I had moved to
another city and had just started a new posting.
Getting to know the area at the same time as getting

to know my patients was a very sharp learning curve and there were nights when I came home thoroughly confused. That dream took me back to the city I knew but gave me the feeling of stress and anxiety that I feel on bad days.

My job is to go round to visit clients in their homes, so this is clearly a dream from work. My home situation is simple. I live alone and moving was not a problem. I am being pushed by the work load right to the limit of what I can cope with. It will get better I hope as I get more used to the place and the patients.

Comment and advice:

Yes, a work dream. Overstress in your new job is the cause of the dream.

But look at the beginning when you push past people rudely to get out in time. Could that come from something you have experienced in the surgery you work from? Do you feel less supported by the doctors in your new surgery than you expect?

For the rest, travelling with no success in getting to where you want is a very common stress dream. It makes you wake with the emotion of desperately trying to catch up.

If you have this sort of dream you should look at your work load and make adjustments if necessary. You can only do so much. Try for more and you will wear out emotionally as well as physically.

• Threatened and Terrified Scary Dreams

The Lions have asked me to dinner or is it for dinner/ It's behind you! Run!

Dreams of being chased or threatened are the most common sort of dreams.

Look at the list which follows for what it is that chased or threatened you and read about other people's similar dreams, what they mean, and how to interpret yours.

Threatened and Terrified Scary Dreams:

Automobiles, Big Animals, Birds, Fish, Nasticreature-crawlupyers (insects etc), People, Small Animals, Snakes, Werewolves and Vampires
These are important dreams that you are meant to remember and act on.

You Wake Feeling:
Pursued or threatened by some known agent, person or animal. You are able to run and do so. These dreams often precede a nightmare. You wake scared, anxious, full of blind panic, wanting to hide, fearful of being found, or found out, breathless and panting and unable to run any further, or falling.
    These dreams are different from a nightmare
1   Because you feel you can move, even if not fast enough!
2   They have strong pointers in their story to show you where your fear and anxiety are coming from.

●   **Automobiles. Cars, lorries, tractors, bicycles, tanks**

Automobile Dream 1
Told me by a mechanic in a garage.

"I'm in the garage with a spanner in my hand and all the cars are moving about as if their brakes are off. It is terrifying. I have to try to make it to the front

138

door and get out but no way am I going to manage, so I duck into the pit which seems to be there. The manager says "The sides won't hold if a tank comes in. You'd better get out before the worst happens." Then I see this Sherman like in an old black and white movie and it is coming towards the pit and I can't get out in time though I am scrabbling at the walls which seem to have got much higher. Then I wake, panting."

Interpretation:

This was certainly a serious scary dream. The cause appears to be firmly rooted in my work. It may be because yesterday the supervisor was talking about management encouraging voluntary redundancy. I didn't say anything at the time but I was seriously worried. I've been there for fifteen years now and I'd find it hard to get another job if they asked me to go. It is always us oldies that are given the heave. It isn't the time either because my son wants to go to University and he'll need money. My wife works. She is out all day. I don't know what I would do if I hadn't the garage to go to. I don't know whether to say anything at the works or not. If they don't notice me they may not pick on me. I haven't told the wife either.

I wondered where the tank came from but I was looking at Second World War films of D-day and the Normandy push the night before and those Shermans made quite an impact clattering up and down through the hedges and fields. I should not have liked to be in one or to service one. I thought so at the time.

Comment and advice:

Just the sort of lifestyle threat that would precipitate this dream. You need to talk it out with someone and your wife is the obvious first. Once another supportive mind has been brought to bear on the problem you will feel less exposed. The tank came from your television watching the night before. That is so often where the scene for a dream originates. What the Manager said in the dream, "Better get out while the going is good", is certainly an option in this situation and it seems that your dreaming brain is already suggesting that you should be looking around for another job while your day thoughts are about hanging on to the one you have. Probably a good idea to do a bit of both, stay put but look around for something without making waves at work. Anxiety is often minimised by bringing it out into the open. You need to talk about your fears to someone you know to be on your side and work out a strategy.

Automobile Dream 2
This one was told to me by a middle aged man who enjoys reading books on historical subjects.

"I was in an 18th century house with Corinthian pillars in front of the front door, possibly by Adam. I was watching from a large room as someone in the hallway, side on to me, was working a light cannon which was being used to reduce a castle in the vicinity, but out of sight, outside the front door. The understanding was that patience and repeated bombardment would get the job done, but the cannoneers were impatient and intended using extra strong powder. This would possibly speed the destruction of the castle but would also have distinct risks including production of poisonous fumes unsuitable for the present indoor situation of the cannon, and also a greater possibility of the thing exploding.

Later in the same dream, I was in another large house and some people were lounging about relaxing in a spacious conservatory. Outside I could see the rubble of a collapsed building, presumably the castle which was being bombarded earlier. I intended going out to use the toilet which was nearby. Luckily, however, I glanced out of the window in time to see a huge JCB-like machine making towards the house, evidently about to smash through the wall. The people in the room seemed remarkably unconcerned for their own safety, possibly just moving to the other side to be out of the line of attack. They were joking that the machine seemed to be making for me and I'd better run for it, which I had started to do when I woke up."

Interpretation:
I know where this dream starts from. The beginning bit comes from my home life. We don't live in an 18th Century house, more like a late Victorian villa, but we are putting in a new central heating boiler. I am very nervous of gas appliances being tampered with, let alone replaced. I do feel that they can explode and turn us all into rubble. So I guess that my unease in the beginning about gas fumes, and explosions all comes from that deep seated worry and won't be assuaged until the boiler is in and I am convinced there are no gas fumes after the gas central heating men have left. Then I needed the toilet in the dream and when I woke that was correct too.

The rest of the dream with the JCB was more puzzling. The people were not from home. Yet I did not feel that they were from work either. I told the dream to my wife and she laughed and said, did I not remember going in to see what the central heating men were doing, and did I not remember being so fussy about them making sure all the pipes were properly connected that one of them said that I should trust them to do it right but if it did go up when they lit it it would be better if I was somewhere else and she had taken the hint and got me out of the room to let them get on.

I suppose that could have made an impression that I had forgotten but my dreams hadn't. In fact they did it very well. I am very sensitive to gas smell and there was none when they had finished. So they did a good job. Maybe they needed my reminder!

Comment and advice:
This is a dream with different bits to it. Most long dreams are. The dreaming brain seems to throw everything in to one dream once it has caught your attention. You must have been reading about cannons and early warfare or seen it on television. There are plenty of historical recon-structions available on the history channels. So your dream made your house the right vintage for a cannon and got on with telling you that your mind was not at ease about your new central heating unit.

The need for the toilet was an add in and then the dream produced something very like what the men said to you to try to get you to go away and not fuss them when they were work-ing. Your brain remembered even if you had forgotten.

Just as well the new central heating boiler works well so you can sleep with peace of mind and not get another dream of impending explosion.

Big Animal Dream 1
This one came from an older lady who travels widely.

"We were out walking, a friend somewhere in the background, a little terrier with us.

There are several sheep fairly far away, crossing slowly from one small island to another through water. The dog was barking. He wanted to cross in the opposite direction and was disturbing them so I seized him in my arms and held on to him while all the sheep crossed. Just then I saw the back of a lioness on the opposite side of the water, walking away. Beside me was a stream with a big waterfall to the left. I thought "Ah! There's safety. I will hide under or behind the waterfall." But I didn't. The dog was still barking and the lioness looked round and then padded towards us, getting bigger and bigger. Suddenly I confronted her, but I saw her through the railings of some sort of balustrade, cast iron and decorated with scrolls, and there were fragments of rock, sharp fragments, lying around. But the lioness was now a woman who spoke and sneered and seized a rock and threw it at me. I wondered, "Should I let the dog go and let him get killed and save myself?" But I held on and took up a stone rather tentatively and somewhat feebly threw it at her, missing. I cried for help and tried to throw other rocks, missing, and then I selected one of them with a particularly sharp edge to defend myself with, intending to hit the side of the woman's head. But then I remembered that it was a lioness that I was fighting and it began to dawn on me that this was serious, that I was actually going to die and I had better face it. I quickly tried to say "Our Father which art in heaven . . ." and imagined my death happening, torn to shreds, all bloody, the huge lion's jaw seizing my head; a slow painful horrible death. I told myself I must be brave, but this was it. I might as well let the dog go. Then I woke. My heart was racing and I was glad I was alive!"

Interpretation:
The dream has to be about something in my home life. The hills where I like to walk were very like the dream, and the opening of the dream gave me a slight feeling of anxiety when the dog barked at the sheep. But it wasn't anything I couldn't handle. I picked up the dog and held him.

The lioness was a surprise but I had been to the zoo a couple of weeks before with my nephew and I remember thinking how powerful those lions were and being glad of the iron railings between us. So what has happened in my life recently to give me such anxiety?

I have a new neighbour. The old lady who used to live next door had become a friend. She was there when we moved in and I remember she brought us both into her kitchen and fed us tea that first day when we were exhausted. We didn't sit in each other's pockets but we were there for each other and after my husband died I used to drop in to see her occasionally and her advice was always sound. However she was getting pretty old and I used to keep an eye on her as much as I could. Her garden was going to seed, and so was the house, and she moved into sheltered housing last year. The new owner is a much younger woman. She works in some sort of accountancy job and is clearly high powered. All Summer, she has horrible, noisy, boozy Sunday lunch parties in her garden. The music from her ghettoblaster is ear splitting. There is only a hedge and some iron railings between us so if I am sitting out I appear to be butting in on her party. They look at me and pass remarks. It has made my life miserable because I used to like my quiet weekends in the garden.

Foolishly I did ask her if she had parties scheduled for every weekend and she looked very threatening and was very rude. I would have liked to have picked up a stone and thrown it at her, but that was pretty childish of me. I know I shouldn't be frightened of her, that I should stand up to her but it is frightening when you are alone. I think that dream was all about that fear. The little dog defeats me except that I had one like him years ago and would hug him when things went wrong.

Comment and advice:
This is certainly the fear left after that traumatic confrontation.

The railings between the gardens are in your dream. The woman turns into a lion and back and eventually comes after you so you are really afraid.

Your dreaming brain is magnifying your trepidation at facing down your neighbour. You clearly dislike her a great deal and that is a pity. But dislike is usually based on fear and so your first job is to get rid of your fear. If you can't beat 'em join 'em is not a bad idea. I suggest you hold a party for your neighbour. Try for congenial people for the neighbour, not only the older set. But have a few of them around too. It is surprising what will happen to your neighbour's attitude if she is exposed to people, whose opinion she respects, telling her what a good person you are, and how even tempered. She may soften. She may even ask you back to her boozy, noisy parties and though you may never really want to emulate you may prefer to be on her side of the fence. Being talked to is better than being talked about. Better to make friends than have bad dreams.

Big Animal Dream 2
A young man's dream.

"I am out on a sort of Braveheart / Rob Roy film set hillside, all heather and long views down to a loch, when I see this big black horse coming at me. I take one look and turn and run. There is a sort of drystone dyke like an old sheepfold and I get behind it. I seem to have a sword and I wave it at the horse which is coming for me. It rears up over me. My sword wilts like a flower stem and I wake. Just as well too. I was about to be trampled. I had no doubt of it. I was busy making up my mind which way to get out. I hadn't given up. I get that dream occasionally. It is always much the same."

Interpretation:
I've seen enough war films from by-gone days to produce this sort of dream picture with no trouble. But the dream is exciting and frightening and at the end I feel very vulnerable and helpless. I used to get it at school before examinations or big cricket matches sometimes. Now I get it less often but I had it the night before I went to interview for a job.

Comment and advice:
This is a sensible young man. You greet challenge with aggression but also caution. Freud would suggest that the wilting sword in your dream suggests

that there might also be the beginning of sexual interest and a nervous wondering how you will perform when you have intercourse. This has got mixed in to the excitement engendered by an examination the next day, or the challenge of a job interview. This dream tells you that you are nervous. It does not tell you whether you want the job or the exam pass desperately. That would be a dream where you would pursue the horse!

- **Birds and other flying creatures**
One of mine:

"I had watched Jurassic Park 3 and when I went to bed I dreamed that the pterodactyls were after me. It was a snippet of a dream. I was running and they were diving and I had my cat in my arms. Then I woke."

Interpretation:
It was time for the cat's inoculations. I had just read an article about it being bad for cats to have too many inoculations so I was very worried about taking him but I knew that if he was not jabbed then he could not go to the cattery. I had a holiday coming up and he was booked in. So I half felt like taking him and running but my sensible side said not to believe everything I read.

Comment and advice:
Dreams about birds are not usually dreams of pursuit. They are glorious creatures and in flight are more likely to derive from contented thoughts or soaring wishes. This lot certainly came out of the film.

147

Fish Dream 1

This one is from a legal secretary who has newly gone back into full time work, having divorced her husband and moved house to a different city with her teenage daughter.

"I was in the sea somewhere in France. I was swimming along with my young daughter beside me when suddenly I see a commotion in the water and everyone is racing for the shore. I hesitate and then the splashing comes towards me and I see it is a huge fish. I shout at my daughter to swim for the shore but she laughs and does a somersault in the water. I am screaming at her and trying to swim towards her and the big fish is after us but she is quite unworried. I am not a great swimmer and I am panting and struggling and getting slower. The fish is almost on us and I am trying to get in between it and my daughter. I am shouting, "Just work a little harder and swim for heaven's sake". But it is fairly hopeless, and when I wake I am still panting and terrified."

Interpretation:

My daughter has a music scholarship which makes it possible for her to go to a private school. When she won it I was over the moon. The school is within walking distance of where we live and the local school is not, so as I work full time this was an amazingly lucky break. She deserved it because we had worked and worked at her violin and she played so well at the audition. I was tremendously proud. However adolescence has struck. She now refuses to play in orchestra or practise the pieces. It is a nightmare. I get letters from the music teachers which are now positively threatening. They will remove her scholarship unless she produces the goods. I don't know what we would do if they took it away. I have to be at work early and I haven't time to take her miles to the local school. My work record would suffer. I don't want to lose my job. I am terrified of what she is letting us in for. She seems to have no idea. I think that dream was about that.

Why we were in France I know not. I had been looking at holiday brochures the night before the dream but we have not been on holiday there though I remember thinking we might be able to afford a week in Brittany now that I had a decent salary coming in.

Comment and advice:
I'd go for that interpretation. You must feel helpless and desperate in this situation. The dream provides all these feelings. You need to be open with your daughter and explain your situation. Teenagers have it hard. They are constantly being asked for more and more commitment at a time when their emotions are evolving and they need time to themselves. However they usually don't want to lose out either, and are plenty old enough to understand family finances. A big carrot called a holiday in Brittany might help. There may be residual hangups from the divorce as well. You have to put yourself in her shoes and remember back to her age. Don't panic and shout.

- **Nasticreaturecrawlupyers such as slimy creatures, wasps, bees, insects and spiders, butterflies**
Dreams about these depend entirely on whether you are afraid of them or love them or have no real feelings about them at all.

The ones in this chapter are ones you feel scared of. Remember it is the emotion they bring out in you that counts. For instance, if you like tadpoles and frogs your dreams about them will be caring and found in "Upper" Dreams or simple Physical Dreams. If they frighten you, this is the chapter to look for your dream's meaning.

First make your mind up whether they point to your work or your home life. For instance if the wasps are in your office it looks as if someone at work is giving you grief. If they are in your kitchen or living room, look nearer home. Now read these dreams for the one that feels the same.

Nasticreaturecrawlupyer Dream 1
From a nurse friend of mine.

"I am lying in bed. It is not my bed but it seems right that I am there. I think it is in France because it seems very hot and I have thrown off the sheet. I see a movement at the foot of the bed and something dark and crawly is working its way up the sheet towards me. I wriggle away from it but it comes on and I see that it is a huge woodlouse which has sprouted a tail like a scorpion. I know if it stings me I will die and I can't make up my mind whether I should move or stay still. I am pondering this when I wake, well covered in my own bed. I stay there until I am sure there are no creepy crawlies anywhere."

Interpretation:
I'd been looking at an old Disney television film on insects so that is where the scorpion came from, that and I was gardening in the afternoon and dug up a nest of woodlice, Ugh! They went everywhere and I am not very partial to them. So I guess the dream

had to be something I am scared of at home. I work as a nurse and there was nothing about hospitals in the dream.

I thought about it and in the end I wondered if it was that my partner wants to get a kitten. I am distinctly unkeen. I just think cats are sly sneaky scratchy beasts and the thought that one might be roaming the house while I am asleep makes me very nervous.

Comment and advice:
The dream is saying, "Do I stay where I am and accept a kitten or do I up sticks and run." It may be that your choice is not as stark as your dream suggests.

You do seem to have a number of things that you dislike – woodlice, kittens – what else? Possibly you are almost obsessionally interested in cleanliness. If that is the case you need to come clean with your partner. Tell him your worries. If you have a good relationship he will not want to jeopardise your peace of mind. If you love him you may want to try to get to know kittens of various breeds in case you find one you can tolerate. It is possible too, to keep kittens in certain rooms only. They seldom can open doors (although I had a Siamese cat who could open lever handles).

This dream follows a pent up horror in your mind. It is destroying your equanimity and should be brought into the open and allayed.

Nasticreaturecrawlupyer Dream 2
From a friend of mine who is paranoid about wasps and works full time as a social worker.

"I am walking along a lane and I see a wasp coming

for me. I swat at it and turn to run but it comes too.
I duck and weave but it is there and it is about to
sting me and I am screaming when I wake."

Interpretation:
What am I so frightened of? The lane reminded me
of the paths behind my house so is it a dream of fear
at home? I thought about that and I am about to
have my mother-in-law to stay and she drives me
mad. She offers to darn the children's socks. My
mother does the same when she comes to stay but
she doesn't say it in the tone of "You do nothing for
your children," like my mother-in-law. She offers to
help me with the cooking too. I feel so put down and
cross. I just can't bear it. I want to swat her. I want to
run.

Comment and advice:
Could be a correct interpretation. This is one fear
that you can do something about. No one wants to
stir up trouble. You have to meet your mother-in-law
half way, defuse the fear and antagonism by trying
to see where she is coming from. Let her darn the
socks and thank her. Tell her how much you appreciate the help. Tell her how busy you are. Same with
the cooking. Stand back. Let her loose and let her
tidy afterwards. It may be delicious. Take her out.
You don't have to like her. You only have to love her.
It is easier. Look at dreams of running and see why
you have to run. Is there an alternative? Always
remember she may be having much the same dreams
about you. The older generation is always in awe of
the young.

- **Small Animal Dream 1**

From an old lady who is a patient of mine.

"I am in my kitchen. I open a cupboard and it is full of mice. They are crawling about. I hate mice and I shut the door but when I look on the floor there are mice there too and they are all over the cooker and I think, "I need to get away, or the rat catchers will come and they'll lock me up for having all these mice." and I am afraid and I wake up."

Interpretation:

It is silly really. My daughter was in visiting last night and she insisted on cleaning out my kitchen cupboards. She said all the stuff was out of date and if I wasn't careful I would have mice everywhere and she threw it all out. Then she started talking about sheltered housing but I knew she meant a nursing home. I don't want to leave my house. I brought the family up here. My husband died here and if I move I shall leave all the good times I remember with him. I get panicky at the thought. Children can be cruel and not know it. I know my daughter meant well and it was good of her to take the time and clean my kitchen. It hasn't looked so good in years. But I was very frightened after she left.

Comment and advice:

This is a dream of fear. The fear is not of mice but of being taken from your house. As you get older you have choices to make. You have made yours and as your doctor I shall try to respect it. I suggest you call a family conference and ask for assistance either in kind or in cash for a home help.

153

She got both I am glad to say. I hope it continues.

So often dreams of fear are brought on by moments of panic. Thinking through the fear may show some way to resolve the problem and relieve the anxiety. Once you are sure you have isolated the fear your dream is showing, you try to resolve it so you have peace of mind. Then the dream won't return.

- ## People and "sort of" people

People Dream 1
From a young man who has a school age daughter.

"I was in a car waiting for my daughter. Two men tried to get in the back and I said "Sorry gents, you're in the wrong car." They got out but then they or two other men got in more deliberately and I realised that they meant no good. I said, "Hey, I'm waiting to pick up my daughter," but immediately had panicky imaginings about what would happen if my daughter got involved with the car jacking as well as me. I gradually woke up as a series of scenarios suggested themselves, such as driving into a scrap yard and trying to make a run for it, driving to a police station, or driving across the road to block the path of an oncoming police car."

Interpretation:
This was an anxiety dream stoked by my daughter wanting to come home on her own. I suppose all parents have moments of panic when their children want to start the road to independence. I had been watching news films of some photographer or news-man being carjacked and it must have fuelled my

general unease. The end bit seemed to be more and more under my mind's control and I thought it might be what is called lucid dreaming.

Comment and advice:
Time to organise things so your daughter can feel she is gaining her independence. You will have to teach her to get home by bus or walking so the first thing to do is to do it with her and then try to get her to come home with a friend. It takes a while and I can remember spending some interminable minutes waiting at the drawing room window, when I realised that one of my children was not home when expected.

By the end of the dream you are trying to manipulate the story to a happy ending so lucid dreaming is probably right. I doubt if you were in REM sleep, more likely stage 1 or 2 non-REM sleep just before waking.

People Dream 2
From a University lecturer in Chemistry.

"I was discussing ethics with two colleagues over the body of a large Frankenstein's monster which was lying face down on a rough bench in a warehouse or farm building. After staying silent for some time and listening to the conversation, I felt I was making a decisive point when I interjected that I was against this sort of experimentation on principle because of being a vegetarian (this seemed a telling point at the time!). Shortly after that, without quite knowing how it happened, I found that the monster had regained consciousness and was up and shambling after me. I took to my heels at top speed, hoping to confuse it by threading a maze of turns through interconnected outhouses. I suddenly came to a turning at which the sunlight flooding in was interrupted by a large rectangular shadow. Was it a harmless inanimate object or was it the monster lying in wait? As I looked harder at the shape, trying to decipher it, I became conscious that I was looking at the rectangular shape of the bedroom door picked out by the faint yellow light from the kitchen downstairs. I had woken up. I needed to go to the toilet and I must say that I was a bit nervous about leaving my bed."

Interpretation:
The family had been watching a Frankenstein film that evening so willy-nilly I was watching it too. At the same time I was reading an article on some sort of ethical dilemma about cattle farming and chemicals in the feed and I remember thinking that as a vegetarian it did not affect me personally, but that it was important that we all had an opinion on the subject, so they got a bit mixed.

The main part of the dream was running away. It was in a warehouse or farmsteading so I think this had to be a work oriented dream and caused by a work oriented fear. I am not naturally anxious about my work but it was coming up to the time when we put in for our research funds for the year. I knew that huge cuts were planned so I have been uneasy about these and I hoped that, if I hurried my results along, it would show that the work was worth funding. Perhaps I saw the commission that will visit as the monster. That could be it.

Comment and advice:
Certainly that dream gives a feeling of quite strong fear of being pursued by something pretty frightening. Something big and unknown is after you.

Yes, probably in a work context. Waking to look at the doorway framed against the light is a common occurrence. It is a bit disorienting for a minute but is due to the effect of the light on your eyes outlining the door edge and being transmitted to your wakening brain. Think round a dream like this. The fear is magnified in your dream but there is something that is making you feel like running away. Look carefully for it. I am not sure that you have the real cause of your fear. It may be something quite simple, like hearing that someone you don't like is coming to visit your laboratory, and you want to get away.

- ### Snakes alive!

Dreaming of snakes? What does it mean? Snakes are specially emotive symbols in dreams so they get a place to themselves in this Section. There must be people who see them as cuddly creatures but they are in the minority. To many people snakes are very frightening creatures.

Anyone who has been brought up in tropical areas where snakes abound has learned to be afraid of them.

I am one of these and for me a dream of snakes is a dream where I am afraid. In the morning I have to work out what I am afraid of, and take steps to neutralise that fear.

Snakes are powerful images and dreaming of them always means that you are troubled by some strong emotion. Sigmund Freud, the father of psychoanalysis, suggests that snakes in dreams, like neckties, are symbols of the penis, the male sex organ. A snake could represent a father, a husband, a brother, or any male figure. For a group of people who had little experience of snakes except through books and pictures or in the zoo, he was probably right but lifestyles have changed and so dream symbols also change their meaning. Snakes may be pets to some people, threats to some and sexual symbols for the male organ as well.

Dreaming that snakes are threatening or invading your sexual areas are sexual dreams and if you are frightened should be taken seriously. Are you longing for more intimate relationships?

Were you half excited, half repelled by the snake, but secretly wanted it to come closer? Were you totally repelled? If so, are you quite content with the partner you are with? This is likely to be a dream of home-based relationships but does not have to be. It could be about a close relationship at work where your colleague is doing something you cannot like or is coming on heavy when you have no such feelings for him or her and feel threatened.

Does what he does, or wants to do, offend you in any way? If you have just met, is he going too fast into physical love for your peace of mind? Is he too old for you, too experienced, too insistent?

Do you feel comfortable with the sort of sex you are having? If not, do something about it. Talk about your preferences, however hard that is. If your partner truly cares for you he will accommodate your desires. If he will not, you have to make your mind up whether you can tolerate what is going on or whether a break in the relationship, even a temporary one, might not be a useful idea.

Is this snake a half perceived threat from some one else who is invading your area? Has your preferred partner cooled off you recently? Do you sense a rival for his attention? The dreaming brain is sometimes quicker to notice small signs that by day you want to discount.

Certainly this sort of dream is to do with relationships and is a significant dream, especially if it is repeated night after night.

If you enjoy the dream of a snake invading your more private areas, it may be that you are looking to be more adventurous in your sexual encounters. You may just be missing sex and have a physical need for it that is being transmitted to your dreaming brain. For further information look at the chapter on sexual dreams. However, dreaming of snakes is not always about sex, whatever Freud says.

Snake Dream 1
Here is one that I was told about by a retired teacher.

"I may be retired but I try to keep myself busy. However, for some reason, this week has been a real rush. Once you give up work you need to have a few things to do regularly or your life becomes featureless and chaotic. I go swimming on Tuesday and play tennis on Thursday. On Tuesday I am with a class of ancients doing water exercises to music and on Thursday I exhaust myself on indoor tennis courts with a cohort of my age, encouraged by a young thing who is clearly anxious that we don't all get heart attacks. My bridge club meets on Wednesday and at weekends I try to walk with friends and change my library books and such like. Use it or lose it is my motto. Given that there is something going on each day it is difficult to fit in extras. Why this should be when I worked full time and never had any problem fitting everything in as well I do not know but there it is. This week has been too full.

There was my routine yearly eye test to go to, my

shoes needed new heels, I had to get my winter coat cleaned and to cap it all the vet sent in his yearly appointment for my cat. I began to work from a diary sheet consulting it two and three times a day to make sure I was not missing anything. I hate to be inefficient. I dislike it in others and even more in myself.

Last night I dreamed I was in a rather bare room, perhaps a bathroom, and two large yellow, almost translucent, snakes came into the room through an open topped pipe that came up through the floor.

The snakes were shiny and full of energy as if filled with yellow oil. They were a bit repulsive but I did not want to kill them. I decided to block off the exit through the pipe by placing something on top of it. It would have to be something heavy, I decided, as the snakes were strong and active and would push anything light aside.

Whilst I was attending to the snakes and looking about for a suitable weight I suddenly noticed that my cat had stolen and eaten a piece of Dover sole and was about to start on a piece of haddock.

When I woke I wondered what it was all about."

Interpretation:
The dream gave me an exhausted feeling. I woke thinking that I needed another pair of hands. I think that is what it was trying to tell me.

Comment and advice:
Good interpretation!

This is a lady with more on her plate than she can manage.

Snakes don't frighten you so I expect you were not brought up in a tropical country where they are generally considered frightening creatures that creep round, appear unexpectedly, and have a fatal bite.

These snakes seem rather jolly, appearing out of a pipe and bounding around with enormous energy rather like the yellow tennis balls you play with once a week at your tennis class.

However you realise that you must keep control of them and stop them disappearing so you take sensible steps to do just that.

However just as you are concentrating on that, your cat is making off with your favourite lunch. It is clearly a case of not having enough hands to deal with the situation.

The vet's appointment appears to have been the last straw and so that is why your dreaming brain has been overwhelmed by animals, all of which you seem to quite like.

You need to ask for help with some of your activities so that you no longer feel pressurised and this sort of dream will not return.

What does it tell us about you?

That you have a well of sympathy and kindness to animals. You see no threat in the snakes. You want to protect them. You are not too upset by your cat thieving the Dover sole. You may regret it but you have no desire to chastise the animal, more a resignation that this is cat behaviour. You are clearly fond of your cat.

It also shows that you take on more than you can realistically perform, probably from a kind heart, and so, when you have overdone yourself, your dreams have to remind you that you are destroying your peace of mind.

The answer to this sort of dream is to simplify your lifestyle. Don't let people put upon you more than is comfortable for you. Ask for help when it all gets too much.

Snake Dream 2

From a middle aged gentleman who lives alone, is coming up to retirement, but who has always taken his holidays as tours to different parts of the world.

"There are two animals about to fight with each other. One is a small mongoose-like creature, a stoat I thought at first, but then I thought more like a pet. My first impulse is to keep it from harm. The other animal is a big snake and when I first see it I think, "Oh! He will kill the weasel or whatever it is, with his fangs and I wonder if I should take up a stone and smash it. But then I decide quite definitely that I must not interfere, that matters must take their course, that this is nature's way etc . . . When the ferocious fight begins they seem to be quite evenly matched. The snake's fangs are not poisonous and the other creature's sharp little teeth try to tear bits of the snake's skin off.

They fight quite a long time, but it doesn't look a deadly fight. I am not frightened and I wake up before it is decided."

Interpretation:
Well, the snake in this dream was a bit of a frightening creature. Snakes don't make me terrified but I am a bit afraid of them. This one makes me feel alarmed. The other animal engenders a feeling of protectiveness. I thought about this kind of double set of feelings. It is like watching a boxing match where you support one of the fighters. When I thought about it like that, I was forcibly reminded of the quarrel two of my friends are having about a company that they have been asked to invest in. George has been asked to be chairman of it and so he is keen to invest but needs another backer who

162

will be a sleeping partner. He sold the idea to my other friend, Hamish, and it was all set to go when Hamish got cold feet and pulled out. George was furious and tried to get me to get at Hamish. I thought they pretty much deserved each other and I decided to stand back and watch the fur fly. Funnily enough George is a bit of a slimy one and Hamish is a quicker snappier little chap, more like a terrier than a mongoose, but there are similarities. I had been looking at brochures for holidays in India and thinking of Kipling and his Jungle Book stories the evening before the dream.

Comment and advice:
The feeling is not strong enough to suggest that this is an argument that involves your family. The feeling then would be far far stronger and you would not decide to to hold back as you do in the dream. Your own family have a profound effect on your emotions that is mirrored in dreams.

Here you decide eventually that you must not interfere. That is your dreaming brain's decision and clearly, having slept on it, should be your own decision about whatever fracas you had been contemplating entering.

The snake is a powerful opponent. You must have felt when you went to bed that whoever it represents, a person or a company, was formidable. However as your dreaming brain mulls it all over it comes to the decision that the apparent underdog will do very well and that is what that dream is telling you. This is the sort of advisory dream that is well worth paying attention to.

Keep your nose out of the disturbance. It is nothing to do with you. If you wake with the strong feeling that you should stand back from some fight, look at what is going on around you. Go over in your mind all the disputes you might be getting involved in and think well before you throw yourself in on one side or the other.

Snake Dream 3
From a well-established assistant producer in a television company, who had been brought up in India.

"In my dream I am walking out into the scrubby jungle behind my family's home in the Punjab. Very soon I can see snakes beginning to wriggle about in the grass by the path. Soon I am walking amongst them and I am terrified because they twine themselves round my feet and I know that, if I tread on one, it will bite me and then I will die. I come to a stop. I cannot go forward. I cannot go back. I am terrified of treading on a snake and arousing it to kill me. Yet I can see that the snakes are getting more and more active around me. I just know that in a minute one of them is going to bite me and then I'll die. I try to call for help but I can't get any sound out. My boyfriend wakes me and tells me I am making dreadful squeaks and groans. I am thankful to wake up and find myself safe in bed with him."

Interpretation:
I never knew why I had that dream. It was my boyfriend who worked it out. One morning, after another snake dream, he said, "Do you realise you only get these dreams the night after you have come in complaining that your producer has been getting at you?"

She is trying to get me sacked. I know it. When she starts on me I get very frightened indeed because this is the work I love and where else would I go?"

She thinks I am no good because I want to bring an ethnic slant to the programmes. She says "keep it simple", but I am convinced we could double our audience if we angled the chat shows to include more minority speakers. She has been trying to get me fired by maximising any little mishap that I am involved in and I get very worked up and anxious because this is all I have ever wanted to do and I don't want to be sacked.

Comment and advice:
It may be simplistic to say that you see your supervisor as a snake in the grass but it is very close to the mark.

You feel threatened, helpless and frightened every time your supervisor gets at you, so much so that you come home and dream about it. It is interesting that you do not dream about problems at work. This must be because you feel no anxiety about what you are doing. It is only the threat from one woman that worries you.

If you come home upset by yet another confrontation, talk it out with your boyfriend and try to get it in proportion before you go to bed. It is unlikely that, after years of work with the same company, you are liable to be fired out of hand. That thought must give you security. You might also get to know other producers whose thinking more closely approximates to yours, and see how your ideas appeal to them. By widening your field and making your thoughts more generally known, without appearing biased or pushy, you might gradually influence those who matter.

Snake Dream 4
This is one of my dreams.

"I am getting ready to go out, changing into an evening dress and nothing is going right. I trip over the dress and get frightened that I have torn it. Then it seems too small a size and I know I am going to be late and everyone will be cross. As I pick up my scarf to put it round my shoulders it becomes a huge boa constrictor snake. The iridescent scales wink and shine in the electric light of the room because it seems to be dark outside. It slides over my arm and I am rooted to the spot in terror. I don't want to go anywhere. I wake up still frightened."

Interpretation:
I know what that dream was telling me. I had to go to a meeting with some NHS officials and I don't like the chief one at all. I think he is a two-faced slimy chap who has his favourites and I am not one of them. I was unhappy about going. I knew that nothing I suggested would be acceptable and could only cause further bother for me in the long run. I already realised that I should take it very easy at the meeting, say nothing and agree nothing but appear to be compliant. I scarcely needed that dream to tell me to be the last person to leave the meeting room, so he could not bad mouth me!

When I dream of snakes I am always upset by the dream and over the years I have come to associate these dreams with awareness that I am facing serious opposition and calumny from someone. Sometimes by day I have no idea what is going on but, when I look more carefully, I always eventually find that I am being seriously criticised by someone close, just as that television assistant producer found. Big

166

snakes, big problem; little snakes or only one small snake, little problem, but always a problem that needs care and attention to avoid hurt to myself.

Snake Dream 5
Again one of mine.

"I was walking along a little path beside a stream with one of my grandsons. He was about seven and lagging behind then rushing ahead and I was keeping an eye on him to make sure he did not fall in the water. As we went along I noticed something moving out of the corner of my eye and when I turned to look it was one of those green jointed plastic snakes that children delight in and I dislike. I backed away and it went rattling and leaping past me on the path and then it turned to face me and hissed, its mouth wide open and two long white fangs showing. I was petrified but my grandson said "Just love it a bit more and it will disappear." So I picked it up and it curled round in my arms and became a warm furry yellow mass, very like my yellow eyed Burmese cat whose wide yawn now looked just like the open mouth that the snake had shown me."

Interpretation, comment and advice:
Now I knew that one of my colleagues was giving me a hard time at work because I had suggested that she was not pulling her weight in the Practice I work in. I did not need that dream to tell me that she was lobbying all the rest of my colleagues and trying to turn them against me. I knew I would have to be very circumspect yet very firm until it all blew over.

However this was a mixed dream in that I was also being reminded of my shortcomings in ignoring my cat. He is a yellow Burmese and a very companion-able animal. He likes to be with me if I am in the house. But when I am at my computer I shut him out of the room and he hates that. However, if I let him in, he sits on the keyboard and I hate that even more. So lately he has been missing out on affection and my dream was reminding me of my omission. When I woke my conscience agreed with my dream, so I took him for a walk in the garden at lunch time and played with him and let him curl up on my lap all evening. I put a contented cat to bed that night and my sleep was also dreamless.

Make these dreams work for you. If you find a dream that recurs in certain situations remember it. It may provide useful pointers in the future. If I dream of snakes I walk warily.

Snake Dream 6
Another of my dreams.

"I dreamed I was looking for ripe mangoes. It is years since I have seen a mango tree full of fruit but in my childhood there was one in the garden. Each year I would climb into it and reach for the close-in fruit. I was not walking in a garden however. In my dream I was in a jungly kind of place with big trees round me and there was a dripping sound as if it had been raining. Behind me I saw a huge snake fall from a branch. It turned and came for me and I ran. I seemed to run for ever and I could go no further. The snake was almost on me and I woke panting and sweating."

Interpretation:
The duvet was too hot for a mild night and I threw it back to cool off. So the dream sweating came

from a feeling of too much warmth in the bed. But that was the least of my problems. Somewhere someone close to me was miscalling me, stirring up trouble in a big way. This was a big and hostile snake.

I lay and thought round the possibilities. The jungle did not suggest that the problem was at home. So possibly at work? I could think of nothing pertinent but the next morning the dreaded brown paper envelope from the Health Board arrived on my desk. Oh yes! A formal complaint from a patient!

Doctors hate them, rightly too because they are born out of venom and hate. I consider I have failed my patient if that is the feeling I have allowed to grow in a patient's mind.

This one was probably not going to give me too much grief. She was a bit of a herb and joss stick burning freak, but she did have a serious chronic condition in one ear. I did not know her well and when she came to me with a flare up I looked back into her notes and found a consultant's letter which said clearly that if she ever got worse she must be referred forthwith to his department, or she could lose her hearing altogether.

I told her I was going to refer her and she got very cross indeed and told me that she was going to treat it herself. I had tried to persuade her to accept a referral. She became abusive. I begged her to see my point of view. I would be negligent if I did not get her the specialist care she needed. She was rude. In the end I said that it was up to her what she did with the appointment to see the consultant but I still felt I had to refer her. That argument must have lingered in my mind.

Comment and advice:

My dreaming brain must have known that I had not satisfied her; that she felt real dislike of me and my decision and had a desire to hurt me in any way she could. Writing an account of the incident, quoting the consultant, sending it all off takes hours of work that could be better spent seeing patients. It upsets the whole surgery because they all get anxious if one of their doctors is being complained about, for whatever cause. My dream had been the usual warning system.

When I dream of snakes it is always because my subconscious has picked up a threat to my peace of mind from some other person, so much so that when the dream happens I greet the morning with "Who hates me now?"

Look at your dreams and see if you have a threatening dream that recurs only when you are facing trouble from some colleague or friend. If so use it as an early warning system. Defuse a troublesome situation that is building. Assuage mounting anger against you. Make sure you are not treading on someone's toes without meaning to. These are helpful dreams. Take heed of them.

● **Werewolves and Vampires**
(Very very scary dreams but not yet nightmares)

Werewolves and Vampire Dream 1
Told me by a young man who had trained as a hairstylist.

"I started a hairdressing business a year ago. I did it all by the book; took a haircare diploma, worked my passage under a real misery guts of a cutter (but, boy! Could he shape the fuzz), wrote a business plan, applied for grants, persuaded two mates from college to join me and opened my own salon not far from where I live so my Mum could send all her girl friends with a promise of discount if they were old enough.

We are still in early stages but we are building a list of regulars who come for six-weekly cuts, and even better weekly wash and sets, though probably the person who uses the equipment most is still me for me.

In this dream I am visiting my Mum. "Hi! Mum," I shout as I walk in the door and breeze into the living room looking round to see if there is something to eat. My Mum makes ace cakes so there is usually something lying about. Her particular mates are gathered there, sitting in a row on the sofa. I've known them all for years, wash and set them weekly now, so I give them a nod. "I'll put the kettle on," says my Mum and she shimmies out through the door to the kitchen. The trio on the sofa watch her go and when they turn back to me they have changed into werewolves or vampires or whatever, sabre tooth incisors dripping blood, hair straggling over their shoulders in need of a good cut and all.

They get up off the sofa, their long fingernails curving in my direction. They don't look as if they are asking for a discount for washing those greasy streaming wierdo hair styles.

I back off, but they follow. "Hey" Hey! What is this? I'm out of here." I turn to run. "Can't stay for tea, Mum. Must rush now."

I am away out the door with the harpies after me. They drift over the furniture like a bucket of water tipped over the floor and they are growling something horrid. I am asthmatic but you should see me go. The werewolves are gaining, however, and I am panting. Then I wake. I need my asthma spray but I am still shaking with fear.

Mostly I forget my dreams but this one is still with me at breakfast."

Interpretation:
This is a dream about work. That's clear enough. I think it was triggered by a council tax bill that came in yesterday morning. Funnily enough it was on top of a colourful pamphlet advertising some Werewolf film or other, all gory faces just like those women turned into. They are my Mum's best friends and they come to get their hair done, but often I think they just come to see how I'm doing. Any sign of failure and they pounce, like if there is no one in the salon. They make remarks and I gnash my teeth a bit. But that's life, I take their money and stay polite.

I was breathless when I woke, so I think that chase was all about a physical feeling of breathlessness.

Comment and advice:
So do you really love your mother's friends? I think not. I bet they sit and mutter together about young Hamish over reaching himself with all this entre-preneurship and getting his own business stuff. I bet you know it too. Your mother will have told you.

You are right about the asthma making you feel breathless even in the dream. You would need your inhaler when you woke.

Why the dream?

Could have been the council tax letter. One extra call on your slim resources and possibly one that you had overlooked. You are so anxious about your ability to pull your hairdressing enterprise off. If it were all in your hands you would feel less troubled, but your success depends on other people coming in to get their hair done. You must sit and wait for them; that is not easy to live with and you must often have panicky feelings through the day.

If you have had a particularly bad week and the returns are only just breaking even or perhaps not quite reaching the weekly level you know to be necessary, you will go to bed with the fear of debt collectors at the door. This threatening pursuit has been reproduced by your dreaming brain most accurately and colourfully enough to make you remember it.

"Do something to bring yourself peace of mind," your dreaming brain is telling you. "Don't sit like a frizzy perm on a partially sighted client and ignore the problem. Make a feature of it! Put a notice in the window offering a lunch-time walk in quick cut. Stay late on a day when you know people want their hair done after work and most other hairdressers are fully booked. Think of something to make you feel more secure financially, and by night you will sleep dreamlessly."

It is interesting that you don't see your mother amongst the vampires. There is a clear distinction. You see your mother as supportive, getting you a cup of tea, looking for cake. You obviously have a good relationship with her.

Werewolves and Vampire Dream 2
Told me by a University girl student, studying Mediaeval History.

"In my dream, I was walking back to my room across the Quadrangle. The University and residences are in a series of squares with open courtyards. I saw my tutor, Dr. James, across the courtyard and I turned to wave. I like the old buffer.

So in my dream there I was waving to Dr. James across the quad and he looked straight at me and recognised me and his face changed. He turned into one of those gargoyles that they have in Mediaeval churches, the ones with open mouths to drain the rain water off the roof, and terrible frightening faces. Then he came for me. The black gown he wears to lecture in swept out on either side of him and he was flying across the quad at me, his teeth shining and long and his mouth pale pink and dripping blood.

I turned and ran for my room, in the door, up the stairs and along the corridor. My door wouldn't open and he was right behind me and I knew I was going to die and I woke, screaming."

Interpretation:
It was very embarrassing. The girl next door came in and asked what was going on. I said that Dr. James had turned into a werewolf gargoyle from Montmartre Cathederal and was chasing me, with his black gown making him able to fly, and she started to laugh. I didn't feel like laughing. I was still shivering with fear. However I did know why I had dreamed it. I was simply not shaping up and I was terrified at the possible consequences.

Up till the morning before my dream he only humphed a bit when I put my essays in late. I never seem to get them done in time these days. It's having a real boyfriend at last that is the difficulty. We meet every afternoon after class and somehow the time passes and the library is closed and I don't get the research done in time so how can I write it up? John is a mathematician, so he seems to carry it all in his head. He doesn't like it if I say I am not going to meet him. Anyway that morning Dr. James had given me a bit of a shock. He said I would fail if I couldn't get the set work in promptly and have it fully researched. I had never been threatened like that before and it upset me a great deal. You see I really need this degree or I won't get a decent job with a reasonable salary. That's important because my mum and dad aren't rich and are already talking about retiring.

So I was rabbitting on in my mind about how unreasonable Dr. James was being to me and what an old misery guts he was, and I had been watching Scooby Doo, a cartoon that I am partial to, and it did have a werewolf chase. I think the television programme gave me the story for the dream but it was my conscience that hit me with the story line.

I knew what to do. I didn't enjoy it but I told Ron I had to work every afternoon and he drifted away, but I got my degree and I got over Ron and married another history graduate in the year ahead. We were always the last two in the library and somehow we started going for coffee together after we were ejected. He understands about research time.

Comment and advice:
You are right. This dream was only one stage before a nightmare but it shows clearly that it is about your work situation. You found your world turned upside down by your tutor and you turned him into a threatening figure. You did the right thing. You changed your lifestyle to prevent these circumstances persisting. Did you have dreams of grief when you lost your mathematician? Perhaps your next boyfriend came along too fast!

Werewolves and Vampire Dream 3
This dream was told me by a young P.A. who has newly started in a demanding office job as assistant to a marketing manager in a big firm.

"I am walking along a corridor carrying some papers. The lighting is not too good and the walls are a muddy green. I hear someone behind me, her heels tap, tapping on the pale wood floor and I look round. It is another P.A. in the office I think, though I can't immediately put a name to her or say which department she comes from. As I prepare to smile at her, her face changes and she turns into a sort of vampire woman and starts coming on towards me faster and faster. I turn and run. My papers fall from my hand but I am not going to stop. She is gaining on me and I am breathless and despairing. I know I can't escape and suddenly I appear to be running in treacle. My legs won't move. A heavy weight presses on my chest and I try to scream but no sound comes out. Then I wake. I am shaking."

Interpretation:
I guess I brought that dream on myself because I watched a Vampire movie on late night television before I went to bed. It wasn't too believable when I watched it but it was scary in my dream.

I am anxious about this new job. Every day is harder than the last. There is so much to do and remember and the office is suddenly really busy. I am afraid that I won't measure up and they will ask me to leave. I am on probation for six weeks so they can do that. My supervisor is not helping. She kind of creeps up on me and if I am not hard at it she clicks her tongue and fades away.

Comment and advice:

This starts as a really, really scary dream and goes on into being almost a nightmare. The change comes when you are suddenly unable to move and you feel a heavy weight pressing on you. Both these feelings are typical of a nightmare. Before these you are able to run away and indeed are trying to. It is very common to start in a scary dream and go on into a nightmare, or to have repetitive scary dreams in the nights before the nightmare. A nightmare is after all really the final stage in sheer anxiety and fear. You can usually avoid nightmares by sorting out your worries as soon as they are beginning to give you bad dreams. After all your dreaming brain is only trying to get you to address your worries during the day so that you may have dreamless rejuvenating sleep.

I would say to this young girl. "You have landed this job because they liked you and thought you could do the job. At the moment it may appear to be very like early driving lessons, where the instructor seems to think you can look ahead, look in three mirrors, watch your spedometer, hold the steering wheel in two hands and use your signal lever as well as your gear lever all while operating three pedals with your feet. You remember thinking, "He must be joking", but now it is second nature and you cannot perceive any difficulty.

Similarly, your work routine in the office will become second nature. It is hard if there is a sudden burst of activity while you are becoming accustomed, but it will make you proficient sooner in the long run. Go to your supervisor. Tell her you really enjoy the job and ask her help in establishing a routine now, so that you know all the things you have to do. She will be flattered to be asked and she may well have shortcuts that you could use. You will no longer feel you are battling alone and have no support. When your worry diminishes you will not be prone to nightmares.

• Nightmares

What is a nightmare?

It is a really terrifying dream from which you wake so frightened that you are scared to get out of bed. The fear stays with you. It is often unspecified, creeping after you, a heavy weight pressing you down. Your legs won't move when you try to run. You have a very real fear of imminent horrible death from something that you don't see clearly.

Nightmares come to you in dream sleep (REM sleep), just like other dreams. They are not the same as night terrors or sleep walking or sleep talking which arise in non-REM sleep (see Section 2, page 16 of this book for a description of these).

Nightmares usually are nonspecific. They may be preceded by a scary dream that pinpoints where your worry is coming from but once you are in to the nightmare it is just a powerful feeling of terror and impending doom.

Sometimes a nightmare will replay an awful happening in your life. These are special nightmares and are part of what is called a post traumatic stress disorder. I will describe this further after describing some nightmares that people have told me about.

Where does the word nightmare come from?

The second half has nothing to do with horses. It is from the old English word, "Mara", a monster from Hell who, in mediaeval times, was thought to range round the country by night and where possible, enter your bedroom while you slept. He would leap upon your chest, suffocating you while he tore your throat out, or raped you, or both. If you woke in time "Mara" was scared off. Our ancestors woke feeling that they had had a narrow escape. That feeling of being lucky to be alive after a nightmare still affects you without needing to believe in spectres.

A visit from "the night hag" or "a riding by the witch" were phrases that used to be used for nightmare. The French word for it is "cauchemar", the "fiend who tramples".

In the Middle Ages fear of being associated with witches or Hell-spawned beings was very real. The clergy tended to stress you to destruction. If they thought you were a witch they burned or drowned you and considered that they had purged you of all evil. If they were wrong they felt that they had merely expedited your passage to heaven. So people put up with bad dreams, especially nightmares. They kept the horror to themselves and therefore little work was done to alleviate them until Freud and his fellow psychoanalysts brought dreaming back into the symptomatology of medicine, thereby making nightmares an acceptable thing to complain about to your doctor.

Nightmare 1
This is one of mine:

"It was my third night of having an anxiety dream and I did not wake fully. I had a terrible dream of a high official of some kind who told me that I would have to resit all my medical examinations the next day, despite my pleading that I needed to revise, look up text books and smarten up my knowledge. I half woke, sweating and had enough time to remember saying to myself "Oh no! Here it comes!", when I was gripped by sleep again and found myself walking along a hospital corridor.

Modern hospitals are all high-tech, with windowed passages and pleasant decoration. Where I trained was an old Victorian hospital whose wards were light and busy, if crowded, but whose internal corridors, high oblong boxes with curtained ward doors, were lit at night by forty watt bulbs that left a shadowy effect. In my dream it was even darker than that. The greenish paint on the walls did not help. It was not a corridor I knew but it felt familiar. There were doors off it, presumably into wards, but I felt hesitant to take them. I did not know what was on the other side of the doors and they had no numbers or nameplates. They were not for me. As I went on the corridor narrowed and became less high. I could suddenly sense something very frightening behind me. I started to hurry but I found I could not. I appeared to be walking in treacle. Nothing would move though I struggled to run. There was a weight on my chest pressing me down and the something behind me was very very close. I made a superhuman effort to run and woke with a jerk, panting and shaking and still afraid. My heart was doing nineteen to the dozen and it took me several minutes before I dared sit up and look round to make sure no one was there."

Interpretation:
I deserved that nightmare. I had an imminent deadline for a book and had not been giving it all my attention. My family commitments and my music agency had been taking any extra time after my ordinary day as a family doctor. So I had been having anxiety dreams and I had not been doing

anything about them. This was my dreaming brain's final warning. I took it and got on with the research I needed for my book and slept the better for it. In the first instance though I used one of my anti-nightmare techniques (see page 191 for "Treatment of Nightmares"). When I looked at the picture my nightmare conjured up, that dark corridor, other childhood memories of dark verandahs began to surface. I was brought up in Sri Lanka in a lonely bungalow on a rubber estate that my father managed. Night falls at about seven o'clock, so children are often still up and playing about at that time. I used to be a little fearful of the dark and the silence and the odd sounds of what I thought were wild animals beyond the rather frail lights in the house. That fear remains with me, though now I am able to ignore it as silly. My nightmares however obviously make use of that fear to make me terrified.

Comment and advice:
Nightmares are the final and strongest message your dreaming brain can send you that you are anxious and insecure or have some fear or guilt that is overwhelming. The interesting thing about them is that they have afflicted most people throughout time and are documented since dreams were first talked about. That is at least three thousand years ago.

Nightmares are classified as sleep disorders, unlike anxiety dreams which are not. They tend to decrease in intensity and frequency with age, though women continue to report them into a later age than men. Perhaps men become more self confident with age!

Everyone knows the horror of having a nightmare. It is the dream that turns into a terrifying experience with monsters, dreadful people, or just a menacing presence never seen but creeping up on you as you try to escape. Whereas in your dreams you can move freely, in nightmares you cannot. You try to run but your legs won't move or move so slowly and with so much effort that you scarcely cover ground.

In Rapid Eye Movement sleep, which is the main time when dreams occur, your limb muscles lie almost paralysed. I believe that this message is being interpreted by your dreaming brain as an inability to run. There is always a mounting sense of terror and usually an enormous pressure on your chest which makes you gasp for breath. This feeling, I believe, stems from the fact that your ancillary muscles of breathing between the ribs and in the shoulder girdle are also immobile in REM sleep just as your limbs are. Usually just as you are about to be engulfed you wake, sometimes with a wild movement or a yell, as your limbs and voice become unlocked in wakening.

Nightmares are not forgettable. They stay with you and if recurrent, make you unhappy about going to sleep. They may be so frightening and threatening that they overwhelm your mind by day, blotting out the anxiety or guilt that caused them in the first place with a growing apprehension, as the day draws to an end, that you will have to face another night with its attendant horrors.

Nightmare 2
From a woman of about twenty one.

"I seem to be walking to school. I have a backpack on and school shoes and a skirt and blouse so I must be younger though I don't feel any different from usual. I am passing this house, it is the last in the row before crossing the road to the school and I know it is full of frogs. I hate frogs, nasty slimy things, so I walk past very quietly so no one opens the front door, because I know that, if they do, the frogs will pour down the path towards me. Yuk!! So I tiptoe past, holding my breath, knowing they are pressing against the door trying to get out and get me. Then I cross the road and suddenly I am in the school corridor. It gets narrower and narrower and now there is something behind me that is simply awful. I don't look round. I am much too frightened but I try to run and my legs won't move, or very slowly. I try to scream but nothing comes out. I feel my chest tight. I can't breathe. I am about to be extinguished by whatever is behind me and I wake, shaking in every limb. There is no way I am going to move from my bed. It takes me twenty minutes to calm down and put the light on and search the room before I'll even try to sleep again."

Interpretation:
It was a real nightmare. I haven't had one like it since just before my big exams at school. I had one then, much the same. I guess I am heading towards another crisis in my life. My boyfriend wants us to go backpacking for six months in Indonesia. I don't want to lose him but if we go I have to give up my job which I like and am in line for promotion in and start again. He can pick up a job anywhere because he is a qualified electrician. It isn't the same for me. Besides I hate hot wet places and nasty creatures. I like walking, which is how we met, in a climbing club on the top of a hill. I don't have any desire to go to Indonesia. I can't think why he does. Just the thought of it makes me sweat with fear. You hear such nasty stories about back packers in these tropical places. I know the brochures show a different picture. I know I may be being silly but I am being pushed into a corner and see no way out."

Comment and advice:

It is a nightmare situation and it reminds you of your last nightmare situation which was at school. There is a typical lead in following a dream of acute anxiety where you are threatened by the frogs and then you are in the nightmare, unable to move with a heavy weight on your chest and something awful behind you. While you are still in your anxiety dream it points towards your problem with going to Indonesia. The frogs waiting to get you are very suggestive of your thoughts on tropical travel. Once you are in the nightmare, you are just in a terrifying situation, and you have dredged that up from your last big crisis which was at school. You may well have the same nightmare throughout your life, though the lead-in anxiety dream will be different and reflect the current situation.

You are very very anxious. On one side you have a boyfriend whom you love and want to be with. On the other you have your own career to look out for. The scene is further complicated by the fact that you have found a major dissimilarity in goals and life-style favoured by your chosen mate. Nightmares give little clue as to your real desires. They just show you you are afraid of the next step.

You have to bring your fears into the open. You have to level with your boyfriend. If he understands and cares, he will sort things out. If he wants to travel and see the world you may have to choose whether you go with him or not. He may settle for a three month trip and you may be able to get your employer to hold your job. He may wait a bit so that you can achieve a qualification that you can use to get a job when you get back. It looks as if you have been going along together with different aims and ambitions that you have not shared. Now is the time to get closer to each other by sharing your thoughts. Love is a great welder. Even the most rigid ideas can change in its heat. You may gain security in his care and he may understand your worries and make provision to allay them.

Nightmare 3
Related by a middle aged man.

"I am bicycling down the main road towards my house. I know it well and suddenly the bike goes over and I am thrown over the handle bars. I wake as I am about to hit the road and I know I am about to be very badly hurt. I lie still when I wake. I am seriously shocked by the episode and it always takes me a while to recover."

Interpretation:
There is no particular trigger for this dream. It happens occasionally and usually when I am more stressed than usual. I did fall exactly like that when I was very much younger. Same place too. I broke my arm and the pain was pretty shocking then. I still remember it. I must have been about twenty at the time. When I get it I get over the shock and then I think round anything that is really worrying me. There is usually something and I know to sort it out. It is not that I get that dream often.

Comment and advice:
This is the sort of nightmare that you get with post traumatic stress disorder. This nightmare is the repetition of the accident that caused the disorder in the first place. Many people have accidents or terrifying incidents in their lives, but not every one gets PTSD

and the nightmares that repeat the causative accident or horrifying occasion. These nightmares repeat the incident that has been so terrible, so frightening or so abnormal that the participant has been overwhelmed by the experience. An example is being the only survivor in a car crash, being a rape victim, or witnessing a murder. Soldiers in action see and participate in horrors that remain with them. Every war has thrown up men who could never forget the horror. In the First World War doctors called it "shell shock". In the Second World War it was "battle fatigue". Post traumatic stress describes the condition better. The sufferer has flash-backs of the incident or incidents which can occur at any time. Also at night he has nightmares that are severe, and recur, and may make the sufferer unwilling to attempt sleep. This makes it all worse.

Behind the condition is often an answering childhood fear that is exacerbated by the accident. There is also a hefty dollop of guilt and anxiety. The anxiety is understandable but the guilt less so. It is often completely irrational. For instance a rape victim will feel that she could have done more to prevent the attack. Perhaps she is even afraid, in retrospect, that she initiated or somehow caused it. The same happens with a car crash. The survivor, instead of feeling lucky to be alive, feels that in some way he is at fault because he is the survivor. In war this irrational guilt is even more marked. "Why did I live through it when my friends died beside me?"

In a smaller way some heart bypass or transplant patients are unable to assimilate their good fortune. Patients have said to me "I was really dead for quite a while. I can't accept that I am alive again."

Guilt is irrational and damaging. It needs to be

assuaged by full exposure and you yourself pardoning yourself, because you see clearly that you could have done no more than you did in that circumstance.

I see this most clearly in patients who come to me demanding the abortion of an unwanted pregnancy. At the time all they want is to be free of this incredible, shaming, disruptive remembrance of a self indulgent moment. They have their own agenda for their life and it does not include a baby. They want a menstrual period to occur instead so that they may go back to classes, continue their modelling career, become a lawyer, or a computer whiz, or a senior manager, anything but become a mother and lose earning power and a desired lifestyle.

Sometimes this matters. Their whole life would be ruined. They acknowledge their mistake but surely it is easily rectified? Yes it is, but at a cost.

The cost is knowing that they have taken a life, however vestigial. I may counsel my patient that she must think about the options; that she is now, however unwillingly, in a different ball park with different rules. She must make her decision, knowing that at the time she makes it, it is not a whim but a serious decision; that at the time she makes it, it is the right decision and the only possible decision for her. Because, sure as houses, when she becomes richer and settled, and even has her own family, she will look back to that episode and feel guilt. That guilt is unassuagable later. It is only pardonable by yourself by being very, very sure that you have made the only possible decision at the time it was made. With that to hold on to, your conscience will let you sleep easy without nightmares. It is harder to achieve that peace of mind coming at it later, because the memories of the agony of decision at the time are blurred, and seem less acute when you are comfortably off and could support a child without difficulty.

A gentle regret as you cuddle your baby in a comfortable house does not beget nightmare if it is accompanied by self understanding and self acceptance that at the time there was nothing else to do.

It is this late occurrence of guilt following therapeutic abortion that makes me support the "morning after" pill. That way you never know if you have conceived so there is no guilt attached. Maintaining peace of mind is often trickier than it seems.

Can Nightmares ever be useful?

Some people like to live dangerously and enjoy their nightmares, even make them work for them. Artists and poets and authors have been known to welcome them to provide inspiration. Not for them techniques to turn off the experience. Some of the more alarming pictures I have seen might well have had their origin in a nightmare.

If nightmares are a recurring lifelong experience for you and you have grown used to them you are likely to have an open trusting nature and a creative artistic mind. Literature suggests that you are the sort of person who is more gullible and likely to be taken advantage of, as well as being more sensitive to life's stresses and therefore more readily upset by reverses of any kind. It is not that you are more phobic, or fearful or hostile. It is more that you are thin skinned. Rigid, solid obsessional characters are not usually so affected by nightmares. Their way is clear to them and other people's feelings are not so important to them. They are more self absorbed.

If nightmare has been your constant companion consider a long look at yourself. Do you need a course in self assertion? Do you need to strengthen your own sense of self? Should you encourage your ability in an artistic field and in that way give yourself the self confidence and knowledge that sets you free from vulnerability? Above all, look at your nightmares in depth and try to remember if they are highlighting any childhood episode of vulnerability or fear. So often some episode in childhood can be remembered and from an adult perspective may be both understood and dispersed.

One woman friend who suffered nightmares remembered being five years old and standing with her mother at a railway station waiting for the train that was bringing her father home after an absence of a year. Her mother was clearly over the moon with excitement but she, who wanted to be as happy, was terrified that she would not recognise him and that he would be disappointed.

In the event it did not matter as his identity was made plain by her mother leaping into this big male presence's arms and then she was hugged in her turn and was happy to be loved. But that feeling of anxiety coloured much of her childhood, she told me. She always felt vulnerable before new jobs, parties with new people, new places to go to and often had nightmares before these things, although afterwards it all worked out and the nightmares did not recur. She needed to strengthen her self confidence, thus allowing her to understand her own anxieties about how she would manage in unfamiliar situations. She found techniques to use so that the old feelings of insecurity could be forgotten and pushed back into her past memory, where they no longer arose to trouble her. These changes reduced her nightmares as well as increasing her day time enjoyment of new challenges.

Vivid, frightening, escalating dreaming may precede a psychotic episode, especially if associated with increasing insomnia. With someone who has had either schizophrenia or manic depression, and is in remission or is well controlled, a change for the worse in sleep pattern, accompanied by nightmares, should sound a warning bell and suggest that a visit to the doctor is advisable to recheck on treatment.

Treatment of Post-Traumatic Stress Disorder

It is essential that these irrational feelings of guilt are eliminated and the continuing anxiety allayed, before trying to disperse the nightmares. They may not all be completely irrational. Perhaps a car crash survivor had some unease about himself as a driver. Was he tired? Had he drunk any alcohol in the previous few hours? Was his eyesight as good as when he was younger? Could he have noticed that child running off the pavement sooner?

It is easy to blame yourself after an event, even if no one else is doing so. It takes specialist therapy, in many cases, to make you comfortable with yourself after a traumatic episode and it is worth seeking it early so that healing is not delayed. Sort out the nightmares later.

Generally it is thought that those who suffer PTSD have, in their past, a fear that is mirrored by the feelings of the traumatic event. Perhaps in childhood the sufferer from a car crash hated speed and used to feel "Stop! Stop! I can't stand this" when he was being driven by his parents. The crash itself, if speeding was to blame, brings out all that well hidden and forgotten fear and begets the guilt that says, "You should have insisted on going slower.

Then everyone would still be alive." This despite the fact that he may well have asked for a slower speed and was ignored. Guilt is irrational and damaging. It needs to be assuaged by full exposure, with you yourself pardoning yourself, because you see clearly that you could have done no more than you did in the circumstance.

Getting back to the bicycle nightmare (Nightmare 3, page 185). Was the chap afraid of falling off as a child? After all, he had fallen before and been hurt and terrified. It is probable that he was anxious about something at the time of the dream. That anxiety was serious enough to mirror the unease he felt on a bicycle at the moment of the accident. He had never come to grips with it. He stopped bicycling. So the nightmare of falling off, repeating an actual occasion, recurs when his anxiety reaches that level. It is likely to become less frequent in time anyway, and he uses it as a reminder to make sense of his stress when he gets the dream. So perhaps he is content to leave it as a sign that alerts him to real distress. Post traumatic stress disorder is a special case where the feelings of grief, guilt, and anxiety inherent in the episode should first be dealt with. The nightmares themselves may then disappear, or be dealt with as a separate entity. This condition needs the professional help of people who are trained in treating PTSD, so see your doctor and if he does not feel qualified to take on your care he will be able to refer you to a specialist who can.

Treatment of Nightmares
Unlike bad dreams, nightmares are listed as Sleep Disorders as they can lead to a state where you are afraid to go to sleep. Ways to prevent them have been discovered.

Obviously it is necessary to get rid of the acute fear and anxiety that caused the nighmare in the first place. The nightmare itself does not usually highlight the stress or guilt which lies at the root of your problem. It may not give clues as to what the precipitating problem is. It merely gives you a really frightening time and allows you to wake distressed and remember the fear so that you will be motivated to do something about it. Punishment by your brain, if you like, for not having cleared the causative problem earlier.

If you look again at the dreams I was having before Nightmare 1 (page 179) their message was perfectly clear. I wish all dreams carried such a simple message. I even verbalised the problem to my examining agent. "I need time to work and prepare for my examination," I complained in the dream. "How can you expect me to do well if I don't get a chance to revise?"

In the nightmare itself fears and memories from childhood are often involved, also guilt and anxiety. These feelings need to be explored, reasoned, pardoned or just plain understood. This is not always immediately possible so, while you are working on it, try some of these techniques to stop the nightmare.

Affirmative action
As soon as you wake, retreat into relaxation and try to retrieve some fragments of sleep. Summon up the picture of the place where your nightmare occurred and then, while feeling some of that terror, make a way out for yourself and take it. "Leave" and find yourself with friends. In the case of my nightmare, I take myself back into that hospital corridor and then I give it a door that I push through. There I find a room with people I know who are working at

a side bench. I join them and go out with them into the restaurant, or to the car park on my way home. By then the dream is really just a daydream but I have recovered from fright. The fear from the nightmare does not linger. It is also less likely to recur. This is not really lucid dreaming where some people feel that they can call up a dream they want. It is more a retreat to stage two sleep, the sort of relaxation you reach with transcendental and other meditation techniques.

Fighting Back
Use the same technique of remaining in light sleep but attack your aggressor and vanquish him, her or it. Give yourself a weapon or a shield or a flame thrower and blast whatever is creeping up on you. Children sometimes find this technique attractive.

Children do seem to have nightmares, especially when faced with a serious anxiety. We adults expect our young to take new situations in their stride, but what about a new school, going camping with a school group, or on a project with other children they are not comfortable with? The continuing hurdle of examinations that perhaps they feel less than prepared for are all stressful issues which may provoke anxiety and, thereafter, nightmares.

Home situations where there is bereavement or the instability and noisy recriminations of a marital break-up are even more severe stressors. Children are so powerless. They must feel frightened.

If the stress is transitory, the nightmares will stop after the stress is gone. In fact if the child does well in the test he feared, or enjoyed the camp he was apprehensive of, he will be more confident when facing the next challenge. If the experience was horrendous it leaves a pathway for more rapid recurrence of the same sort of horror if stress returns.

These days with television characters, both real and cartoon, locked in mortal conflict with every kind of monster, there is no shortage of dream content for a child's nightmare. They need not just fear advancing darkness closing in on them. These days children's nightmares are full of blood pouring all over themselves, weapons of destruction and some very fancy monsters. Commonly a cartoon seen the evening before is involved.

Children are mostly very ready to day-dream a huge sword into their hands to behead the monster or imagine a magic carpet at their feet to soar out of reach. They will draw their monsters, and cut them out, and play with them till they become familiar and non-frightening denizens of the night. They learn how to deal with them.

One seven year old I know had nightmares about skeletons chasing him in the dark. The only recent significant thing that I knew had happened in the family was that his younger brother had been diagnosed as having a bone disease and had to have an operation. The older boy had gone with his mother and brother to hospital and had been present when the doctor had shown his mother the X-rays. The little chap hadn't liked them. He was, however, perfectly happy to consider digging a ditch behind him as the skeletons came at him and he told me he felt much better when they all fell into his ditch and could not get out. That nightmare did not return. Of course his mother and I took the opportunity of going over the whole story of his brother's problem with him, explaining that the doctors had made his brother better with the operation. It was very bad luck that it had happened to his brother but was something that would not affect him. Children's nightmares have a very blurred border with bad anxiety dreams. I say more about children's nightmares in Section 8, page 270.

Acceptance
Lie completely still and allow the horror to sweep over you. It does so and just disappears. "There," you say to yourself, "that wasn't half as bad as I thought." Interestingly the nightmare often does not return. Older people are more courageous at using this method. It may be that fear of death is part of their nightmare and peace of mind and acceptance is a more natural reaction in old age than when youthful resistance to threat is strong.

Medication to stop Nightmares
Drugs that suppress dream sleep such as the benzodiazepine anxiolytics and hypnotics. (temazepam, nitrazepam, diazepam etc) give short term relief from nightmare. The effect does not last. It seems that dreaming is very necessary to our brain and, after a couple of weeks, dreaming breaks through again whether we are on these medicines or not. Some anti-depressants have a similar effect.

6

'Downer' Dreams

Leave you feeling: Angry 196,
depressed/worthless/disappointed 199, disgusted 210,
frustrated 212, grieving 222, guilty 236,
jealous/suspicious 242, small 245, revengeful 247,
in fear of poverty/need to save money 251

● **Angry Dreams**

Angry Dream 1
This was told me by a patient who I saw for a routine health check and whom I found to be suffering from high blood pressure.

"I was walking along on this narrow path between palm trees. I don't know where it was. It looked tropical though it was not particularly sunny. A man came the other way. He seemed to be insisting on walking on the crown of the path and there wasn't room to pass. I suddenly had a load of wood on my head, which I was balancing, so I could not step off the path to let him through. I shouted at him to give me room. He shouted back, "Get out of my way," or something like that and I lost my temper and told him what I thought of him. It was dreadful and I woke exhausted. I've been having dreams like that for some time now."

Interpretation:
The dream came from the office. I don't work in palm trees but there is a shady walk outside where I go to cool off when I get cross with my staff. We are assembling computers. It is meticulous work and we have had to take some work experience kids to teach them what the work is like.

Now some are amazing, better than me already, but the lot we have just had were idle. I find it hard to maintain my cool. I don't shout like I did in my dream but I would like to. Instead I bottle it up. I don't wonder my blood pressure is soaring.

Comment and advice:
This sort of angry dream is often associated with hypertension (see chapters on dreams from physical feelings, page 26). Repetitive shouting dreams that end with you waking with a headache are worth discussing with your doctor, and getting your blood pressure checked. For the rest, this dream is showing you very clearly how you should reach peace of mind. You need to avoid getting upset by your trainees. It is always possible to rearrange the work so that unkeen workers are sidelined into simpler jobs. They can then qualify for promotion by showing their expertise.

A young relation of mine told me that in art class he was sent to pick up litter in the playground, a chore he and the teacher infinitely preferred. He has no desire to outpaint Picasso. Wandering around the playground gives him peace to compose music for his guitar group in his head and practise his bowling action (he is very keen on cricket).

Angry Dream 2
From an older lady whom I met at a party.

"I wake up speechless with fury – trying to verbalise my anger. Two painters have come in and redecorated my living room. They say they had been asked to do so by my son who had not asked my permission. It looks terrible, more like a saloon bar with red-brown walls and an orangey ceiling and crude green brushed on designs. I am absolutely livid. How could he have done this! He has no right! (and how carefully had I decorated it before . . .)."

Interpretation:
I woke feeling incandescent. In fact no one had been in my house but two painters had been working on the house next door for almost two weeks. They were painting both the inside and the outside of the house. I could hear them talking in the garden. I didn't really like them. They seemed a rough, hashy sort of pair and I thought I would not wish to have them working in my house.

So why the temper? I don't know. I don't usually fly off the handle. I tend to bottle things up.

Comment and advice:
You are right about where your dream came from. But why did you wake in such a temper? I would want to take your blood pressure and I suggest you get a routine check from your own doctor. That sort of waking fury is often associated with high blood pressure.

There may be more in the dream. Your son, or some other man close to you that your dreaming brain may have muddled up with your son, has clearly done something that has annoyed you so much that it has erupted into your dreams. You need to stop bottling things up and talk to your son or whoever has offended. Clear the air.

- **Depression / Worthlessness / Disappointment**
You wake feeling let down, no good at anything, unable to get up and go.

These dreams may be associated with your physical health and so you should pay particular attention to any physical feelings in the dream and look them up in the Physical Feelings section of the book, page 26.

Depression/Worthlessness/ Disappointment Dream 1
From an elderly lady who had enjoyed hill walking in her prime.

"The postman brought a padded envelope which was torn at one side. I was sorry to see that but I opened the rest of the flap and a dried red flower fell out. The other contents were a small diary and a returned letter. The Post Office had put them all together and sent them back. "Henry is no longer with us" said a note on the diary and it gave a date of death. I was very disappointed to hear this news and woke quite depressed."

Interpretation:
I don't know any Henry so I really have no clue why news of his death came into my dream. No one I am fond of has died recently either. It just gave me a feeling of being down and tired and upset. I did have a faint memory of sending a dried red flower to someone years ago. I must have found it when I was walking on the hills somewhere and picked it and dried it. I did that for a while when I was younger. I

still have a book of dried flowers somewhere. It made me feel depressed too as I have not been able to walk as I used to for some years now. That dream seemed to colour my day with depression. The next day, however, I got flu and felt perfectly awful so maybe it was just early infection pulling me down.

Comment and advice:
The dream has a nostalgic depressed feel to it. It appears to remind you of times and pleasures that will not return. You are depressed by that. In fact you may be right about it being precipitated by an infective illness that made you feel down in just that way. If you have further dreams like that, you should look at your lifestyle to make sure you have not allowed your pleasures to slip away leaving only the depression of old age. You could talk it over with a friend or relative or even your family doctor. You need fresh ideas, new things to concentrate on, new friends to get to know. This is where your family could help by taking you out to something regularly so you have at least one night a week to look forward to.

Depression/Worthlessness/Disappointment Dream 2
This dream came from an eighteen year old girl who lived at home.

"I was going to this party. It was a sort of disco inside a huge hall and all my friends were going. I got ready though it was difficult because nothing was where I expected it. My skirt was under the bed and had to be dusted off. I hoped no one would see the marks. My top didn't quite fit but I pulled it down in front and it seemed all right. My mother drifted by and said something about starting a new fashion which alarmed me for an instant, but I could not find another top so hung an orange feather boa round my shoulders.

By then I knew I was late and ran most of the way, though there seemed to be a great number of splashy puddles and I hoped I wouldn't look a mess when I arrived. I comforted myself that the place would be so full that no one would see my legs.

When I got there there was a huge man at the door. I could see my friends dancing behind him through the open door and I shouted to them that I was coming but they didn't hear me. The man was asking for my pass. "No pass no dance!" he said. I hunted in my purse and there was a list of my GCE results which I showed him, shaking them in his face.

"Not good enough! Where is your real pass? Every one else has one." He turned away and went inside and shut the door and I knew the rules said I could not get in without his permission so I stood there in the rain and I woke almost crying."

Interpretation:
I know where that dream came from. I had just been turned down at interview for a temp's post in a law office. It would have been so convenient, that job. I had it in my mind that I would get it. Walking distance from my house, and everything. I had my hopes built up. The chap who interviewed me wasn't a bouncer. But he was much taller than I was. I could see the office behind him when he came through to see me. The girls were all sitting at computers and looked cheerful sort of souls. He seemed to like me and I was doing well till we got to my exam results. I had a good pass in English but my IT was not my greatest-ever result. I think it was that that did for me. I got the "I have to interview

other applicants but I'll let you know as soon as possible by post," routine and the girls at the job centre said that was the kiss of death.

I got the refusal letter yesterday and I felt depressed all day. Somehow after the dream I felt a little better. It was nice to know I wasn't standing out in the rain crying. Mum had got me a pear for breakfast, my best favourite kind and we talked about their refusal. She said they would have been lucky to get me. I know it is all nonsense but having someone on your side is comforting, if irritating. She said what about doing a course in computers at the local college, and trying again? But I'm going to try the plumbers down the road. They want a secretary who is good on the phone and that I can do. I can learn more about computers once I am earning.

The dream was funny in that I did have trouble getting dressed for the interview. My white school shirt was too small and I undid the sleeve buttons and put a blazer on top to hide the gaps. It was raining when I came out of the interview too and I stood and looked at the place and felt like crying because I knew it was a no no.

Comment and advice:
This is a passing disappointment that leaves a small memory scar, but you have a supportive family and have survived the disappointment without lingering trauma. You have a sensible view of your own capabilities too and have angled your next job interview to suit these. There is nothing like success and if you get a job you will not have this sort of dream again. If you can share your feeling of disappointment it helps. A sympathetic listener will be able to boost your self worth. Your dreaming brain is always trying to soften the pain, so, if you sleep well,

your memory of the misery will be that much less.

Depression/Worthlessness/Disappointment Dream 3
This one came from an old gentleman whose wife had died about five years previously.

"I was in some sort of factory. It was a dreary empty dusty place with poor lighting. I was dressed in a white overall and had my shoes and my head covered in those blue plastic bag things which you see the nurses and doctors wearing in television on the medical programmes.

I seemed to be trying to find my office where the equipment I needed for an experiment was. As I wandered on, a man came out of a door that I hadn't noticed. "You will have to get moving if you want to catch the train. The boys are all on it," he said and suddenly I was on a platform and the train was beginning to move and I started to shout and run after it but it was dark and no one saw me and there were dead frogs all over the platform that had been squashed by cars and I didn't want to put my feet on them in case I should fall and break a hip. I was pleased to wake. I got up and made myself a cup of tea as I didn't want to go to sleep again in case that dream returned. I sat and thought that there wasn't anything to do."

Interpretation:
I suppose I know where the frogs came from. I saw one on the road as I was driving home yesterday and thought, "Yuk! What a horrible way to die."

I think a lot about dying these days. There isn't anything else to think about, is there, at my age? I miss my wife. She always had ideas about what we should do. I had been to visit my daughter but she was busy getting the children's supper so hadn't time to talk. Her husband gave me a whisky but he was watching Celtic playing some foreign team and might as well have been part of the furniture. I used to go bowling with the wife. She loved it and the chat and a drink afterwards in the club house. It wasn't the same after she went and I stopped going. I don't need the lunch club either. I get microwave meals and eat when I want. I suppose that empty factory was pretty much what my life is just now. As for the train, I've certainly missed the boat as far as having friends any more. No one drops in to see me now the wife is gone. My neighbour fell on the ice last winter and broke his hip and had a hip replacement but he has not been the same since. I don't want to be like him.

Comment and advice:
This is a typical depressive dream. Empty dark spaces. Flat echoing halls. Nothing interesting to look at. A sense of having missed what is going on. The squashed frog just helps to set the scene of yukky boredom. If you get this sort of dream you may well be clinically depressed and should certainly see your doctor about it. You need to be encouraged to find an interest, in fact interests. Some should be inside the home because you are older and not all that mobile, as well as outside interests where you meet other people and make relationships. Freud would say that missing a train usually means that you are afraid of death but thankfully you are alive, as the train with all your friends pulls out of the station bound who knows where? But in this case I believe that though you may be depressed by the fear of the unknown, most of your emotion is depression at having been left stranded by life.

Footnote:

The trouble with this sort of dream is that the dreamer keeps it to himself because he is depressed and so no one notices, or, if they do, they just think he has become a cross old man. In this case it was not the dreamer who came to me about his problems but his daughter. She may have been busy getting the children's supper but not so busy that she didn't notice her father's depression.

"He used to help with the children when Mum was alive," she told me. "She used to push him in to it and he did it well. He was never close to Allan, my husband. They just don't have the same interests. Dad used to do DIY all the time. Allan likes football. But they get along. They just don't go out together and I haven't the time to push him like Mum used to."

"Could Allan go to woodwork classes one day a week and take your father with him? He could say he needs his help to begin with. He will have to be quite firm with your Dad." They did that and when I saw her next she laughed about it. "Dad was resistant but Allan said he needed to learn so Dad went along. Now Dad is doing inlay work and Allan has learned to make a stool. It has changed him and I don't mean Allan! Dad has gone back to the lunch club too and he goes on all their outings. I can even get him to hear the children's reading when he visits."

When I saw the old man for his annual check up I asked about his dreams and that was when he told me the one above. I am glad to say he is not dreaming that sort of dream any more. Medication would not have helped that old man. Getting back into the human race did. He needs to keep contact with people, build up friendships. But he needed help to do this and his family were best placed to offer this help. Of course if he could meet a lady and find a friendship that leads to love he would be well placed. Sexual desire is an amazing spur to smartening yourself up, mentally and physically. You are never too old for love. You just have to take care that your partner will stay as caring of you as you are of her.

Depression/Worthlessness/ Disappointment Dream 4
From a single mother with three pre-school children.

"I am walking through the desert and the children seem to be with me. I certainly have hold of one of them and I keep telling the other two to keep up. We pass an orchid flowering beside the path and I want to stop and show the children but it just seems too much bother so we go on. There are sand hills and one of the children says, "Can we play?" I say, "No!" but they rush over to it anyway and I know we will be late and there won't be enough bread left for breakfast."

Interpretation:
The desert came from my habit of not getting to bed till late and sitting watching old films. This one, "Ice Cold in Alex", was a Second World War movie set in the desert with the hero staggering down sand dunes just like we were in the dream. I remembered thinking that the kids would have loved to play on them. What the orchid was doing I don't know. It certainly wasn't in the film. I've always wanted an orchid. I stand and look at them in flower shops and stores but of course I can't afford one and if I got one the children would ruin it in no time and that would just upset me.

Otherwise it was a dream that made me feel hopeless and useless and late for everything, just as I do most days when I am going anywhere with the children.

There is never enough bread for breakfast. The kids always eat it all at supper and then I have to get my neighbour to keep an eye on them while I rush out and get some. The neighbours get annoyed by my asking them at that time in the morning, and I hate doing it, but what else can I do? Life is pretty miserable just now. I guess it showed in the dream.

Comment and advice:
Yes it does show. You are a depressed mother and your dreams are showing you that you feel worthless and miserable. You have to seek help, by organising your own life more appropriately. For instance, you could buy an extra loaf of bread and put it in the freezer, so that you don't have to expose yourself to your neighbour's remarks, but more so that you yourself feel competent and on top of the situation again.

Bringing up three children is very hard work. When they are pre-school it is a twenty four hour job. That is the time to find yourself a friend with young children so you can share the looking after. It is easier to look after six children with two adults than three with one adult. The kids play with each other and it is nice to have a bit of grown up conversation, even if it is an exchange of moans. Once nurseries and schools take the children for part of the day you can get time to yourself. At that point you can contemplate outside employment. It is amazing the self worth and confidence that even a two hour a week job brings with its pay packet. Humans need other humans of their age group to talk to. It seems to allow them to retain an emotional normality. Trips to the health visitor, mother and toddler groups, local church societies, all take organisation to get to but are worth the effort. Sinking into the isolation and depression that your dream suggests is not the way to continue. Make sure your health is tip top. Make new adult friends. Don't let your home become a ghetto.

Depression/Worthlessness/Disappointment Dream 5
From a middle aged man who works in the City.

"I was in a gloomy mansion late at night, talking to my daughter through a grille. She was sitting in the centre of a darkened circular chamber, reminiscent of the star shaped central entrance hall of the Chateau de Fleurac in the Dordogne valley. I was trying to have a reassuring conversation with her about ghosts, mainly because she would be sleeping here on her own and might be worried that such an old building might be haunted. She asked me if ghosts did exist and I replied that if they did then they certainly wouldn't move about from one place to another – they stayed put and haunted one spot, as far as I knew. To me this sounded reassuring. Then I said that I thought people believed in ghosts to give themselves proof of an afterlife and that if ghosts did not exist there was probably nothing after death at all. Somehow this seemed to be just the wrong thing to say under the circumstances. My daughter burst into a bout of bitter sobbing, either because the idea was frightening or because it reminded her of her parent's mortality. I immediately woke up feeling spooked and went to the toilet with a creepy feeling of apprehension."

Interpretation:
I had been feeling depressed most of that week. Two of my colleagues had died suddenly. Heart attacks I believe. I didn't know one of them well but old John had been a friend at the end of a phone for years and we met at all the get togethers that happen in the City. I shall miss him.

I went to his funeral. It makes you remember your own mortality. I thought back to when my mother died and Dad. It does make you feel spooked, just as I felt when I woke. I holiday in the Dordogne most years and know it well. Although it is only three weeks a year it is the only time I really get with my daughter to talk about her life and what she wants to do. She had just told us she might go off with another girl on a walking trip instead this year. Now that she is at University, of course, she must do as she likes. But that made me depressed too. I seem to be getting old without noticing it. Time is passing so quickly now.

Comment and advice:
This is the sort of depressed dream that older people are said to get. They may do so but only if their own lives are unfulfilled and dull. In the end we are ourselves and we need to keep that persona lively and looking forward or life is very boring.

You have the double blow of your daughter, who brought joy and enthusiasm and ideas into your life, abandoning you and your old friend leaving you too. You have been relying on others to keep you happy. You need to look around for other interests, find other hobbies. Make your own life rich; do not depend on others to enrich it for you.

- **Disgust**

You wake feeling disgusted, mentally nauseated, sick (sometimes at yourself).

Disgust Dream 1

This one came from a middle aged lady whose older sister lives along the road from her. Though the older one is getting less able, she will not allow her sister to help her.

"I was walking up the road wondering what to have for lunch and decided to get a sausage roll from a baker. His bags have a well known logo on them and I put it on the table. I seemed to go away for a while because I came back into the room, and opened the bag, and there was a dead rat. I felt disgusted and sick to my stomach. There it lay, long and grey and beginning to rot, tail and everything. I have not been able to eat a sausage roll since."

Interpretation:

I had had a bit of a barney with my sister that day. She would not let me tidy her house and I remember saying to her, "The next thing you'll be getting is mice." She won't let me bring her a good cooked meal either. I feel disgusted with myself because I am doing so badly with her. I get frustrated and my irritation makes her more resistant. That I should have been so silly as to start a row makes me feel sick to my stomach. She is clearly living on bought in food which I suppose is nourishing. But she never used to and I hate to see her getting so old and incapable and yet refusing my help. I could have kicked myself when I flew off the handle at her. It just made her more determined not to let me help.

Comment and advice:
This is much deeper than frustration because your heart is involved. You are disgusted with yourself for handling the whole issue so badly. That you did it merely shows how much you want to help and how distraught you are to have that offer rejected. The dream gave you an OTT picture of how upset you are. Make sense of your relationship and accept that your sister needs her own space. If you are worried about how your sister is coping, ask her what she would like you to do or what she needs help with and take it from there. Later you may be allowed to increase your caring input.

Disgust Dream 2
A snippet from a girl who worked as an assistant in a dress shop.

"I was walking along a pier with my boyfriend when suddenly I found my feet slipping about and when I looked down there were fish guts and bones everywhere. I had a huge feeling of disgust and horror and I woke wondering how I would get the smell off my shoes."

Interpretation:
It happened the day before. My boyfriend and I were at the fishmonger and one of them was filleting fish. He was scooping the bits into a bucket beside him and I could scarcely bear to stay in the shop and I didn't want to touch fish afterwards. I know it is silly but I have always been like that.

Comment and advice:
Phobias about slippery, slimy, squashy things are not uncommon. This was a simple memory that made

an impression and may have been reinforced by having to cook the fish that night. If your boyfriend likes fish you may have to find it ready prepared and microwavable or from a packet in a supermarket. Pity, though.

The way to cure a phobia is to gradually get used to the idea little by little. Start with pre-prepared, and, if you enjoy it, tell yourself how much better it could be if you prepared it yourself and take it from there.

- **Frustration**

Frustration Dream 1
From a civil servant with teenage boys who play rugby, so he goes to their school matches as well as taking them to District and Club matches.

"I was walking down Dundas Street in Edinburgh New Town which I know well. It is a sloping street down from Queen Street and has shops below Georgian houses. There in the gutter was a great white pig. It was sitting on its haunches and I went over to it at once. I like pigs. This one had the name of a famous Scottish prop forward of my younger days. I don't know how I knew that but I did and I at once addressed it by name and began to teach it how to sing. It tried very valiantly to follow my lead. I kept stroking its chin which it held up obligingly and it did try to stay with me and in a little we were not doing too badly but I felt very frustrated that it simply wouldn't do it by itself. It needed me to sing along. Then I woke."

Interpretation:
I told the family about my dream. I wish I hadn't because the interpretation was so obvious and it

212

created such trouble. I had been trying to teach my youngest son a piece on the violin. He is really very good indeed but this piece seemed to give him trouble and I am no expert. I just kept singing along with him in the hope he could get it right. It was so frustrating. In the end I gave up and told him to tell his teacher. Of course he knew what to do. He changed the fingering and it all became easy but I didn't know how to do that. I had had an evening of total frustration and irritation because I felt the boy could manage easily if he wanted.

However I will learn to keep my dreams to myself because my son was mortified to be likened to a great white pig, even if he was called after a famous rugby player, and the family have never let him forget that dream.

Comment and advice:
People close to you can often help with interpreting your dream. If it might involve them, think before you speak. You had an evening of total frustration, with yourself for not finding the way for your son, and with the lad for not managing as well as he usually does. Your dream used your interest in rugby to show that this frustration was from your home situation, even suggesting it came from your children whom you watch playing every weekend. You had not far to seek for an interpretation. Your family got it in one.

Footnote:
I told him that it did show his pride and delight in his son's ability to play and make music. The pig sang beautifully and he had enjoyed the music it made in his dream. He replied that the amusement of the rest of his family was only matched by the

hump his younger son had taken. Half of them were laughing at him and the other half weren't speaking to him. Dreams can show more than we want.

Why a pig? He had been at an agricultural occasion where the star of the show was a prize white pig who refused to come out of his pig transporter. Civil servants are equal to anything and having come from a farming family he told me that he liked pigs and so went in to the transporter and crooned to the animal and tickled him behind the ear and encouraged him to come out and show himself to the cameras. That occasion where he struggled with an animal he rather liked was certainly in his dreaming brain, tucked away in recent memory and ready to be brought in to add a story to his feeling of overwhelming frustration with a child he loved. A pity for his son really, who was not amused.

Frustration Dream 2
This dream came from a friend of mine who is a male nurse in the accident and emergency department of a big hospital.

"Two hunters were blanket shooting an area where two other hunters, knowing they were coming, decided to sit it out in hiding. Afterwards I checked under a double bed which appeared to be situated in the strawberry patch, which seemed entirely normal in my dream. I found them there both dead! They hadn't got away with it. For some reason we could do nothing about them straight away, possibly having to wait till daybreak. When we checked again one of them was moving. Obviously he wasn't dead after all, but gravely wounded. I wasn't at all sure that I didn't see the other one move as well. I realised

I had to call the emergency services, first the ambulance and then the police. I went outside where some Cockney taxi drivers told me we were in Reading, although the house and garden looked much more like one I know in Ireland. Then I started trying to phone 999 but couldn't get through, sometimes being answered by police in Glasgow, sometimes getting a recorded message, etc. I tried different phones and mobile phones. Once I got a recorded message saying, "Here is the direct line to the Police. O! No! I'd better not give you that one." My brother was guarding the bodies and came in to tell me that I had been trying for two hours. I realised as I woke that if there had been any chance of saving the wounded hunters it was gone now."

Interpretation:
My frustration as I woke was enormous. It was so much the sort of feeling I am left with some days when nothing goes right in the hospital. The day before the dream had been particularly irritating. Nothing had gone right. People had been left on trolleys. There had been a very nasty gunshot injury which had taken up a great deal of medical attention. The doctor picking out the pellets said at one point, "Pity you could not have ducked." "Wouldn't have saved me, doc. He had the damn thing unbroken and no safety catch on and tried to climb a fence. It was lucky I was bending double in the strawberry patch. It's just my bum that he filled with lead."

The police were everywhere. Then they all went away and we got in a rowdy one, and I couldn't get on to them for ages and I was badly needed to help. We had an exchange doctor from Montreal for six months once and he used to tell us tales of the hunting season in the Canadian outback. That day reminded me of his stories. He said that the hunters there wear bright red coats, and the farmers paint "Cow" on the side of their cattle to try to save them from being shot.

It was such a frustrating day that I guess my dreaming brain was trying to get me to cool down all night.

Comment and advice:
Too right. Frustration is a strong and hurtful emotion that is hard to remedy. You need to go back into the episode and think what you could have managed better. You need to accept that you did in fact do the best you could at the time and pardon yourself for not being superman (who is after all?). Then your frustration will begin to cool and you may regain the peace of mind that your dreaming brain is trying to get for you.

Frustration Dream 3
A middle aged man who worked in a Civil Service department told me he had this dream.

"My wife had entered me to play in the Pro-Am Golf Tournament and I tried to explain to her that my handicap was just not in that league and everyone would mock me. She wasn't listening. She went off and came back with a teeing off time. I was getting quite het up when I suddenly found myself in Japan in a very fancy hotel. I think it was the New Otani in Tokyo because it was an extremely luxurious bedroom with a computer in one corner. I was trying to send an e-mail home and was having some difficulty. It wasn't made any easier by a lovely young Japanese girl who kept chattering to me. Eventually when I had geared myself up to ask her to leave me to concentrate, an older lady seemed to take her place and I thought, "Oh no! Not more distractions." But she showed me how the computer worked and I was just about to get the darn thing off when I woke."

Interpretation:
I knew exactly where that dream came from. The frustration was trying to get my tax claim filled out and sent. I had been doing it all the afternoon before. My wife had suggested golf but I said, "No, I really have to get this form filled in and sent off."

Then who should visit but my daughter-in-law and grand daughter? The little one appeared at my side and wanted to talk and I didn't like to send her away because she is such a dear little thing. It seemed mean to do it. Then her mother, who is Japanese, arrived in the room and she is a computer whizz and puts me right when I get it wrong. She must have been the older lady, though I had aged them both about ten years for some reason. I probably felt about ten years older myself after struggling with the tax claim.

My wife is always giving me impossible tasks and is so confident in my ability that I wouldn't have put it past her to have entered me into an impossible golf match. However I finished the day frustrated because I had not finished the tax return and had remained polite through a great deal of interruption. I seldom dream but this time my feelings spilled over into my sleep.

Comment and advice:
Frustration occurs because you suppress your real feelings and put up with other people taking your

217

time and your energy and wasting them. Prevent frustration by being truthful from the start even if it means saying "No". There is always a nice way of going about it. Think how you could have managed the episode better for the next time.

Frustration dream 4
This one came from a young woman, a patient of mine.

"I had this pain in my tummy. I hoped it wasn't anything bad, but you never know. So I thought I ought to bring it to let you see it, Doctor. But all evening I worried about ringing up and making the appointment. When I ring your surgery I often have to wait a week for an appointment, then they say every one else is booked. They make it really difficult to get in to see anyone, and if you are worried you just feel so frustrated and desperate after a phone call like that. I kept thinking of things I could say, of things they would say, and I worried away at it all evening. Then when I went to bed I dreamed I was trying to catch a train. I got to the station, but I had to let my family know I was coming, so I took out my mobile but there was no signal. A woman standing beside me said the pay phones were over the line on the other side. It was a country sort of station with no stair over. You had to get over the line further down. I walked down the platform to where she pointed and there seemed to be a number of people waiting for my train so it was difficult walking between them. I got to the spot though and then I had to wait because a train was in the station. Eventually it moved out and I could cross, but I was getting upset because time was moving on and I had to make the call and get back to my platform before my train came in.

However I managed and went into a booth. There were three side by side with glass walls and they were full of people and now there were more people waiting outside in a noisy group. I knew I had to hurry but the type of phone was strange. I couldn't find the slot for the money. Then I saw it and tried to open my purse but the change fell out and went all over the floor. I had to try to bend in that small space and pick it up and put it back. But I had parcels now and there wasn't much room and it was getting very difficult. Then I managed, and got some money in the slot and lifted the phone, but getting the number was almost impossible as the numbers kept moving their position. Then I seemed to hear my train coming so I had to try to get it done even more quickly. I was beginning to despair and I was saying to myself, "This really is quite impossible," when I woke in a sweat of frustration."

Interpretation:
I knew where that dream came from. It was a perfect picture of my feelings about ringing the doctor. I had had it all the previous day but I didn't think it would pursue me into my dreams. It was silly really because when I did ring the receptionist said you had a cancellation the next day and here I am. I wasted a lot of mental energy all for no good reason. I suppose the train came into it because I am booked to go on holiday at the end of the month so I am anxious that I will be able to make it because I have paid for the tickets.

Comment and advice:
I was able to reassure her about the pain. She got her holiday. I made sure that there were no dragons at

the end of the phone. We had a training day for all of us on phone technique. Receptionists in a general practitioner's surgery can give an impression of unhelpfulness if there are no appointments to offer. But we have set in place other emergency surgeries and telephone times when patients can speak to a doctor. So she should not have any further frustration dreams from the surgery!

Dreams can teach you a great deal, even other people's dreams can be educational. That was a useful dream for all of us but I was sorry she had to suffer it.

Frustration Dream 5
From an ex-district Nurse who was a patient of mine. She was happily married and had a little girl of about three years old. I had always found her to be a sensible well adjusted woman.

"I am having this dream of being in a maternity hospital and I am on a surgical plinth in an operating theatre waiting to have a caesarean section. There is a green cloth draped screen in front of my face so I don't see what the surgeons are doing and I have just had an epidural injection so I can't move my legs.

The surgeons come in and are about to start. They are all capped and masked so I don't recognise any of them. They take up their positions. I suddenly realise that though my legs won't move, the anaesthetic has not taken full effect and I can still feel my abdomen, just where they are about to make a hole!

I try to stop them. There is a nurse at my right hand, holding it and I pull on it and tell her to stop the surgeons. She tries to reassure me. I shout out loud but no one even turns to listen. I can see the surgeon picking up a scalpel and I know it will be a disaster and I try to tell the nurse by my side again. She just makes soothing noises. I could shake her. I make a huge effort to be heard but it is hopeless. Just as they are about to cut I wake."

Interpretation:
(I went through the dream with her to help with her interpretation.)

I expected to feel fear when I woke but I didn't. That must be significant. I felt an overwhelming frustration only. I have had this dream three times now and I am beginning to feel nervous about going to sleep. So the dream must be important. So what is so important to me just now that is making me feel totally frustrated?

Put like that there is only one answer. My little girl's third birthday party. You know we live in a Victorian tenement block with two flats to a landing? Well the lady in the flat opposite has just died. She was very old and frail so we cannot be sad for her but we all liked her. My daughter and I used to take her in meals and a selection of any good baking that I did and she enjoyed that even though she got meals on wheels. She liked the chat too. Well, her funeral is later this week but my daughter's birthday is in two days and I wanted a party with her nursery school friends.

I had mentioned this to the lady who lives downstairs and she was horrified. "You can't do that when the relations are all over the flat and all dressed in black and miserable looking. It just isn't right." It is clear that I will offend the rest of the tenement frightfully if I hang out balloons on my door! I don't know what to do. Sometimes I think

I'll go ahead. I have already made the cake. Sometimes I think I'll have to cancel. I am just so frustrated.

Is that the reason for the dream?

Comment and advice:
Certainly it is. It is interesting because that sort of dream in another person in other circumstances could have been a dream of fear of falling pregnant again, or wishing for another pregnancy. In this case it is neither of these. This lady wants to return to work once her daughter is at school for most of the day and has no thought of another child just yet. It shows the importance of interpreting your own dreams. Only you know what they really mean to you.

In this case she was frustrated because her daughter was to be denied a party for what she felt was no good reason. Her dreams told her this repeatedly. By day what her neighbours said had more weight with her. By night her dreaming brain showed her how frustrated she was.

"Move the party to the Zoo," I suggested. "Get another mother or two to help. Take the cake. Use the restaurant for the party. They sell lovely party boxes of kids' food." She did and the dream never recurred. She was delighted because she had been a little anxious about that dream's significance.

• Grief
You wake feeling sadness, a sense of loss, loneliness, you wake in tears.

Grief Dream 1
I heard these next three dreams from a friend whose much loved cat had died. They came in the order I have reported them.

"Whiskers (my deceased cat) appeared inexplicably, sniffing my foot. I called urgently to my wife and daughter to come and see but they didn't. I was afraid to touch him because somehow I knew very well that he wasn't real and I was afraid to do anything that might make him disappear again. I had a mental image of being the only one who could see Whiskers and of foolishly demonstrating to my family the empty space next to my foot, with them in turn assuming that I had gone mad. During the dream Whiskers did actually appear and disappear like a hologram a few times."

Grief Dream 2

"I was in the kitchen and there was a strange noise coming from the cat room. Whiskers, my deceased cat, was disturbed by it and wandered out into the hall so I opened the door for him thinking it would be better to get him to safety before investigating. When I opened the door into the cat room I was surprised to see that the work surface between the sink and the cat basket had a sort of oven hob inserted into it and that there were flames coming up although there did not seem to be much danger."

Grief Dream 3

"I had a phone call from the hospital laboratory. Twin kittens had been handed in. The donors had the idea that they might be used for medical experiments but the laboratory was not set up for this and the animals would have to be destroyed unless someone took them. The caller had heard that I might be interested. I immediately resolved to accept them before consulting anyone!"

Interpretation:

The first dream was somewhat comforting. I seemed to feel the loss of my cat less acutely. Having him back, even for a short time was all pleasure for me, and though even in my dream I knew he was ephemeral, a sight of him made me miss him less sorely.

The second dream was less easy to understand. I guess my wife had been thinking of ways to use the cat room now that it wasn't where Whiskers slept and had his food. If we put the cooker in there she said we could free up the kitchen as a dining room. That may have been part of it. I can't account for the fire. I wasn't worried by it in the dream. We gave Whiskers to the bin men. They made a special call and treated his little body in its box with great respect. It seemed the right thing to do. I knew they would burn him but cremation has always seemed a reasonable end to our lives so may be that was the fire.

As for the third dream, that was pure wish fulfilment. My wife might be talking about re-doing the kitchen but I realised after that dream that I really wanted another kitten or even two, one to keep the other company as we are both out a lot now, working, as our family are older. I might have been agreeing with all her plans for the cat room but in my heart of hearts I needed a cat in the house. I realised I should break this to her as soon as possible so that we could discuss the idea.

Comment and advice:

Grief goes through stages, almost like a minuette or a Scottish Country Dance. You feel intense sorrow and loss, guilt at being the one left alive – "Why was it him?" " Why did I survive?"; anger at the person or animal lost – "How dare they leave me!" This cools into resentment at being left and having to manage by yourself, gradual acceptance, and in the end, independence and nostalgia and self posession.

The stages are the same whether it is loss of a child, loss of a partner through death or a divorce, or any sort of loss that causes you sorrow. The vital thing is to continue through the stages and not stick in any of them because then you may become depressed. Bereavement counsellors are always available to help you along with advice. Your doctor can recommend one, so, if your dreams seem to show you that your thoughts are becoming fixed on one of these emotions, go and talk to him about it.

Grief Dream 4
This came from a friend.

"I was peeing in a public toilet in a cubicle when I heard Z's voice outside, chatting casually to someone. I went out and confirmed that it was indeed him. He was washing his hands with his back to me. I knew he was meant to be dead and I suppose I expressed some puzzlement but during the whole episode I had no sense of anything strange going on and I woke with the dream unresolved. I hadn't spoken to my friend, just seen him there with his back to me washing his hands in an everyday sort of way."

Interpretation:
It was a bit of a shock to hear that Z had died. He was my age and a fit looking man. He was not a very close friend, more a colleague that worked in the same firm; a sort of "Good morning Z, how are the family?" kind of acquaintance. I knew he ran a good department and was respected. We met at

interdepartmental meetings. Seeing him there just as usual seemed to take the shock element of his death away. In the morning it all felt more natural. I woke wondering if perhaps he had had medical problems we knew nothing of. That was comforting somehow. Now that I think of it, I expect his death was a startling reminder of my own mortality. I know my will and my provisions for my family are in order so I was not fussed about those. Thinking on from that, I wondered if I shouldn't go to my doctor for a routine check up sometime.

Comment and advice:
I think both these interpretations say it all. If you think of your emotional make up (your ability to love) as a sort of octopus with all sorts of lengths of tentacles sticking out of it and all necessary to the octopus, it is easier to explain grief. Big tentacles represent a big love such as you feel for your children or your partner, your father or mother. Smaller tentacles represent the love you feel for your pets such as your cat or dog or horse or hamster. Smaller or larger tentacles, depending on how much you care for them, represent your house, your garden, your books, jewellery, bank balance and that sort of thing.

If one of these dies or disappears it is as if that tentacle is cut off. The wound has to heal. It takes a longer or shorter time according to the extent of the cut and your healing power and determination.

So if you lose a husband or wife, partner or parent, this is a big wound in your emotional make up. Your dreaming brain will try to lessen the loss, usually by allowing you to dream about that person in ordinary situations so that the complete severance that you have suffered seems to be less acute. Some people find this very comforting. Their loved one often says things that make them feel at ease with the idea of dying.

This sighting of your dead loved one in your dreams is very common after bereavement. It gives you a chance to say things to them that you always wanted to, tell them how much you valued them, get off your chest the things you did not tell them in life but wanted to. These dreams should become rarer as your emotional wound heals but people you were attached to will return on occasion to give a strong feeling when your dreaming brain is trying to get a powerful message across.

There is a grieving process which goes through various stages, first, panic and rejection of the whole idea of separation, "I can't bear it"; then guilt, "Was there something I could have done to prevent it?"; revenge (mostly felt by divorcing partners); insecurity, "how will I manage?"; tentative return to society; and eventually serenity. Your dreams will highlight all these stages.

Trouble ensues when a person gets bogged down in one or other stage. Guilt can descend into depression unless the life force of the individual or his life pattern of activity keeps him going until he moves on by himself. I have seen many a patient who says that, after their mother or their father or sibling or wife died, they became depressed, never returned to work and had been on antidepressive medication for years. The depression is hard to treat at this stage and their dreams are depressed dreams of dark passages going nowhere and horrid things met with on the way. You can tell how you are convalescing from bereavement from your dreams. If they stick in any one phase for too long you should take your doctor's advice or visit a reputable bereavement counsellor recommended by your doctor.

Revenge dreams are all about catching and hitting back. Revenge is a very normal, very strong part of the grief reaction, especially following the break up of a relationship. One or other partner feels betrayed and let down and wants to hit back. There are television programmes made of discarded wives who cut their husband's Porsche in half or spray paint it pink with blue spots. Revenge is a wholly natural, wholly unhealthy and self damaging emotion and is best got over as quickly as possible.

To quote the bible "Revenge is mine, saith the Lord." I'm not sure where it comes but it is none the less valid for all that. It is surprising how one's victim finds his own hell if left to himself, to the extent that you are almost sorry for him or her in the long run. Enjoy the immediate release of doing something outrageous if you have to. Our natures are all different. You may have guilt dreams about it but they will pass. Then forget revenge and get on with your own resuscitation. "Nursing your wrath to keep it warm" makes a pig's breakfast of your life and ruins the possibility of any long term betterment for yourself. Just get on with learning how to get along with yourself.

Grief Dream 5

I was told this by a young woman who had been left by her long-term partner and was grieving dreadfully for him. She came to me first because she was having nightmares, which had a clear basis in the anxiety and fear she felt at being left on her own for the first time in her life. Her boyfriend had been a school chum before they moved in together. Luckily, soon after, she got promotion. She told me she found relief from her thoughts because she had to work late learning the new job and it was completely different in that she now had to travel and meet people.

"Since the new job I have stopped having nightmares. But last night I dreamed Alan and I were walking on Arthur's Seat, just as we used to do on summer evenings. He was just as usual and I told him I was going into a new life and a new job and do you know what he said?

"You'll do it very well and the people will be just as grown up as you are"."

Interpretation:
When I woke I missed him but he appeared to be further away and I did not need him in the same way. I began to wonder if I hadn't grown away from the way we used to be. He was always pretty juvenile and liked to go out to the pub with his mates and get a bit pie-eyed. I used to be just like him but then I found I had a headache the next day and work was dire and I stopped going out to the pub except at weekends. I guess he met someone else on one of those weekday evenings and felt they were more in tune. But you can't stay mind free for ever. I wanted to get on. I thought he did too.

Comment and advice:
In relationships you often take for granted that if you start together you progress at the same rate. You have grown up and your boyfriend has not matured in the same way and your dream highlights that quite cleverly and allows you to feel good about it.

You always have some anxiety on leaving a steady relationship even if you have outgrown it. But is a natural progression and you have no need to feel guilt. It is far worse to be shackled to childhood scenarios that no longer interest you. You may feel guilty at getting out, but in this case there is no need because your boyfriend has already chosen someone to fit in with his needs and plans so you were already redundant if you but knew! So this is an "all's well that ends well" situation.

Grief Dream 6
Falling out of love related by a twenty year old girl who was a patient of mine.

"I was in a sort of empty warehouse and I seemed to be walking across the floor towards a door but it was always a little ahead. It was half dark and dusty and I felt very lonely and tired as I plodded on. There was nothing to see, nothing to do. I walked on a bit and woke up."

Interpretation:
That dream is just what I felt for the first week or two after we broke up. The phone didn't ring for me. I kept taking out my mobile and realising I had no one to text. I felt down and miserable. Then the girl who works next to me asked if I would like to come to her birthday party. I didn't really want to but I said, "yes". It felt strange going alone but it was great fun once I got there and by the end of the evening I had had a good time. I didn't dream that dream again.

Comment and advice:
You are describing a typical dream from the depressed miserable stage of grief. Falling out of love is a grief reaction that can happen at any age but is usually of short duration.

In my younger days I seemed to fall in and out of love with remarkable rapidity. In fact being of a scientific turn of mind I began to quantify the process and on average it took three weeks. Of course at that time falling in love was not always routinely accompanied by sexual intercourse. My guess is that once that has occurred the woman feels more committed and after a break up the grieving process takes longer. But I well remember the break up and the sense of loss, accompanied by no phone calls, no sighting of the loved one and the pain when sighting did occur.

My dreams at the time were all about running down dark places or empty rooms searching but never finding. These became less frequent as time went on and in about three weeks my usual dream pattern re-established, dreamless sleep alternating with the usual student anxiety dreams of sitting exams they had not prepared for! I was then ready to fall in love again.

Deep emotional ties, if severed, leave scars that are always tender. They heal more readily if you force yourself to work on at other things. Later it is also a good plan to leave the place you associated with your partner for a short while. The Victorian habit of going away for three weeks to somewhere quiet had reason. You come back, usually having been monumentally bored but you have a different perspective and you can make clearer decisions. Work and necessity are great healers thereafter, though it is often hard to take the first step back into the community. A helpful friend or employer who appears to need you to return is very useful.

Grief Dream 7
This one came from a middle aged lady who was a keen member of a mountaineering club that organised hill walks most weekends, so the members knew each other well.

"I was attending some sort of celebration in a church. Outside, in a small square some amateur performers and musicians were giving a show. A relative of mine was about to play something and was giving instructions to the drummer while a small audience gathered. They began but I could not hear my nephew for the din being made by the drumming. After a bit I realised they were playing a ceremonial fanfare. Some black clad councillors processed by and walked into the church. I followed them but, when I got in, there was not as big a space as I expected, but a series of small complicated rooms. I decide not to stay for the service. On my way out my nephew is standing with some money in his hand. He tells me it is not enough for his rail fare. As I go down the steps of the church a man comes up to me and to my horror it is my neighbour who is talkative and a great bore. He puts his arm across my back. It feels very warm and I comment on this. "Ah yes," he says, "I have just finished a bath." Then I wake and find that my little duck down pillow has got itself tucked into my neck just where his arm lay and it is extra warm there."

Interpretation:
My good friend Heather from the mountaineering club had just died in a hill fall. I had sorrowed for her all the previous day but she did not come into my dream. A friend had rung to say that they would be having a church ceremony of remembrance. I hate these but I felt I would have to go. The last funeral I watched was in Italy where I had gone on holiday with my sister and her almost-student son (he had just finished school). We were in a little square very like the one in my dream when some

musicians started to play, very badly, and this procession of men in black suits and a coffin appeared and went into the church. Later, after they had left, I visited the church but did not stay for a service which seemed to be starting. I don't know why my nephew had not enough money for his rail fare unless it was something my sister had said when she told me he was coming with us: "He couldn't afford the train journey himself" she said. "So I am going to treat him for the last time before he becomes a student and lives on his own income."

Comment and advice:
You have been able to give way to your sorrow, so it has not damned up inside you and therefore has not come into your dream. However, you feel rotten about having to go to a formal ceremony of remembrance. This gives you a strong sense of bottled up misery, and frustration that nothing is quite right for you. This comes out in the dream with your irritation about the awful music, not being able to hear your nephew play, having to wait for a funeral to clear the church and being approached by your garrulous neighbour. Everything is wrong about your life just at that minute, and your dream is picturing that for you.

You are probably right in your memory of your sister's words about your nephew and maybe the thought has often struck you that young people have it hard and you wish you could help. The physical feeling of a warm little pillow has obtruded (see Touch Dreams, page 70) into your dream as well.

Dreams highlight feelings you have been unable to express. So, though you have been able to grieve fully and go through the stages of loss, you still have a general feeling of missing your friend which will become less acute in time. You have no problems with guilt or resentment or anger because you have not been so closely involved with your friend or her death. The feelings that ruin your peace of mind are frustration and irritation. You have to attend and conform to other people's notions of what is the right thing to do, which you do not share, but equally feel you can't mention. There is little alternative. Once you have been to these ceremonies you will stop feeling cross about them, may even find some comfort despite your reservations.

Grief Dream 8
This dream was told me by an old lady.

"I was swimming in a bit of sea between rocks, rather like the scenes in travel brochures for the Mediterranean islands and I saw a golden orange fish pirouetting about in the water. I swam right up to him and stroked him. He didn't mind but he seemed to have a metal plate attached to his back and I thought this could not be good for him so I took him to the technicians, two large men in grey jerseys who seemed friendly and offered to unscrew the plate. At this point I found I was participating in a film and my daughter was also there. She was quite ruffled because they had asked her to play the piano and she had done so, sight reading the music. Then they told her that they had recorded it. She said that for recording she needed time to rehearse the music. To record a play-through was nonsense.

So we climbed out of the water onto the rocks to get changed, but there was no way back to the shore from the rocks, and we saw that we would have to jump in again and swim back. The rocks, however had become very high and my daughter jumped and fell flat on to a rock shelf only just covered in water. I could see she was badly hurt, she lay so still, and I hurried to be with her. She lay very white and had a painful elbow. I woke, sobbing. I was so upset."

Interpretation:
My granddaughter fell off her bicycle yesterday and fractured her collarbone. Children do break things and most of them have done something silly but the little girl had not. She just fell badly. I am pretty stoical about breaks, having nine grandsons. It is usually the mother who needs treatment for shock. But when I saw the little girl asleep in her bed, all bandaged up and lying so still and so pale I was heart sore. I woke to that feeling magnified. I could have wept. She is a musician, plays the violin. But I do have a daughter who plays the piano and that bit seemed pretty accurate too. She would not record anything unless it was perfect and has always railed at me because I made a tape of her playing as a demonstration. It was so popular that a firm took it and marketed it, but she tells me that there is a passage in it that she does not want to hear, and that it gives her grief every time it is played. She has always begged to re-record but the firm won't. They are happy while their tills click up the money. The recording sells.

As for the fish. Who knows? It reminded me a bit of my yellow cat playing in the sunlight. Certainly I stroked it the same way. Maybe that was what it was doing in the dream.

I went back to see my granddaughter the next day with a present and felt a great deal happier because she was looking so much better and remarkably cheerful. She even liked the doll I'd brought her.

Comment and advice:
A calm day of everyday things topped off with a strong grief which disturbed your sleep. It allowed you to continue to sorrow the next day and to return to look at the little girl. Finding her so much better assuaged your grief, and your bad dreams should not return. You did right to take her a present and allow yourself to participate in the healing process because it will heal you too.

• Guilt

You wake feeling embarrassed by what you did and wish you hadn't done it. You are thankful it is just a dream and needs no putting right. You are glad no one else knows about your dream. (Guilt comes into dreams of many other main causes so look at the Sexy Dream chapter (page 77) and the Nightmare (post traumatic stress disorder) part of the Scary Dream chapter (page 178).)

Guilt Dream 1
A single girl living on her own and working in a supermarket told me this one.

"I was in some posh, OTT hotel lobby going up to my room and there were all these bottles of wine stacked by the lift door. I picked one of them up and was looking at the label as I shuffled foreward and I was in the lift with the doors closed and the bottle still in my hand before I realised I had just stolen a bottle of wine. I looked at the other people in the lift with the sweat pouring off me. It wasn't a really expensive bottle, the wine was pinkish which I am not all that addicted to anyway. But there it was in my hand and all round me these flunkeys dressed in penguin gear and starched to their eyebrows, and men in suits all looking ahead but at any minute I felt they were going to turn and look at me accusingly.

I rush to my room and put the bottle down on a table and wonder whether to ring the manager, or drink it and get rid of the bottle or just throw it out of the window. The trouble with the last was that there were people and a swimming pool down below. Then there is a knock at the door and two or three bellboys bring in my luggage which has grown to seven or eight suitcases which they have to find room for so they walk all round the bottle on the table and don't seem to see it and I woke, wondering what to do and feeling awful at the embarrassment I was going to feel when they did see it and ask me about it."

Interpretation:

I sit at a check out all day just beside the wine shelves so I see wine bottles all the time. I guess this is a dream about work. I have never taken anything from my employers. I can assure you of that. Yesterday, however, when I went in, I put my outdoor things in a locker and changed into my working overall. The next-door locker door was lying open, across mine. Ella always does that. She never bothers closing it properly when it is empty and it is very annoying as it swings across automatically unless she does. She says she would forget the key if she locked it. I keep mine pinned to my overall pocket and then in my purse. It is perfectly easy. Anyway I was cross and I slammed her door and the top hinge broke off. I should have told her or the manager. I should have told them that she had been a nuisance with that door for ever. I should have said something at once but I didn't. I didn't want to get into trouble for breaking something and I was afraid the manager would take it off my wages, so I got on with changing and went in to work and said nothing. No one seemed to notice at the time. By the end of my shift there was a new hinge on her door and it was closed and Ella was at work. I was thankful and hoped I had got away with it. But I felt bad about it for most of the day. I had forgotten about it by night which was odd because I am pretty sure that dream had something to do with it.

Comment and advice:
The dream was even more evocative of emotion than the actual event. That is usual for dreams. They give a florid picture to catch your interest and memory, as if your brain wants you to remember the emotion. After a dream like this you have to make your mind up what to do. Do you clear your conscience by telling, or do you sit it out? Either way you will forget it in time because the whole episode is finished and was not so extreme that it will linger in your mind. However at present it does appear to sit like a hob nail in your peace of mind and so my advice is to get rid of the guilt by confessing.

As a single girl I would guess you often feel a little vulnerable in a new hotel when you go on holiday and nervous of doing the wrong thing. I do myself and the grander the hotel the more nervous-making the staff seem to be, until you get used to them. So the dream setting is one of instability. Then comes the simple action of picking up a bottle and looking at it, something you must often have wanted to do from your seat at the checkout. The trouble stems from there. You are right to place it in the work situation. The bottles are a give-away despite the holiday atmosphere.

Footnote:
She took my advice to go to her manager and to her surprise found him sympathetic and sensible and grateful for her honesty. He did not dock her wages. He said it had been entered in the accident book and there it would stay. The lockers were due to be replaced, anyway, he told her and they were going to upgrade the female staff changing room. She told me later that on upgrading, the lockers were reallocated and she found herself with a corner one and a careful neighbour. She had clearly profited from her reaction to her dream interpretation. She did not dream that sort of dream again.

Guilt Dream 2

This dream came from a middle aged lady who is a friend of mine.

"I was visiting my aged aunt's house. She is actually only ten years older than me and if I am as spry as her at her age I shall be delighted, but she lives in a house that is more like an exhibition of antiques than a home. Both she and her husband collect antiques, rubbish my husband calls it. But their rubbish, some of it, is priceless and very fragile. It has always amazed me how they managed to keep such a place and bring up two children while my house with the same number of children in it has been distressed to the point of becoming a tip.

So in my dream I was standing in the entry corridor of her house, which I know well, but it had become much narrower. As I turned, my coat began

to catch on the furniture and the ornaments wob-
bled. I was very anxious and stood still but I wanted
to go to the toilet and started to go there, extremely
carefully so as to not knock anything over. It took
me a long time because I couldn't seem to find any
lavatory paper and then the soap wasn't there and I
couldn't find a towel. At last I gave up and decided
to come out with wet hands as I felt so guilty about
keeping her waiting for me for so long. When I
opened the door she was waiting for me to come out
and she had a friend with her who also clearly
wanted the toilet and I felt doubly guilty at keeping
them out for so long. I picked up my gloves from a
nearby table where I seemed to have left them, and
noticed that they were of different colours and the
two ladies must have noticed. I felt mortified as well
then.

My aunt said that I had missed the antique sale
that they had just been to. I had clearly arranged to
meet them there and felt guilty at having forgotten
that and began to apologise.

My aunt's friend then told me that they had
bought an antique mirror at the sale and they were
waiting for me to advise them where to hang it. I
looked round the walls which seemed to have not
one place to spare. There seemed to be nowhere I
could advise and I knew I was disappointing them
all down the line. It made me feel bad and I was
thankful to wake and find it all a dream."

Interpretation:
The week previous to my dream I had begun to
realise that I had been busy in my own work and
had not made contact with any of my friends or
elderly relations that I usually keep up with by

phone if nothing else. My husband had commented at breakfast, on the morning before my dream, on the fact that I had no news from the "outback" as he calls my gossip circle. The thought had stayed with me all day, making me feel guilty. That dream was a very accurate picture of my feelings when I went to bed.

I followed my hunch about that dream's meaning and rang my aunt. In fact she had been a bit unwell and was pleased to hear from me. I promised to visit the following afternoon though I know that when I get there, the memory of that dream will make me walk warily in the corridor. I rang all the people I could think of that I felt guilty about. By lunch I felt a great deal better.

Comment and advice:
You got it right. You laid your guilt to rest. It was right to get on the phone to the people you cared for and catch up with their doings, see if they were all right and generally get back into the swing of things. It sounds as if you are the lynch pin for a number of people. It is not an easy position to keep going if you are a busy lady. However it is often the busy ones that are the doers, and certainly your conscience is not going to let you give up.

Incidentally that dream has physical feelings in it too. Your need for the toilet would still be with you when you woke (see Needing to Urinate Dreams page 51).

The mortification you felt at finding odd gloves could have come from anywhere. It is possible that it may have been your feelings when your husband reminded you that you had not been keeping up your caring connections. Only you will know.

• Jealousy / Suspicion
You wake, feeling jealous/suspicious.

Jealous/Suspicious Dream 1
Told me by a woman whose husband had told her he was leaving her. She was very upset.

"I knew in my heart things weren't too good at home. At least four months ago I dreamed that I was in bed with George. At least I thought it was George but it wasn't a familiar back that was lying next to me and I said "George why are you so different?" and he turned over and there was someone else, another woman with yellow hair tightly wrapped in his arms. I felt totally bereft and I woke up saying "But George is *my* husband!""

I woke George too and told him my dream and he told me not to be silly. But he didn't laugh like he used to when I told him ridiculous dreams, and that didn't help much. I had a duff day because I kept thinking back to that awful feeling of jealousy and suspicion. It took me ages before I forgot it. I shouldn't have!"

Interpretation:
I think I knew, even before he told me that he was having an affair with Sheila, that things weren't right between me and George. We go out a great deal, to friends mostly and for dinner. I give dinners too. Sheila is the wife of a man who works in stocks and shares or something. She came into our dinner circle fairly recently but she has always been nice to me. Since our little boy went to nursery school, however, I have not been telephoning George so much. He used to like me phoning him at his lunch time on his

mobile if we had not arranged to lunch together, which we used to do a lot. I have not been going out to lunch with him either. How could I? I need to collect Rory from school and see he has a good lunch and get him to rest afterwards. He is tired after the morning. I used to take him in the push chair and he was so good in the restaurant. I always fed him before I set off and we used to give him a chip to chew or something like that.

George is always the life and soul of the party. Everyone loves him. However he has never done this before. I never felt he would leave me. At least during the day I didn't. That dream came back to me after he told me about Sheila and I thought. "That dream left me feeling suspicious. I should have tried to do something then instead of discounting it."

Comment and advice:
Dreams that leave you with a clear suspicion are worth pursuing just a little further even if you are not a suspicious sort of person. Some people live with suspicion. They think the butcher is trying to give them short weight. They think the lady next door is talking about them and saying nothing good. They think the post man is only delivering half their mail. Some of their suspicions may have minor elements of truth in them. That is always the trouble with paranoia! There is often a grain of truth in the suspicions.

Interestingly, the more paranoid you are, the less you are likely to have these clear dreams showing up a single suspicion. You tend instead to have more depressed dreams of dark wide lonely spaces where you are alone and lonely.

It might have been useful to have found out your husband's intentions earlier but by the time a man is on the move to another woman he has built up a head of steam that is hard to cool down. Unless you hold a financial whip that can bring him to heel or can threaten him with consequences that he is unable to accept, such as loss of his job or children, you are on a hiding to nothing. Some women are happy to hold a man to his promise to be their husband for life, despite infidelity and possibly even growing dislike. That is a personal decision. The only thing they can be sure of is that their dreams will show them their real thoughts throughout.

Jealousy/Suspicion Dream 2
This dream came from an old friend at his thirtieth wedding anniversary party.

"I was going along a sort of beach to meet my, then, girlfriend. There were lots of people sitting on deck chairs and I had to walk in and out of them but I could see her because she was standing and they were all sitting. Then a man got up from a chair and she took his arm and went off with him. I didn't recognise him. He had on a pale jacket, one I had seen in a shop and lusted after but it was Armani and much too expensive for me then. They moved away and I was hurrying through the soft sand which caught at my feet and got in my shoes and I had to weave round the chairs too which slowed me down. It was dreadful and I wanted to batter the man and shout at my girlfriend I felt so jealous. Then I woke."

Interpretation:
Looking back it was silly because she had never really given me cause to be jealous. It was just that I wanted her very much and thought I wasn't rich

enough to take her fancy. I told her the dream and she laughed a great deal and has teased me about it ever since. Of course now that we have been married for thirty years I don't get cross about it any more.

Comment and advice:
This is a dream of pure jealousy which had no basis in fact. You may have known that she went out with richer men, and that sparked the feeling, but that is very normal. Telling her the dream was very sensible. She was able to set your mind at rest. If she had indeed preferred another man she would then have had an opening to tell you. You were better to know if she was not going to keep up your relationship. Even in marriage this sort of dream may be a mistaken jealousy or it may be a hint that the dreamer has picked up from his partner, be it man or woman. Telling the dream and assessing your partner's reaction is a very useful way of clearing the air. Morbid jealousy can be very damaging to a relationship and trust is part of true love but a dream like this comes from a fear of being left and, if unnecessary, the fear should be put to rest. Always remember that this sort of dream may have come from a different source of insecurity. You may dream of losing your partner but it may be that she is the figurehead for your jealousy of a colleague or partner at work. Who is causing you to feel insecure and suspicious?

Does the dream picture point to your home or your work?

- **Made to Feel Small Dreams**

Made to Feel Small Dream 1
From a male colleague of mine who is old enough and experienced enough to be self confident at any occasion.

"I was going into a bank. For some reason I was wearing my pyjamas and a dressing gown. The hotel I was staying at seemed to be closely joined to the bank so I could go easily from one to the other and it seemed to me that it was quite in order to dress in this informal way if I was merely looking for information.

However the female tellers gave me disapproving looks as I asked, "Is one of your managers called something like Mr Stamp?"

Instead of simply giving me the information and letting me go on my way, one of them started telling me off, saying that this was no way to dress when seeking a serious interview with a bank manager. I did not get a chance to remonstrate. I just felt so put down I retreated shamefaced, and then I woke."

Interpretation:
I woke feeling very small. I haven't felt like that since I was a teenager and went to a wedding party in what I thought of as party gear, which at the time was a clean T-shirt and jeans and found all the other men in suits and ties. My mother was mortified and so was I.

The other time I felt it was when a friend asked me to golf, not a game I play often and I wore jeans and they asked me to change into trousers before I went on the course. That time my friend was mortified. I was just gob-smacked. So I looked round for a similar incident to bring on the dream.

It had to be something to do with work, because that is where I wear formal dress. Then I remembered. I had applied for a job in another unit and gone for interview there some weeks previously. Actually, when I got there I had found that their work was not in the same line as mine, though the specifications had been written to suggest they were. I went in to meet this Board and clearly they did not like me. I thought it might be something to do with the fact that my tie, my only clean one, is a sort of rainbow of colours. Theirs were all regimental and stuffy.

We did not gel, so their polite refusal was not unexpected, nor in fact unwelcome. Just going for the job made my own unit look at me again and offer me a rise so nothing but good came out of the occasion, but when I walked into that interview room I remembered feeling much as I had on the other occasions when I had been made to feel small.

My bank manager is in fact a very jolly man but the girls behind the counter are slightly po-faced. Those episodes must have been going through my mind the evening before my dream. I had certainly been to the bank that afternoon.

Comment and advice:
That interpretation is one that only you would know to come up with. I think you are right. Your dreaming brain is triggered by the slight unease that going into your bank and facing the po-faced tellers engendered. Then it looked back into your memory banks for memories that needed to be softened or removed to reach true peace of mind and came up with this dream. I think your failed job interview still rankles, however good the outcome. This dream may do much to put that feeling to rest.

• **Revenge Dreams**

Revenge Dream 1
This came from a commuter who travels on the train to work every day.

"I was bent on exacting revenge on the driver of an approaching train. Cunningly I removed a large bracket from the buffers at the end of the line and then waited in anticipation that the train would somehow plough through the buffers at high speed and off the end of the track (it didn't occur to me that the buffers only come into operation in an emergency). However I then began to think uneasily that I might have been observed in the act by means of video surveillance."

Interpretation:
I know where that one came from. I travel to work with the same four chaps most days and we had been talking about a report about boys throwing stones at a train and saying that we hoped they caught them because if the train crashed it could cause such a dreadful loss of life. Then one of us who writes thrillers in his spare time said, "What a way to get rid of an enemy. No one would know if he was one of many." I said it wasn't foolproof and besides he would find it had all been caught on video camera which would serve him right. Then we went to work but on the way back the train was late. The driver said that there was water on the line. "Wrong sort of water, wrong sort of leaves, wrong sort of snow. They always have an excuse. I sometimes hate those drivers." I suppose his thoughts stayed in my mind and invaded my dream. However I did wake feeling guilty at even having thought it so I suppose that showed some sense. I'd rather arrive late than dead on time as the old advertisement used to say.

Comment and advice:
This was a bottled irritation at being late home that surfaced in a dream. You were right to realise that

reality played no part. In real life you would never attack the driver. You know he is doing the best he can with the equipment he has. That dream would mitigate your irritation and allow you to wake with peace of mind having sorted it out. You are only left with a mild guilt at having felt it at all. This sort of dream is acting out an irritation in imagination. The best way to get rid of it.

There is an interesting bit of guilt that comes in at the end, almost as if your conscience is monitoring that dream, and deciding that it should not let you get away with your revenge because it is, in effect, so foreign to your normally kindly nature.

Revenge Dream 2
This one came from an au pair from Sweden who lives with a family but also babysits when free for other families in the road. She is well liked by everyone and has made lots of friends of her own age, mostly from the English class that she attends. She told me the dream herself.

"A group of four or five young men of about seventeen or eighteen years old were railing against someone and had decided to get their revenge. For some reason I went along with them. They made a rocket and gave it to a Swedish ship's captain to launch when he got home to Sweden. A couple of days later, I was jogging down this grassy path between trees and the backs of a row of Victorian houses. Suddenly there was a whoosh and something flew over my head and exploded in one of the houses, causing great devastation. I stood there thinking. "That is where the people live that my friends were wanting to get revenge on. I am not sure that they have hit the right house but it is no

249

wonder when the rocket has come all the way from Sweden. I do hope that no one will think I was part of the plot. It was a terrible thing to do."

Interpretation:
May be this was more guilt than revenge. I don't know.

I cannot think of anyone I want to get revenge on, nor do I feel guilty. I did however want to see a television film about a rocketeer that won a war and because my friends came in to see me I missed it. Maybe my dream was making up for the disappointment. Perhaps it had got all turned round so I was feeling that my friends were revenging themselves on me, or someone near me, by making me miss my film. I certainly had some resentment against them for visiting just at that time and took that resentment to bed with me.

Comment and advice:
There is more guilt than revenge I think. It is the thought you woke to that counts. "They can't blame me" is what you said.

Footnote:
I enquired further and the most dramatic thing in her life at the time was that the little girl she baby sits for had burned herself at a Guy Fawkes party. She had tried to pick up a spent rocket that had fallen off course and got her fingers burned. The au pair had not been there when it happened. She had been asked but was going to her own party that night. Did she blame herself for that?

Everyone feels, "Had I been there I could have done something." They never can. But the thought remains and if strong enough can surface in a dream. Dreaming it will probably put the guilt to rest. (See Guilt Dreams page 236)

The resentment was also there in the rocket coming from Sweden to blow up a place inhabited by her friends. It had got distorted I think, because she herself would not have hurt anyone, even those who had denied her the pleasure of watching the programme she had wanted. Her dreaming brain could not get her to launch a rocket, so it got someone else to do it!

Fear of Poverty / A Wish to Save Dreams

A Wish to Save. Dream 1
Told me by a young man of twenty two.

"I was in a bar with another chap of my age. I seemed to know him well. He had run up a bar bill of £6 but had then left the bar for a short time, a misdemeanour which the harsh bar man told him carried a fine of £10 per half hour away, so that the amount had now swollen to a staggering £36.

I appealed to the barman on my friend's behalf but to no avail. Then I realised that an attractive middle aged woman sitting at the bar might be the owner, and I tried appealing to her softer nature, this time with the desired effect – the bill was reinstated at £6 again. In gratitude I gave her a little cuddle, but this did not seem to please her at all. She said "You are intellectually unintelligible and 32 years old!" I reflected that she had inadvertently paid me a compliment because, dream or no dream, I realised that she thought I was ten years more mature than I was."

Interpretation:
I often feel small in this sort of situation. I am not rich and to suddenly be faced with a huge bill was frightening and embarrassing. I seldom know what to tip people. I find bar men intimidating and they bully me. I know I have to count my pennies. I know I have to stay within my budget and I feel sweaty if I get in amongst big spenders. I expect that it gets better as you get older. It always seems so smooth when I go out with Dad.

Comment and advice:
Right as far as it goes. This dream gives a good picture of finding yourself in an uncomfortable financial situation. It is very much a young man's dream. However it also suggests that you are very well aware of your ability to charm the opposite sex and you do so in this dream. So who provided the memory of the older lady saying, "Get off with you, young man," however flattering her mistake about your age. Your dreaming brain was giving you a sexual pat on the back – a sort of wish fulfilment. A very common one for an inexperienced twenty two year old who thinks he can get away with most things by flaunting his maleness, I should think.

7

'Upper' Dreams

Ambition 253, count your blessings/contentment 257,
elation/showing off/flying 260, strong wishes 264

• **Ambition**

Ambition Dream 1
Told me by a lady television producer

"I was in the snow with a cine camera. It was quite
small so it did not hold me back. I had fur topped
boots and a heavy coat on so I moved quite slowly. I
was trying to photograph a snow tiger . I knew it
was somewhere in Russia but it was just a great open
area with rolling hills of snow and fir trees here and
there in clumps. In fact it looked very like the
Scottish mountains in a good winter. I ducked
behind a fallen tree. The branches were bare but they
gave me some cover. I could see these two tigers
playing on the snowy slope in the sunshine. They
were glorious and I wanted a film of them very very
much. I just couldn't get the right angle. I crept
closer but they moved off. They weren't apparently
aware of me but they moved away. I followed. In the
end I was going after them faster and faster and they

were on the move and getting further away. I woke desperate to get that picture. It was quite a shock to find myself in bed."

Interpretation:
The camera and the subject had to mean that this was a dream about my work. I produce animal films, usually small animal and insect films. I have never done one about tigers, though that dream certainly tempted me. Then I accept that it was a wish for something. My chief feeling in the dream was a desperate longing to get those pictures. So what is it at work that I have a desperate longing for? Put like that the answer is easy. There is a job up for grabs as head of the department I work for. I have applied. I really really want that job. I try not to think about it during the day, there must be others going for the job too, so I don't speak about it. I do think about it though, almost all the time. I remember this dream especially but I dream I am chasing something almost every night. I never used to. This is a new slant to my dreams.

Comment and advice:
Good interpretation. The repetitive dreaming makes the dream message an important one. Clearly a work dream for you. If you had only seen tigers in the zoo when you were on holiday then the dream would have been likely to have been about a holiday wish or a home related wish, perhaps to escape from a situation. But here is a dream of pursuit. You want this job. You should prepare yourself as best you can for the interview. Make sure your portfolio is beautifully presented and your ideas clear in your mind. Give yourself the best possible chance.

She told me later that she got the job and the dreams of pursuing things did not recur.

Ambition Dream 2
One of mine.

"I was walking down the High Street. It looked a little different but I knew it had to be that street because I came to a carpet shop at a corner and went in. There on the floor was the rug I had seen, in fact, the day before. It seemed to glow and I knelt down beside it and felt its silkiness and just wanted it very much. Then I woke"

Interpretation:
I am a bit of a carpet freak. I love old Indian and Middle Eastern rugs with their gorgeous colours and designs. On the other hand, I am also aware of how much they cost. I saw this rug in the window as I walked back from the station yesterday and I remember thinking that I loved it, I also remember deciding not even to bother asking the price. So I did not go into the shop. However my dreaming brain knew my ambition to own it and took it out of the window and on to the floor for me to touch. My dream told me I really wanted it.

Comment and advice:
Sometimes you cannot have what you desire. Sometimes your waking, calculating, brain says no! Your dream, however, is telling you what you want.

In my case I had a birthday handy and mentioned my ambition to own that rug. I'll never know what it cost but I do like having it!

Ambition Dream 3
From a sixteen year old girl.

"It is early morning and I seem to be outside the front door. I see the postman in the distance and I am running after him. He seems to be appearing and disappearing as he crosses the road and back. I am doing it too and it is rush hour and the cars are whizzing about and I am getting more and more frantic because I know he has my results and I want them."

Interpretation:
I had that dream two days before my results were due to be posted to me. It had been hard waiting. I always feel that I haven't done as well as I want to but I did work very hard for these exams. My University place depends on the result and I just couldn't face failing. I have never done so before, so Mum says that is a good sign and I should lighten up. It is not that easy. I shall always be an anxious sort of person and want to do well I guess.

In fact the results were not a wild surprise either way. I got my place to University and we went out to a Chinese restaurant and ate a huge meal to celebrate.

Comment and advice:
Not so much a go getter as an honest worker. You will not give short measure ever. You'll do your best. In your heart I believe you know you have passed. You just desire the confirmation.

The truly ambitious person's dreams are often wider in scope and have huge unusual settings and dream material, more like the woman who was chasing tigers in the first dream. The feeling in them is very strong and the picture harder to pin down because other ambitions are increasing the emotion. This dream is a very specific one, more like a child's wish fulfilment dream.

- ## Count your blessings/Contentedness

Count your blessings/Contentedness Dream 1
From a friend of mine who used to live in Sri Lanka

"I don't know what was making me frustrated and irritated but, when I went to sleep, my dream was all about difficulties. Then I seemed to be trying to push my way over a river. It was quite shallow and brown and muddy on the side and there was a herd of elephants in it, bathing just where I wanted to cross. I told you it was a dream of frustration. However that is where the water was shallow enough to wade across so I set off. My husband was with me and he kept pushing me to go this way or that when I wanted to go another way. But he was right because in a little we got through, with all those great beasts moving and shifting about in a dangerous way, and we reached the other side. Then in my dream I put my head on my husband's shoulder and said "What would I do without you?" And I just was filled with gratitude to him for being there for me. Then I woke."

Interpretation:
The frustration was there but it did not last. What I woke to and the thought that stayed with me for that whole day was how grateful I am for the way my husband supports me in all I do. I do not tell him about this very often but after that dream I do try to.

Comment and advice:
A dream of thankfulness for a lifestyle. A dream to make you count your blessings and a useful dream that reminds you that a marriage is held together by being nice to each other. Telling your partner what you love about him and what he does well is a good idea and can be done as often as possible with good results. A useful dream reminder.

Count your blessings/contentedness Dream 2
From a friend of mine who knew I was asking for dreams.

"My father died when I was in my late teens so he never knew Derek, my husband. I met Derek later and we have been happily married now for years and have two children who are in secondary school. Though I got on with my Dad he has been away from me now for a long time. However, one night not so long ago, I dreamed I was catching a bus. When it came along it was one of those old fashioned ones where you swung on to the back platform and then either went inside the lower deck or climbed the stairs to the upper deck.

I swung on to the platform and who was there standing but my father. I was so pleased to see him. I said to him that I was married and happy. It was like catching him up when I used to come home after a school day. I gave him all the news and then he gave me a big hug, just like he used to and smiled at me so lovingly that I was really really happy. Then he turned and went up the stairs and I knew I couldn't follow and I woke."

Interpretation:
When I woke I felt so comforted and happy. I felt somehow that my father did know and was pleased

for me and Derek. It was an amazing feeling of content and stayed with me all day.

Comment and advice:
A lovely dream to cherish. You must always have had a secret wish that your father should know and share in your happiness and you have always regretted that he died too soon to do that. Dreams will often redress a long held wish. Most dreams frighten the socks off you. It is nice when you meet a healing one. Let it comfort you.

Footnote:
Dreams where you see your loved ones are not the same as the occasionally reported "after death sightings" of a loved one, usually a husband or wife. These phenomena are seldom discussed because the person to whom they occur is overwhelmed by them and often suspicious that he is hallucinating and going off his head. They break all codes of everyday life but are documented in medical journals.

I had a patient once, an old lady, whose husband had just died. I had attended him and got to know them both very well which was why she eventually burst out with the information that her husband had come back to see her. "I think I am going mad," she said. "I saw my husband last night. It was not a dream. He came and sat on my bed for a chat, just as he always did before we turned in."

"What did you talk about?" I asked. "Just little things," she said. "He told me it wasn't bad being dead. I was half afraid, half happy to see him."

"How do you feel now?"

"Comforted," she said, and comfort is the general feeling from these after death experiences. They seem to happen towards evening or when the couple would normally be alone together.

They are not dreams. They have never been explained in medical literature, just documented. It is usually enough to reassure the person having them that she is not dementing or going mad, and that this is a known happening that usually gets less frequent and stops with time. The episodes are nearly always comforting and in medical literature are said always to be so. I only hesitate because the only other patient of mine who reported sighting her husband was one who was not comforted. Again I had attended the family for some years and I knew that the husband was extremely worried about the possibility of predeceasing his wife.

"She is unable to handle money," he told me and he amassed huge savings for her in case he did die first. He knew he had a heart condition which might carry him off suddenly and one day it did. After his death his fears were shown to be all too well founded. Overwhelmed by his provision she set about spending it. She told me that she was troubled by seeing her husband standing looking frowningly at her in the place where he always used to stand. She redecorated her house completely to try to prevent this recurring, presumably by making the place less familiar to him, and she did what he had feared, frittered her money away. She then sold the house and went away so I lost touch with her but I felt that her experience was perhaps closer to a hallucination from a guilty conscience than a true after-death experience.

- **Elation/Dreams of Flying/ Showing off**
You feel a wish to show off, to be admired and desired, ("Look at me! I feel free! I am beautiful!").

You feel invincible / beautiful / clever / happy.

Flying Dream 1
This is one of my dreams.

"In Edinburgh there is a huge area of parkland in the middle of the City called Holyrood Park which is the remnant of old volcanic cores so has cliffs and valleys covered in rough grass and gorse. Salisbury Crags is one of these cliffs. At its foot runs a path hacked out by French prisoners of war from Napoleonic days and beyond it another hillside running down to the valley. In my dream I was walking along the path and for some reason stepped out into the air and found I could fly. From then all was delight. Once I was in the air I appeared to be dressed in a silver fishscale outfit with a long train that billowed out in the updraft and I was able to somersault and swoop and dive and rise above the valley. I had a feeling of weightlessness and delight in my physical wellbeing that I seldom feel after a day of looking after four children and working (at that time admittedly only part time). Mostly I meet the mornings with a moan, my previous day's exhaustion only half assuaged. My dress turned to gold and the sun glinted off it. I could see it trailing after me in the air. There were no other people in my dream. My delight was in myself. Eventually I came back to rest on the path again and woke."

Interpretation:
This dream came when I was about forty I suppose and usually working pretty hard. My days were very full. This dream was an escape. I wondered if my pleasure came from the pretty clothes so very unlike the grotty stuff I usually got into and worked in (I

may have bought a new dress for some thing prior to the dream). At that time I went with my husband to yearly garden parties at Holyrood Palace and they were about the sum of my social activity. It could have been that which triggered the dream. It certainly pinpointed that area.

Comment and advice:
Flying dreams are common to everyone (like teeth falling out and looking for a toilet, though these come for different reasons).

I was speaking to a financier one evening at a drinks party and asked him if he had ever flown in a dream. He was used to travelling all over the world by plane and misunderstood me, saying, "No! If possible I fly by day." When I explained he nodded at once. "You mean levitation," he said. "I often whisk over the country about two feet above ground in dreams. It is a great feeling."

I have never had a report of a miserable flying dream. They all seem to be pleasurable. They facilitate movement, allow you to speed from one place to another at great speed without knocking in to anything or anyone. You seldom seem to fly as high as aeroplanes do. The most I have heard of or experienced has been flight at about tree top level like a bird. In these you get a bird's-eye view of the ground below and see the tree tops clearly. It is the sort of remembered view you get from an upper window or from the top of a hill.

Freud never had a flying dream himself, so the dream maestro thought they were memories of when, as a baby, your parents rocked you in their arms. In fact your movement in the air in high flying dreams is much more like a swimmer's freedom in water. You can dive and turn somersaults and float.

Weightlessness is much the same but flying dreams have been around far longer than space travel.

Flying Dream 2
The man who told me this one is morbidly obese and wheezes when he walks. He has not done more than waddle slowly from place to place for years.

"I dream I am zipping along about a foot above the road. I dodge in and out of the people walking ahead of me. I enjoy the wind whistling past my ears. It is often a road I know and one that I would take a bus down. But not in my dream. I am unstoppable. I am not trying to run away. I am not trying to catch up with anyone. I am just scooting along for the sheer joy of doing it."

Interpretation:
I suppose you'll say it is the thin man inside me trying to get out. I have never been thin and I am not in my dream either but I am one foot above the pavement and it is a bit like being on a skateboard, I should think, only much more manoeuvrable. When I wake I don't feel breathless. I just feel happy at having done it. I don't know what causes this dream but it comes when I am happy and well and not anxious.

Comment and advice:
Freud treated a very short lady with just this sort of dream. He decided that she dreamed it because it made her that little bit taller that she could at last see over people's heads and her long view was not impeded. It was in fact a wish fulfilment, her wish to be able to see more than just the backs of the people in front. In the case of the dreamer of the **flying**

dream 2, his is a wish to be able to move and duck and dive in a way he envies but has not been able to do since he was very young, if then.

- **Strong Wish Dreams**

Wish Fulfilment, Dream 1
Told me by a young mother of two young children that she was bringing up on very little money.

"I was younger and I didn't seem to have the kids along. I was in a hairdresser's and she told me I had beautiful hair. She put it in curlers and sat me in the dryer and I had a marvellous relaxed time. Then she came and frizzed my hair out all round my head like a huge puffball and said I was ready for the catwalk. Somehow the way out of the shop had changed into a stage and I was walking along it and I had my head high. It seemed to be all glorious but I kept feeling I had forgotten something and I woke thinking "But where are the children. Who is looking after them?" and I was alarmed then until I realised it was all a dream."

Interpretation:
I had been watching "Miss World" on television the night before so I guess that this was just a wish to escape my grotty house and life. I used to want to be a dancer but the children put paid to that. It gave me a good feeling though, that dream.

Comment and advice:
A wish fulfilment dream. Escape from the drudgery of living on very little money and always being in charge of two demanding children. Follow your dreams. You may not be in line for the catwalk but

talk to the people you are in contact with, your health visitor, your social work department, your local church. Ask them what outlets there are for you to get out into the world. Crèches abound at training institutions. Even if only one morning a week, learn some craft and gain self worth. Follow your dreams. They are telling you there is a world out there and, if you look, there is lots going on that does not need money.

"Wish Fulfilment," Dream 2
Told me by a young woman who worked in a big firm but was on a basic salary.

"I was dressed in some designer kit that hung off one shoulder and had twinkly things all round the skirt. It was silver and really very fancy. I was in the office going down the corridor and lots of the other people at work were there, as well as strangers. We were all going to the Board Room, where there was to be a dance of some kind. I went in and along one wall was a table covered with the most delicious snacks, smoked salmon, little quiches and raspberries in meringue cases. Everyone seemed pleased to see me and I was entranced by it all and then I woke up."

Interpretation:
I was a bit disappointed when I woke but the feeling of happiness that I felt in the dream lingered.

I knew where it came from. We had been cleaning the Board Room the day before because the Directors were going to give a big party for all the other firms that we work with.

I had been polishing the windows and my supervisor was pleased with it and she said,"It's a pity we can't see it all ready for the party," and I said, "I wish we could be asked too." I really felt it at the time. I suppose I still wanted to go to the party when I went to bed.

Comment and advice:
A Cinderella dream. Many children's stories must arise from fantasy. This one was clearly a wish for a slightly more luxurious life, or even just a treat. The treat is more easily attainable. She should start saving for an exotic holiday.

Wish Fulfilment Dream 3
From an aid worker.

"I was in a township with my wife and children among the tin huts when a group of white men with guns arrived to harass us. The leader stood confidently away from the rest of the group. I chose my moment and then without warning, smashed my huge powerful fist into his face, demolishing him. I took his rifle and began firing at the others, scattering them. Then I realised that I couldn't stick around and I ran in and out through the maze of huts as the white men regrouped and began to give chase. Then I was over the wire fence and running across some scrub land, then over an iron gate, through a small well kept park and into streets of a respectable white residential area. I kept going, knowing that I would now have to stay in hiding. I was walking fast along a more urban street with shops. There were a few people about, mainly white. I was struck by how small most of the white people seemed. A black man passed me, going the other way, and we hailed one another. A tiny white woman crossed the street and gained the pavement next to me, apparently unheedful of the large rifle I was carrying. She was hardly above my waist in height. What happened next I don't know. I woke up. (In fact I am white and this is the first time I recall dreaming that I was black.)"

Interpretation:
This dream came from long ago. I was on my first posting in South Africa and we were trying to bring aid to the township people. It was fairly early in Apartheid and the white South Africans were not very co-operative at that time. The township folk were very suspicious too and at times I wished I could slough off my white skin and let them see that I was with them. My dream caught hold of that wish.

Then I remember going home night after night raving about how small-minded the white population were, how short sighted, how downright hostile. That was shown in the dream. I had wished the white people small and small they were. I am a pretty unathletic weedy looking type so the superman who took on the gang leader was another wish fulfilment. I have often thought as I argued my points with the authorities that I would like to hit them. I never have. We work through getting on with the authorities, being nice to everyone. We are, after all, their guests and we can be tossed out at the drop of a hat so we are trained to be diplomatic. It is however difficult to control one's natural thoughts.

In the end I think we helped and now that I am retired from the work I see such huge strides in friendship between black and white that I am happy for them all. I was watching the young rugby teams playing the other day and they seem so good together. The days of the token black man are over. These were all just young men in a team and they clearly liked each other whatever their colour. Sometimes I am a bit cynical about aid to the indigent but if someone doesn't start the process no one perceives the need to follow it through.

Comment and advice:
Your dream and interpretation say it all. This is a wish fulfilment dream. Your dreaming brain shows you your real desires whatever is happening by day.

Wish Fulfilment Dream 4
From an old friend who has recently started looking after her grandson one day a week so that her daughter can get back to work.

"I was wandering about in the park behind our house when I caught up with an oldish lady who was walking the same way. As I passed her she turned towards me and I saw that she was my husband's aunt. She has been dead these twenty years and more, and in my dream I think I knew that, but it did not seem at all out of place to be talking to her. I smiled and said, "hallo!" just as I would have when she was alive and she smiled back. We walked on together chatting away just like we used to. She used to come to stay with us sometimes when my children were younger and she was everlastingly kind to them, baby-sat them, allowed me and my husband to get out together for occasional evenings out. Her visits must have been hard work for her, though she always said she enjoyed them. They were blissful breaks for me. I don't know that I ever really told her so, so, as we walked, I did tell her. I said how much we all loved her and how grateful we were, all of us. She seemed half amused to hear it as if she really knew it already. We walked on and gradually she seemed not to be there and I woke feeling very content inside myself."

Interpretation:
We never express all we mean to our loved ones and I think this was a wish that had remained on my conscience for years. I don't know why it surfaced then but I was pleased it did because I felt good about that dream all day.

Comment and advice:
Usually the trigger for a dream is a similar wish or similar thought. Now that you have taken to grandchild minding you are doing a very similar job to your aunt-by-marriage. I am sure you find it rewarding, if tough. I think you must often think back to how useful the help was to you when you were younger, and that was where the dream came from.

8

Children's Dreams

Newborn babies slip in and out of mainly Rapid Eye Movement sleep which is the phase of sleep where most dreams occur. Children are said to begin dreaming only at about two and a half years when, for a time, their sleep may become more disturbed.

However I find that they seldom verbalise their dreams very accurately until they are about seven. Even at five, when they are able to tell stories quite well, the dreams they report are more like day dreams or wishes in story form. From about seven on, however, children's dreams show when they are upset about anything. Kids often don't dream for considerable periods when everything is going along well at home and at school, but when exams or home circumstances or school happenings become in any way anxiety-provoking, dreams will be the result.

Children will make up story dreams to please you. You must learn to disregard them. If one child describes a dream at breakfast, a younger sibling will often chime in and relate something very similar just to get attention. Making too much of children's dreams is not a good idea. It is better to allow children to be aware that, if they have a particularly vivid dream that they remember at breakfast, you are happy to listen to it without rushing in to action. That is about the right weight of response. Dreams usually just confirm your own feelings about what is going on at home or at school. Repetitive anxiety dreams need further investigation. Dreams that are forgotten are seldom significant. A child will remember a dream that arises from a real problem just as adults do.

Night terrors, sleep walking and unexplained nightmares are worth talking to your family doctor about. You will get further referral or sensible advice. But simple dreams often crop up. If your child enjoys telling you, it may give you an inside glimpse into what is going on in his or her mind that can help with parenting. Every little helps where bringing up children is concerned!

Child's Dream 1
This was told me by a nine year old boy.

"My grandad bought a Lotus Elite and offered me a ride in it, front seat and all.

"Don't hold me back," I shouted, leapt in and belted up in less time than it would take a ferret to run up my trouser leg. We set off down the road past the railway station and he turned onto the tracks. I did tell him not to but he said, "Shut up and sit quiet," pretty much as he always does when I interrupt.

But I could see a train coming towards us, a huge diesel with rusty bumpers and it was getting closer and closer and I started shouting but grandad just went on driving and paying no attention, just as he always does when I want him to do something different. Then at the last moment he pulls to the side and the train roars past so close that we could touch it. Grandad is not upset. He goes on driving down the line till we come to a bridge. Anyone could see it was old and had huge holes in it but grandad kept on driving until he got to the middle then he stopped. Why he did that I could not think, except then I saw another train coming straight at us. This time the train stopped when it was just on the bridge and, crack! crunch! the bridge gave way and we were hurtling down in the car and I was held in only by my seat belt, just like at the big dipper in the Lammas fair that comes every year.

We splash into this lobster farm and sink and all the lobsters are as cross as anything and come after me with their pincers clacking.

I am out of the car and swimming. Grandad is not and I am shouting at him to come too and desperate because the lobsters are just behind me.

Then I am in France in the sea at a beach that I know, and I am trying to swim for shore but it is too far so I turn over and float. Grandad appears beside me and tells me to head for home so I follow him. But as we reach shallow water the place has turned to Portugal and a huge jelly fish is coming at us. It lashes at me with a great tentacle and I am bleeding but trying to escape.

Grandad says he is going back for the car and I tell him not to but off he goes, paying no attention as usual. In a little he comes back saying that it wasn't a real Lotus after all and in fact it has turned into a sailing boat so I get in. At once there are sharks all round us nudging the boat. It wobbles about. Grandad shouts, "Hold on," but I fall in. However I can see that they are basking sharks and not carnivorous and I just ignore them and set off swimming for home. However once they disappear another huge shark appears and I know I am too far out to get back to the shore in time and I am desperately trying to swim faster but I am tired and the shark has its mouth wide with all those teeth ready to bite me when I wake up. "Whew. It was only a dream." "

Interpretation, comment and advice:
Children's dreams are full of frustration and anxieties and a feeling that danger looms. It is to be expected. They are constantly being introduced to new things, needing to learn new things, do school work better, meet new people. This dream shows both mild frustration, that must be any child's normal companion, as well as anxiety. The boy shows a rather charming desire to keep his grandfather safe and doing the right thing while accepting that his older relation seldom does exactly as he wants or what he expects. The relationship appears normal and happy and I can see him telling his mother, "Grandad and I went for a walk and we came to this boggy bit down by the river and I knew you wouldn't want us to try to cross on the stepping stones but you know Grandad and he was all right but I fell in and he pulled me out, so that's why my trousers are a mess". His mother would remember how it was just the same when she was young, and mutter something about how that old man should be in a cage, and exchange a grin with her youngest that said everything about grandfathers in general and their one in particular. That sort of escapade would trigger that kind of dream of mild anxiety and frustration.

For some reason dreams are always more vivid than the episode that precipitates them.

Child's Dream 2
This dream came from a little boy of seven. He had it the night after his class had been taken to see the local fire station.

"I was in the school playground. It is sort of concrete stuff that you can run on but is sore when you fall. We were all there, the whole class. They had asked us to line up to see the fire engines and they came in and parked so we could look at them. The one nearest us was the water tank one. We were all looking and talking and then suddenly I was alone as if the teacher had said, "Go back to your class" and I hadn't heard her. That does sometimes happen, so it's not a new feeling. Then the one of the fire engines that was nearest to where I was started to go back and forwards in the playground. I suddenly saw that it was coming closer and closer to me and I was trapped against the wall of the school building and could not run away.

I just stood there petrified and it went back and forward, back and forward, getting closer and closer. I knew it was going to squash me on the next run and I was very frightened. Then I woke."

Interpretation, comment and advice:
This dream shows a great deal of anxiety and definitely points to a school environment. Mum should ask his teacher if he is finding the work difficult. Is it all mounting up on him?

It is probably not bullying as the other children are not featured at all except in the beginning of the dream where they seem to act as security around him.

The dream was obviously coloured by his visit to the fire station. To a small boy, a huge shiny red fire truck must seem very large and dangerous. So, when his dreaming brain looked for an image to show him that he was feeling threatened because he was not understanding his school work, and was not able to keep up, and felt that his teacher would be cross with him, the picture of a looming truck was very apt.

Child's Dream 3

A mother told me about a dream her ten year old had reported. His class had been learning about William Wallace and she had reinforced the lesson by taking the little chap to see the Wallace monument which lies outside Stirling in Scotland. "We were lucky," she told me. "We climbed the hill to the monument. At the moment we arrived, a history student, dressed like Wallace, showed us how to use his huge sword, and how to manage infighting with dagger and shield, and all the other dreadful weapons they used then. It was very dramatic and made a great impression on both of us.

That night he told me that he dreamed that he was with Wallace, looking down on the English troops crossing Stirling Bridge and on the word they swooped down to attack the advance party which somehow just disappeared. He found himself standing alone but very pleased that they had won the battle without a fight. But then, when he looked round, there were the English forces, right behind him, and a huge man had his great two handed sword raised above his head. Her son said that he had just time to think, "Woopsie. Here's trouble!" and then he woke and was really very relieved."

Interpretation, comment and advice:
This is very much the sort of dream that children get. The dream material comes from very recently

seen dramatic scenes that have been read, seen on television or witnessed.

"Woopsie! Here's trouble!" is about the right degree of seriousness of this dream. The sort of thing that it overshadows is a big match that he is not confident about playing well in, a test in school that has been less than adequately prepared for, even a party where he is not confident of his reception. He will almost certainly be able to tell his mother what it is and she may be able to reassure him or help him to face the trial with greater confidence. Another thing that it also illustrates is that scenes immediately before bed are often used by children in their dreams. It is well worth monitoring what younger viewers watch on television, especially just before bed. If they stay up late they may be exposed to violent scenes that lead to frightening dreams.

Bullying may be suspected from dream reports long before children actually confess their misery to their parents.

Child's Dream 4
From a little girl in the upper primary school.

"I was running across this purpley-blue kind of endless plain and there was a pack of wolves after me. I knew they were wolves but they looked like the dogs from next door that yap a lot every morning when I am going to school and Mrs Soames lets them out in their garden. Then I was in a corridor and still trying to run but the bigger children were pushing me and I thought they were going to hurt me and I was trying to get to my locker but they were shouting at me and I woke."

Interpretation, comment and advice:

This little girl was indeed being bullied at school. She was naturally timid and her mornings usually started in fear from her neighbour's dogs. She clearly sites her dream in school and there is a real feeling of fear as she is pushed about by bigger bodies and shouted at. She felt safe when she had her face turned to her locker and could pretend she wasn't there. Sometimes her persecutors would not notice her.

Her mother went to see her teacher and the bullying stopped. The teacher gave her the names of two or three little girls who were in her class and were happy to be friends. Asking them home to tea seemed to de-fuse the situation. She had friends. She was no longer alone at break time in the big purpley-blue tarmacadam playing space. She was able to walk home with another child, her age.

Even more successful was her mother's approach to the next door dogs. She had a word with her neighbour who was appalled to think that her dogs were terrorists and asked them both in to play with the animals until she felt able to pat them and talk to them. She still let her dogs out every morning to rush round her garden but the little girl now paused to have a word with them on her way to school and asked her mother if she might be allowed to walk one of them someday. This sort of dream just stopped coming. Children are very conscious of their surroundings despite apparently living in a world of their own.

Child's Dream 5

A nine year old boy whose parents had parted company and who lived with his mother and younger brother told me this dream.

277

"I was in my bedroom and Allen, my brother, came in and started fiddling with my things and some of them broke. I gathered all the things I really liked and went into Mum's room, and hid under the bed clutching on to all my belongings, and I felt safe. Then the shadow wife came in and I knew she was going to kill me and I lay very very still. She came nearer and nearer to the bed, and then I woke."

Interpretation:
"Who is the shadow wife?" I asked.

"I used to dream of her when we were in my last house," he said. "I don't know who she is. I've never really seen her. I know she is there. I stopped dreaming about her when we came to this house and I thought she had gone away but now she is back. She is very bad."

I asked his mother if she could help me with making sense of the dream. She said that she had indeed parted from her husband at about the time when the shadow wife had first come into his dreams. There had been rows at that time, that her son might have heard, though they had thought the children were asleep.

Now suddenly her husband was demanding that the children be sent down to him for weekends and it was clear that the boy was not yet ready to go off on his own into unknown country. The dream had started innocuously enough with the younger brother being a nuisance as younger brothers often are. But it had gone on to summon up memories of fear from a previous time, and that was serious.

Comment and advice:
I suggested she offer longer one day visits as a beginning and see how her son reacted. Who was the

shadow wife? His mother did not know. May be the fear of Social Worker involvement taking him away from all he knew and valued. Children get the weirdest notions, and television programmes offer a feast of detail to little minds. The shadow lady did not recur after it all settled back to much the same as before.

Child's Dream 6

Children can have dreams of happiness, especially after a really good day. I remember one little boy telling me that he dreamed that he and his friend were in a field in the sunshine telling each other jokes and laughing fit to burst. It had been a good dream, he said, with no nasty follow on.

I wish they were all like that.

Child's Dream 7

A fifteen year old boy told me this dream. His mother was divorced from his father, and he and his younger brother, Thomas, lived with their mother.

"Thomas and I owned a company called l'Oreal Juice Company which sold shampoo from vending machines. When coca-cola tried to buy us out they used small robots to eat our machines. This is a picture of their robots. See the big grinding teeth!

So we sold all our machines quickly to get some money. We then infiltrated the coca-cola H.Q. but the guard was Steven Hawkings the amazing mathematician who is wheelchair bound. So Thomas took over Steven Hawkings body but, of course, he got it wrong and ended up with a rabbit's head. It was a Video game rabbit's head and I thought it was just like him to get it wrong.

Then we came to a glass door and Thomas was on

the other side of it. Dad came out of a room beyond the doors with an oar from a boat and he killed Thomas with it. He then advanced towards me muttering in a sarcastic fashion, "I saw you so much" over and over again. I knew he had the intent to kill me so I took this musket off the wall next to me and just as Dad opened the door I shot him at point blank range. His head exploded and I was showered in blood which went all over my white top. His torso then slumped to the ground and began gushing out blood. At the end of the dream I felt quite good with myself."

Background:
Darren has newly taken on a paper round (first job) which has not been easy to complete even with his brother's help so he is anxious. L'oreal are the sponsors of Club Mickey, a children's club on the beach that both boys have attended on the two summer holidays they spent in France. Steven Hawkings was recently on television and Darren has difficulty with maths so feels he is a wizard. The rabbit is Arthur in a maths based video game. Darren complained to his mother that his father was insisting on washing him and Thomas in the shower when they went to stay with him. She suggested that their father was just trying to get them clean and had not realised that they were now private individuals. She did however tell her husband that his children had outgrown a parental need for supervision in the shower and he took umbrage.

Darren, however, was equally cross. He had previously received at least one phone call a night from his father on the mobile that his father had given to him. He now switched it off. He told his mother that he was pretty fed up that he has a father he can't relate to and rely on like his friends can to theirs.

He appears to be becoming protective of Thomas, whom he thinks soft but clever. There has been no contact with father since, and this sort of dream has not recurred.

Comment and advice:

This stands out as a serious dream on two counts, first that the dreamer has cast one of his parents as the bad guy. This is very unusual. It can happen on a rare occasion when a parent has over-chastised a child and caused it fear. Normally the parental bond is so strong, and so confident, that it takes a great deal for a child to hate a parent in his dreams, however unreasonable he may think him or her by day.

He also sees himself as a necessary champion and therefore his anxieties need to be taken seriously. It may be that with no father figure in the house Darren is now beginning to take on that caring role for his younger brother.

All children, as they mature, begin to loosen the parental bond. Up to about five or six a child will crawl into a lap to be cuddled and kissed and comforted. After that, although a kiss on the cheek or a hug from mother seems to remain acceptable for life, children begin to value their privacy and their own space. They are not so keen to have parents watch them bathe or shower, certainly not to wash their more private areas. Parents need to rethink their behaviour. This father still thinks he is dealing with the babies he used to help look after. It is easy to understand how that can happen; perhaps it is not all that uncommon when normal day-to-day contact is intermittent, as in a broken marriage. But he is wrong. He is doing something that offends them.

Footnote:
After a cooling off period, contact with their father restarted. He has learned to respect their space and they are wary but happy to have made contact again. In broken marriages it is hard for children to keep up with both parents. In this case Darren has cut himself off from his father's advice although he will accept his friendship again. He will have to rely on his maternal grandfather and uncles if he needs a man's view of things. This is a case where a dream brought a real family problem to light.

We very seldom see our parents in a frightening role. They are a bulwark in our lives and for all our life. If, however, they appear as werewolves, or someone who wants to do harm to us or to someone we are protecting, look closely at the relationship. This dream is so unusual that it must mean some sort of parent-child relationship break.

If a child reports it on more than one occasion look at his or her relationship with that parent. Make sure that there is nothing threatening the child, real or perhaps only perceived, and put it right. Being so afraid of a parent that you dream you are being pursued by that parent, and will be badly hurt if caught by that parent, is a terrible feeling for any child and should not be allowed to recur. It is rare.

Being pursued by siblings is not so rare and usually means some bullying is going on. That is much more easily addressed by talking to the child and finding out his or her problems. It may not be anything to do with their siblings. It could be happening at school and the dream picture is using a well known face of about the right age on the threatening figure. So if you are a parent trying to find out what is the matter, don't immediately accuse the figure in the dream of bullying. First find out more about what is causing such distress at night.

Child's Dream 8
Told me by a very active seven year old who is often in trouble for making a mess at home.

"My big brother and I are being chased by the police. We run to this castle tower that has scaling ladders up it and we climb them. At the top there is a gun and we take it and shoot at the police and kill nearly all of them but one comes on and captures us and makes us do awful things like clean our shoes and put everything tidy."

Background and comment:
His mother told me that she had threatened him with the police the day before when he had refused to put on his seat belt. It had worked. She had refused to drive until he had done it. This chap finds taking orders quite difficult. Not all children do but, for those that prefer carrots to stick, it is wise to use the kinder approach if there is time. The trouble is that sometimes there is only time for an order, not explanation and suggestion. This dream does give a picture of his feelings towards authority. He runs and fights back. However when the chips are down he does accept that he cleans his shoes and tidies his room. The funny thing is that he actually likes doing these things if he is in the mood. It was his reaction to forcing him to do what he was told that sparked

the dream. The dream material is pure television cartoon channel.

Child's Dream 9
Again from a seven year old.

"I was walking into a petrol station. It seemed perfectly normal concrete, but as I went, I suddenly found that the floor was all petrol and I fell in and it was over my head and I was drowning. Then I woke and I went to see Mum."

Background and comment:
The day before he had been to a party. I suspect he found himself very anxious there for some reason. He does not like parties with a lot of other children and I think he felt swamped and afraid.

This is a real scary dream. Children get them quite often in the early years of school and socialising by themselves. Perhaps a mother should just hang about these occasions more often, unless her child tells her that she doesn't need to.

Child's Dream 10
This dream was turned into a poem and won a prize for a nine year old boy.

"A huge and fearsome beast lurked beneath my
      bed
It ate my sister's toes
Then it ate her head.

A few days later
Down in his tummy
He got a secret message
To eat my lovely Mummy.

This did not fill the fearsome beast
Because my Mummy is quite petite
Then he looked in the house again
And ate bananas ten by ten.

My Dad was angry!
He got a knife
And swore an oath
To revenge his wife.

But he was unfortunate
The knife was blunt
And he got eaten
With one loud grunt!"

Interpretation, comment and advice:
I know this boy. He has a wicked sense of humour. I should guess the dream came from a wish fulfilment following a mild reprimand from his parents not to tease his little sister. His parents never rise to much more firmness than that. It is interesting because his younger brother is uninvolved as he almost certainly was not in the episode.

This chap is growing, and his admittedly small mother will soon be small to him too, so she made only a little mouthful. It shows parental support for one another. He expects his father to look after his wife. In fact it is a rather sweet riposte to the time honoured "Don't tease your sister".

9

Drugs and Dreams

Dreams are very sensitive to the foods you eat and the scents you smell as well as to herbs and medicines. These things also affect your sleep pattern. Some increase dream sleep; some prevent it.

Where dream sleep is suppressed it seems to resurface or break through after a week or two and then your dreams may be quite wild, as if your dreaming brain is having to make up for lost time.

When you stop the medication that suppresses dream sleep, the same thing happens and you spend longer in REM sleep than normal. This appears entirely rational if you believe that REM sleep is the time when your brain is sorting your memories.

- **Beta blockers (medication for high blood pressure and sometimes anxiety and panic attacks)**

Take the beta blocker group of drugs first. These are usually used to treat high blood pressure and angina. They often cause nightmares, especially the fat soluble (lipophylic) members of the group.

They may also cause disturbed sleep with a tendency to wake often.

In small doses these beta blockers are also offered

to patients to treat anxiety and panic attacks. Though the medication may steady its taker by day, it may exacerbate their dreaming by night. As the dose increases, however, these medicines suppress REM sleep and so dreams are at first prevented, and then gradually break through into your sleep. If you change your medication to a different group of medicines to treat high blood pressure or angina, your dreams would return in a cascade of night time fantasies. This would again give you disturbed sleep until things settled down and you had made up your dream time. This desire of your brain to make up REM sleep and so make up dream time after it has been suppressed, is the clearest sign you have that dreams are essential to your brain. It happens after you stop any drug that prevents REM sleep. It is clear that your brain is working hard during this part of sleep. It resents any suppression of activity and tries to make it up as soon as possible.

- **Amphetamines**

Amphetamines are seldom used as medication these days, though some of the medication for hyperactive children is from the same family. Amphetamine-like drugs such as speed, cocaine, etc., are drugs of abuse. They decrease the amount of REM sleep and dreaming you normally have. They also tend to keep you from falling asleep. Ecstasy is of this family of drugs and completely suppresses REM sleep, so for this reason alone is harmful to those who take it.

- **Caffeine**

Caffeine, which is also a stimulant substance found in tea, coffee, and some fizzy drinks, has little effect on REM sleep or dreams, although taken at night it may tend to keep you awake. Its effect is enhanced by grapefruit and grapefruit juice which may be a welcome boost to your wakefulness in the morning. But start your dinner with grapefruit and finish with coffee and you will remain awake longer than you may want to.

- **Antihistamines (used to treat hay fever and also sometimes as a sleeping aid to get you to sleep)**

Some antihistamines suppress REM sleep so if you are on this sort of medication for hay fever you may notice that you lose your dreams while you are on them. When you stop, your dreams may be quite troubling for a week or two. Some antihistamines are sold over the counter as sleep aids. These will have the same effect.

- **Benzodiazepines (prescribed to allay anxiety and to promote sleep)**

The big anxiolytic family of benzodiazepines all suppress REM sleep and dreaming. As part of their immediate anxiolytic effect they will stop your anxiety dreams for a short while. This may give you time to work out your problems. Even if you get more dreaming on stopping them they may not be upsetting dreams because you have reached peace of mind. If you continue to take benzodiazepines you will find that a few dreams begin to break through again. You will, however, still face disturbed sleep for some nights when you stop them.

Temazepam is a member of the benzodiazepines. It is a well known sleeping pill and is widely used. It does suppress dreams. This may not be a bad thing in all cases. If you are having repetitive nightmares, some nights of peace from them, coupled with a good sleep, may be enough to allow you to work out the cause and prevent it recurring. In addition, seriously ill people occasionally have dreadful dreams. I remember a very ill lady telling me that she dreamed she was on her knees in the snow in front of a snow plough that came on inexorably. She could do nothing about it. She felt too weak to move. She felt very frightened. Miserable dreams like this that mirror the clinical condition should not be tolerated. Even a small nightly dose of temazepam would prevent their recurrence.

There are sleeping pills that do not change your sleeping pattern. These are to be preferred when getting to sleep is a problem and dreaming is not. Examples of these are Zimovane (zopiclone), Stilnoct (zolpidem), and Sonata (zaleplon), which are now commonly prescribed in most countries. They have no effect on dream sleep so there is no rebound of disturbed dreams when you stop taking them.

• **Antidepressant medication**

Many anti-depressant medications, especially the sedative ones that need to be taken at night, suppress REM sleep and dreaming. If you miss your night time fantasies you can ask your doctor to prescribe an antidepressant that does not take away your dreams. In depression your dreams become flat, infrequent and sad, and one sign that you are beginning to improve is when your dreaming increases and becomes florid again.

• **Alcohol**

Alcohol decreases REM sleep and dreaming in the first half of the night but in the second half, if you have drunk more than a little, you may suffer increased dreaming and disturbed sleep. Alcoholics who stop drinking suddenly may face a sudden increase in dream disturbed sleep and may even go on to have hallucinations and delirium by day.

• **Nicotine**

Smokers have few dreams. Nicotine suppresses dream sleep. Regular smokers must get some dream break-through, but their dreams seem attenuated or only occur when some monumental happening in their lives spills over into sleep. Disturbed dreaming follows abstinence from tobacco as REM sleep is made up but occasional dreams of deprivation from smoking may persist for years. Smokers miss the night time give and take between day time feelings and night time dreams that I feel is a natural and useful body mechanism.

• **Steroids (sometimes prescribed for asthmatics)**

Steroids reduce REM sleep and dreaming. Asthmatics who are put on short courses of steroids may sleep deeply as a result. As their dose is prescribed to reduce gradually, they may not suffer a period of dream disturbance when they stop.

• **Opiates**

Opiates are strong pain killers and sleep producing medication. When first given they may suppress REM sleep but if taken regularly their effect on this sleep stage tails off and dreams return in an almost normal fashion. Opium addicts can have huge amazing dreams and in Coleridge's "Kubla Khan" poem we can share those dreams.

- **Aspirin and Paracetemol**

Aspirin and paracetemol have no effect on dreaming or REM sleep.

- **Levodopa (prescribed for Parkinsonism) and Baclofen (a muscle relaxant)**

Medications like these can precipitate nightmares that do not wear off, and the medication needs to be changed to allow the taker a reasonable night.

One patient of mine who was taking baclofen because he suffered the muscle spasm of multiple sclerosis reported that when he started the medication it did relax his muscle spasm but he started having nightmares. These were so severe that he woke from a terrible dream and turning over went back to sleep to be engulfed in the same nightmare which just powered on as if it had never stopped. I found an alternative medication for him, which gave him similar muscle relaxation without bad dreams. Other people get no bad dreams from the same medication. It appears to be a personal reaction.

- **Mefloquine**

Reports I read in medical journals suggested that mefloquine, a commonly used anti-malarial medication, could cause increased dream activity and disturbed sleep. As this is often taken by tourists entering malaria-infested countries as a prophylactic, there may be many people who think that their dreams and poor sleep were due to the holiday or the food or anxiety when in fact the cause could just have been their anti-malaria pill.

Any medication that either stops dreaming or causes bad dreams is a cause for concern and should be reported to your doctor so that he may change it for something that gives you normal sleep.

Homeopaths suggest that nux vomica, aconite or ignatia prevent the disturbed sleep that is associated with nightmares. However, to use these correctly you really need to see a trained homeopath who can advise you. Modern herbals no longer emphasise the need to prevent dreaming and mostly concentrate on offering herbs that encourage sleep.

- **Passion flower, hibiscus, camomile, vervain and lime flower teas**

Infusions of these herbs are used to promote relaxation and sleep. Many of them may be found in supermarkets and chemists. However, if you suddenly begin to dream more, or if you find your dreams have deserted you after starting one of these herbal teas, consider stopping them and see if your dreams return to normal. If you then re-try your herbal drink at night and your dreams disappear again or again become florid, you will know that it is the infusion that is affecting your sleep pattern and you will be able to use it appropriately. They may affect different people in different ways. I find that I do not dream much after taking vervain tea, a brew which certainly encourages me to sleep. Lime flower tea, passion flower tea, and camomile do not affect my dreams.

I know that in France I began to dream in a very florid manner. I could not think why but in the end traced it to a butcher's sausage which had a high quantity of nutmeg or mace, a herb I scarcely ever use at home. It is an interesting experiment to try out various herbs and spices in your cooking and see what effect they have on your dreaming. Herbs are taste stimulants but they are a great deal more than that as the doctors of long ago knew well.

Aromatherapists suggest that narcissus, mimosa and cedarwood scents increase dreaming. I must confess I did dream very freely when I was last in Madeira, walking by day in the mimosa groves. I had previously put it down to the different food but it could have been those lovely yellow flowers.

Any food or drink may have an effect on your sleep. Little research has been done on the effect of food and drink on your dreaming. Cheese is said to encourage dreams as are red wine and chocolate.

I suspect that most people find out what gives them disturbed sleep and avoid it at night and never talk about it to anyone. This is a pity as I suspect there is a great deal of useful research material going abegging.

10

Interpretation Overview

Before you feel confident that you can interpret dreams you have to develop some personal theory of what you are dealing with. Freud had a vision of a buried sea of passionate infantile desires that could be hooked out by a present day wish, rather like a fisherman in Canada in winter with a line through the ice to the lake below. Jung seemed to think of our minds more like a see-saw, always trying to get back in balance by loading one or other end of our conscience.

At least part of the purpose of your dreams is to retrieve peace of mind lost in the day or days before. I believe your brain seeks peace of mind all the time because it is a state in which your bodies work best and most easily. All day you do your best to make pigs and whistles of your equanimity and all night your dreaming brain tries to right the situation. When the condition you have got into is too upsetting or anxiety provoking, or there are strong feelings lying around that your brain cannot mitigate, you wake to a dream that you remember.

This is not coincidence. The dream is there for you to think about, find the meaning of, and do something about in the day time to change the situation.

Then your dreaming brain has peace of mind and can carry on slotting away memories and sorting out your daytime thoughts as it is programmed to do. If you like, it is as if, having swept the floor, your brain is left with a pile of detritus that it can neither file nor pulverise. It opens the door into your daytime state and brushes it through with a "sort this out by tomorrow" notice. But that is just one of the things that happen at night.

I like the theory that your brains are powered by a sort of intrinsic calculating machine that goes along at the pace that is normal for each one of us. Some of us have a lethargic machine and think slowly. Some of us have an active mind process and think at a great rate and can encompass many thoughts at the same time and make sense of them. Sometimes this intrinsic machine becomes faster and faster because of some imbalance in, presumably, the hormonal or chemical control of the rate mechanism, and then you get a schizoid type illness where bizarre thoughts overwhelm your waking state and you are apparently lost in dream country all day and night. Sometimes the machine becomes very inert, again presumably due to chemical imbalance within your brain, and you suffer depressive symptoms.

Both these states are subject to the curative power of medication that restores your normal power base by changing the chemicals that control your brain back to normal levels for you. This theory is not mine. It is the idea of modern psychologists working in the field and when I read it, it seemed to tie in with my ideas of what is going on in your dreaming brain. I am happy to accept their theory and use it as the base for my own ideas.

I believe that at night in dream sleep your brain is involved in sorting and storing memories. I think everyone now agrees with this. How your brain stores memories is still unknown but it is clear that it is not alphabetic as we do filing in the office. The office of the brain works differently. From my experience I see in my mind a sort of huge old fashioned telephone exchange where the enormous area supplied by the convoluted cortex of the brain is used as a storage unit. I think that memories are stored there by age of memory, that is when it happened in your chronological age, as well as by importance to you. There may be no actual linkage between stored memories but it does appear that, if one memory is triggered, others come up with it, sometimes memories that you had thought you had forgotten or which had not come to you for years. That happens often enough in your waking brain but more so in your dreaming brain. It is because, if something is being slotted in to a certain place, the memories round it are also disturbed.

The enormous increase in blood supply with its increase in nutrients and oxygen circulating through the brain in dream sleep facilitates this greater mobilisation of memory material. That is the purpose of that part of sleep, memory re-setting and storage. It may even assist with memory retrieval. Who has not gone to sleep worrying because they could not remember a name or a place from long ago only to find it easily available the next morning? There seems to be a time lag in the storage system, in that you do dream of things that happen to you the day before you sleep and then not so often until after three to five days have passed. You can see what memories are thrown up by talking about some long ago memory that was powerful at the time. I tried this out on my husband who never dreams but has been so supportive over this book and clearly wanted to help.

We had been babysitting and I said that it was time we enjoyed our retirement together more, doing the thing that we had talked about in our working days, seeing the world together.

I had been reading a travel book about the Middle East where we had had a really good holiday before babysitting took over our lives. I discussed it with him. Then I reminded him of our first journey together, out to India, where I had thought I had a throat growth and was told by a very sensible doctor that it was just a neurotic reaction to having recently lost a baby. I looked back at those days, and remembered what a pain in the ass I must have been, but did in my own mind accept that, for me, losing the baby had been a horrendous experience. If you are a young doctor you not only think the worst when you have a real symptom but you also feel very betrayed by your calling when things like having a baby go wrong. In retrospect being told by my doctor to take up knitting and get on with life was not ideal though it was certainly a very sensible thing to have done if I could have. My mother's attitude which was, "Better a dead baby than a lifetime looking after an abnormal one" put an end to any real hope I had of discussing the whole thing with anyone. My husband had been posted abroad (in those days compassionate leave was not what it is now and phone calls abroad were a non-starter). I was stuck with an overwhelming sorrow that I did not verbalise and reaped the consequences.

Now I am sorry for that rather foolish young person that I was, and very sorry for my poor husband who had to mop up the results and did so with a great deal of kindness. I understand and have forgiven myself and said so. We went to bed but when I rose much later I tripped over the bed in getting up, and woke him.

"I've had a dream," he shouted. "Tell me. Tell me." I begged. "Don't move. Tell me everything or you will forget it."

"We were on holiday by a beautiful lake," he said. "Where we were was idyllic with orchards and green fields running down to the water though further up the lake were oil wells with tarry smells." (That evening we had also talked about coal tar soap and its distinctive smell as being part of our childhood.) "Your mother wanted to come with us but we had managed to be by ourselves and we waded out to swim. Mostly we swam under water so we got lost and surfaced by the tarry oil wells where we came ashore in front of a lovely hotel, just like the one at Latakia in Syria. A maid told us that a European woman was waiting for us, but I suspected it was your mother. I wanted us to be by ourselves so I just went in one door of the hotel and out the other. You came with me. Somehow I was eating a piece of cake and as we left we had to get over a wall. I dropped the cake as I reached to take the child you passed to me over the wall. She was clearly a grandchild, and you reproved me for then picking up the cake and finishing it." (I am sure I would in normal life too, especially in front of a grandchild.) "We then had to go home and you were told to go by road and I was to swim and I looked at my watch and told you what time I would expect to arrive. I left without waiting to see your mother and I wanted you to do so too."

I was much struck by the way talking about that time so long ago had brought all those thoughts to his mind. I understood the idyllic holiday spot. Our Syrian holiday had been a delight and his dream had reproduced the hotel by the sea that we in fact had stayed in. Talking about the travel book of the same area had clearly brought that material to mind. But what about the rest? We obviously still felt we had baby-sitting responsibilities but why my mother?

"Why was my mother in your dream?" I asked. "I guess I always thought your problem was not so much losing a baby as leaving your mother."

I had never thought of that. Fifty years later I wondered if he had not got a point. I was a very dutiful daughter. It took me years to be myself. It might have had a part in my jejune reactions. I was totally fascinated that, in his mind, these memories lingered together in his filing system. They were not in mine. Maybe they will be now. I don't know. This was not a dream of any importance. It was a triggering of a few wishes, the wish to travel, the wish to be by ourselves, the wish to go somewhere beautiful. But the links joining the material filed in his brain brought together that bad time for both of us with the person he thought responsible for my reaction. There was colouring and pictures from thoughts he had had that evening and that was really all. It was a dream that he could make sense of but no one else could.

I believe that is the case in most instances of dreaming. You are the only person who can really interpret your dreams and have any idea of their significance or importance. In addition much of your dreaming is material very private to you and you do not want other people prying. I have let you know enough of my personal history to understand this dream because it all happened so long ago and I am no longer troubled by it. I have forgiven and understood that rather silly girl that I was and so has my husband. We have moved on. You may not be in that position. You may not want to bare your soul to your analyst or your friends who tell you they understand how to make sense of your dreams.

So, how do you set about interpreting your dreams on a day to day basis to help you with your normal daily life?

First go over your dream when you wake. Try to remember as much of it as you can. If you have a problem with that, write down the salient facts. In the middle of the night note down enough to remind you of the dream. You can then turn over and go back to sleep. The time to mull it over is in the morning at your convenience.

The best way of getting the full flavour of a dream is when you wake with time to spare and can lie and go over your dream then and there. Your emotions are fresh and clear and are still quite strong within you. This is fine if it occurs in that last part of the night when you are approaching the time to get up. It is not sensible in the middle of the night, when you should be getting back to sleep in order to get the right amount of sleep for you to have a good day. Then you must just jot down a fact or two, clear your mind and turn over.

This is a very real problem as you get older. After about the age of fifty, instead of going into stage one and two non-REM sleep (as bridging light sleep passages between more deep sleep or REM sleep), you tend to wake. This is annoying but natural as you get older. The trick is to get back to sleep as quickly as possible. If you have to go to the toilet do it without waste of time. Do not let your day time worries obtrude. Try repeating a simple word and concentrate on it. Try telling yourself a story that you use to gain sleep entry at the beginning of the night. Try counting sheep but don't let yourself waken.

The trouble is that if you have woken to a dream

300

you will forget it if you go right back to sleep. That is where a jotter by the bed is a necessity to a dream diary. Jot down a few words to remind you, and then put the whole thing out of your mind. You should have enough to be able to recall the dream when you wake.

This business of forgetting dreams is a very real hindrance to dream interpretation. Dreams are ephemeral, evanescent whiffs of consciousness. They appear so strong when you wake, but you will lose them entirely if you do not go over them to reinforce them in your memory, or record them on paper or tape. A visit to the toilet and you will not have a dream to figure out.

On the other hand as you get used to running over your dreams you will find that they seem to become more and more obvious. Their meanings are clear. As you sort out the troubling thoughts that threaten your peace of mind, the things that matter stand out. In addition, as you clear up long forgotten troublesome memories, your dreams become so much simpler as they only contain current problems. You reach that stage where, each night and morning, there is give and take between your working brain by day and your dreaming brain by night. This is how I believe it should be.

So, the first thing to think about is what emotion you are left with when you wake. Is it anger, anxiety, frustration, fear, resentment, joy, peaceful remembrance, horror or a mixture of some of these or other feelings? Once you have isolated the main feeling within your dream, look into your waking lifestyle to see where that feeling stems from. You may have many things frustrating you or causing anxiety. Go over each of them and see if some of your dream pictures highlight a particular problem.

For instance, if you feel anger, with whom were you angry the previous day? If you were angry with several people, who appears to be involved in the dream? Is it a dream of work environment or home? Are there hints about the dress or behaviour of the person in the dream that remind you of someone who you were angry with? Have you had a slow burn anger mounting for some days? Was there something to trigger this dream? Your dreams do throw up the problems that are really important to you. You will find in each dream that a lot of the pictures come from something you have seen or done on the previous day. You may recognise scenes or people from a television show that you saw before you went to bed. I remember one of my dreams was played out in a dusty wilderness, in bright sunshine, after having watched a Western on television. I knew the scene was of no significance. It was just an easy picture readily available. The meaning had to be in what was happening in that desert. You may meet people you met the day before. Again they may just be extras popped in to receive the message your brain is trying to get across.

Your brain storage system appears to pool recent experience and sights and leave them swilling around in a retrievable morass for about twenty-four hours. After that, your mind appears to be sorting them and filing them and they are not so easily available for a day or two. You seldom seem to dream of things that you experienced in between about day two and day five prior to a dream. After that your memories again become available to your dreaming brain and it may show you pictures that go right back far into your childhood; so far, in fact, that you may not recognise where they come from.

Some of the things you do and see in your dreams

may appear to be completely new. They seldom are. You do not dream what you have not experienced somewhere, either vicariously by reading, on film or actually. The memories may be a bit different, names of places and people are changed but you can often discern where the memory came from.

The scene itself may be coincidental, though you should look at it in case it helps you isolate a problem. For instance, you might find yourself on a beach shouting at a stranger who has stolen your picnic. He tells you his name is Tony but you don't care. You wake from screaming at him full force, and you feel the definite desire to shout at someone. The previous day you were at the hairdressers and your coiffeur cut your hair expensively, but not well, and not as you instructed. Looking back at the feeling in your dream you will recognise your angry frustration when you looked in the mirror. At that time you did not feel you could make a fuss, so you bottled your fury and left. Your unrelieved anger, however, remains, and has shown up in your dream because it was so strong. Your dreaming brain could not ameliorate it and soften it into peace of mind.

Why did you dream of a beach and a man called Tony? If you remember the hairdresser's salon was very warm and the lights were bright like sunshine. Looking back the feelings of the place were not dissimilar to those you experienced in your dream of the beach. What about Tony? There was a big poster on the wall of a long-ago lady with a Toni perm. Perhaps even the sort of hairstyle you wanted. Certainly there are signs pushing you in the direction of your hairdressers, even if you had not recognised the origin of your anger. So what do you do about it?

Take a long look at your new hairstyle. Is it perhaps perfectly all right, if not what you wanted?

Do you feel a bit foolish now and begin to feel glad that you have not made a fuss? Can you say to yourself, "This style has possibilities and could be beautiful? I feel good about it now?" If not, and you still feel aggrieved, ring up your hairdresser and explain that you are unhappy with the result and ask him if he will rectify it as much as he is able without further cost. Both these courses will allow your venom to subside and you will sleep the easier for it.

This is a made up dream but it shows the way dreams work to give you hints as well as leaving you with the feeling that needs your day time attention. If you do not manage to give yourself relief from your slow-burn anger, you will probably have another similar dream the next night, and on, until either your dreaming brain eventually manages to store the memory as time makes you forget, or you sort out the feeling by doing something about it by day.

Reaching acceptance or accepting an apology and restitution will give you peace of mind. It would be different if you had sounded off in the hairdresser's and caused a scene and felt thoroughly ashamed about it. Then you might have been left with such a feeling of embarrassment that you dream of losing your clothes at a party, and you would have had to come to terms with that emotion the next day instead.

So, dreams that you remember are an ongoing way of showing you the problems you have not come to accept during the previous day or days. Your brain in dream sleep is storing memories, sorting them, resorting them, bringing some out from long ago, arranging fast track memory paths for things you need for your day to day work. It can only do this where you have peace of mind. Different researchers have differing theories of how this is done. Until we know exactly how the various chemicals that monitor brain action act and interact we will not have the answer. However peace of mind is the key. Your brain does not work well when it is distracted by negative thoughts that go round and round your mind like a rat in a trap, seeking a way out.

Hate, anger, guilt, resentment, stress, anxiety, sorrow and fear are all negative emotions. Overwhelmed by one of these, your dreaming brain may try to soften the emotion but it will also highlight it by producing dreams that you wake to and notice.

Emotions like love, happiness, even ambition if not tainted by stress and anxiety, do not upset your peace of mind in the same way. Your dreaming brain will not trouble you with these emotions unless there are negative attachments such as jealousy or guilt connected to them. Peace of mind is an instinctive search. Every religion speaks of it as a blessing and offers it as an ideal state. Everyone knows within themselves that they are happier if they are not worrying about something.

"Sleep on it" is not just a phrase. Feel guilty or ashamed or anxious about something before bed time, and waken again after a few hours, and the acuteness of the feeling is still with you. If you sleep again and travel through that part of sleep when you dream, which is usually in the second half of the night, you will wake with the experience softened. You will feel more able to look at it objectively and begin to find some sensible reaction to it. "Sleep on it" is good advice. Your brain in REM sleep is trying to bring you mental equilibrium.

If you are woken by a noise in the middle of the night, just as volunteers in sleep laboratories are, you may remember a dream but it is unlikely to be of any

305

importance. You may think, "There is nothing to do about that dream, no feelings to sort out. It was just banal."

It probably was. The brain appears to use dream pictures in its memory sorting process. REM sleep is full of coloured pictures and dream sequences that are of importance to that part of sleep, and ultimately to your memory banks, but need no action from you. I see this in my mind like stumbling in to a room full of smoothly working machinery, from which you get a glimpse of all that is going on, but you are not needed. As soon as you go back to sleep again, the brain just gets on with its nightly work.

Your brain sees to it that you wake to the dreams it wants you to remember and do something about. It makes them sufficiently colourful and bizarre to stimulate your memory. It is aware that your dream is likely to be forgotten otherwise, and then the purpose of putting it into your conscious mind for sorting is lost.

After you have gauged the feeling of a dream, what should you do? Work out some way of relieving that emotion so that it does not affect you so severely. If you feel stress then you must address the problem behind it. I have described stress relief techniques you might use, and relaxation exercises. Anger and resentment should be worked through to give you peace of mind. Guilt accepted and pardoned. Grief takes time to work through but there are trained counsellors available as well as friends with listening ears. As for nightmares, they follow serious anxiety and may require expert help from your doctor if they become repetitive. In the main you can undertake these self-cleansing tasks during the day.

One important fact about dreaming belongs especially to children's dreams. Youngsters have troubling dreams where the border line between nightmare and anxiety dream is blurred. Their dreams, which younger children find difficulty in telling you about, are full of monsters and fearful things. As they get older many children have told me that their dreams have material from the television programmes that they watched immediately before going to bed. I believe the same thing happens in younger children so it is very important to monitor what your children are watching before they go to bed. Frightening games and frightening pictures on television may give them a bad night with shocking dreams. It is not enough to think, "Oh my children just watch cartoons. That must be all right". That is not necessarily so. Many cartoon characters are very fierce looking and out of context can appear and terrify a youngster. Dream disturbed sleep does not make anyone feel well set up for the day. You feel duff, tired and upset. Make sure your children are not having bad dreams and if they are find the cause and deal with it. It may be a combination of what is happening to him or her at school, or at home, coloured by horrible monsters from late-night television watching.

It is easier to analyse your own dreams. Children can seldom report dreams accurately until they are over six. If your dream itself was wild but the feelings left when you wake are slight and apparently unimportant, look for a more obvious cause. Was the dream about pain or swellings or some physical problem? Does it isolate some part of you body? Do you feel discomfort in this area? Is there something in your body that can account for it? In fact, is it a dream brought on by your physical condition, an intrinsic dream? It does not have to be a pointer towards disease. It could just be a desire to go to the toilet.

You cannot miss the dreams that come from deteriorating heart problems or chest disease. The long slow marches over difficult country; pushing heavy loads up slopes. If you suffer from heart problems and your dreams change to give you a miserable time at night it is time to alert your doctor to the problem. He may be able to alleviate a worsening situation and you will dream more comfortably. If you are thirsty you will dream of water and drinking. Diseases that first show with the symptoms of thirst may throw up early warning dreams of this kind. If you are hungry or slimming you are likely to dream of eating or seeking food. If you have a headache you may wake from a dream where someone has been crushing your head. I dreamed my nose was being squashed. It was not painful but I did not like it. I woke to a nose bleed which surprised me but made me remember the dream.

So, after assessing the feeling you wake with from your dream, check to see if it has its origin in physical factors. If it does, keep an eye on what is going on and if the dream is repetitive consult a doctor. Your body may be giving you an early warning. On page 61, I discussed a feeling of leaning over a billiard table in a dream on the first night after the dreamer had cracked a rib. I was in no doubt her dreaming brain had noticed. However, although it remained sore, especially at night, she did not dream about it again. Her dreaming brain obviously felt it was not significant. Repetitive dreams are of significance and should be acted on.

Then, assess how much of the dream comes simply from outside stimuli. For instance the dream about having an arm wrenched off while driving down a lane, described in a previous chapter was purely caused by a kitten licking the dreamer's armpit. It was not significant in any way and, however emotional, could just be forgotten.

See where the material originates from. Was it just a television show the evening before? Was it last summer on holiday in Greece? It may be significant. It may just be colour and detail for the dream. You will know as you mull it over. If it does not strike a chord, forget it.

I have no expertise or experience in the dreams of people who have abnormal mental states. Research suggests that the dreams in worsening schizophrenia and hypomania become more bizarre and those of depression become flat and sad. But dreams that visit paedophiles and those who desire abnormal lifestyles or who have antisocial leanings are not within my expertise. My guess is that if you are aware of a wish to do wrong you will suffer dreams of guilt. If you are in prison you are likely to suffer dreams of both anxiety, anger and frustration unless there is some programme to alleviate these emotions that you can undertake. I would fear that if you have no conscience to tell you that you are doing wrong then you will not suffer this sort of dream, because dreams are there to maintain your peace of mind.

Go over the subjects in each chapter in this book and consider whether your dream comes from any of these sources or a mix of them. To gain peace of mind you may have to discuss problems your dream has highlighted, settle emotional upsets, change your lifestyle and approach to your family and work. Your dream shows you what is sticking in its mechanism to achieve peace of mind by night. You have to think out how to remove that block by day. After you start to analyse your dreams you seem to dream more. It is as if there is material dammed up for years that at last gets a chance to surface. Deal with each dream in turn; analyse and deal with the main features.

There is little point in delving too far into every minuscule part of each dream. That way you will start making things up to fit the case. The main features of your dream are usually strong and obvious.

After some months of regular dream analysis you will begin to find you have a sort of dialogue going between your day mind and your dreaming brain. Incidents by day are rapidly thrown back as dream pictures and minor upsets to your general peace of mind are highlighted. This is what I believe dreaming is there for. It is, in a way, another sense working to help to keep you stable and content through life.

If you can keep a diary of your dreams, with a note of what you thought they meant at the time, it makes for fascinating reading. It may help you to analyse a complicated dream which has similar features to one you dealt with previously.

Can you influence your dreams?

With medication, you certainly can, as described on page 286. Where medication suppresses dreaming you tend to get an overspill back into dreaming after a few weeks. This is a necessary body function that cannot be fully stopped in the long term. You also suffer an increase in dreaming, usually of a bizarre nature, once you stop any medication that has suppressed dreaming. Where medication produces nightmares, stopping it may be the only way to prevent bad dreams. But only do so with your doctor's permission. If you start taking a medicine and lose your dreams you should ask your doctor if the drug you are taking has an effect on REM sleep. Recurrent nightmares may be prevented in the short term in this way and may give you respite to work through the problems that are causing them. Pills will not stop the bad dreams for ever.

Old herbals list plants that prevent dreaming, mostly to combat those dreams of sexual deprivation that attacked a celibate clergy and were thought to emanate from the temptations of Satan. Nowadays this is not such a major problem. You may accept dreams of physical desire as a natural reaction to deprivation and resurrect your peace of mind by sublimation or having sexual intercourse if it is safely, lovingly available.

Any illness, especially one associated with fever, has a profound effect on your dreams. They become bizarre and difficult to interpret. Returning health is heralded by normal dreaming or deep sleep without dreams. It is sometimes hard to tell whether it is a medicine or the disease that it is treating that is affecting your dreaming. In the short term, in an acute illness, this distinction seldom is of importance. Renewed health and cessation of medication go hand in hand. In a chronic illness starting a new medication with the onset of wild dreams is usually easily recognised and the medication can often be changed to one that lets you sleep easy.

Treat your dreams as the sixth sense they are accepted as in many Eastern countries. They are there to pinpoint the problems your waking brain has fashioned and which your brain in REM sleep cannot ameliorate or store by night in order to allow your body and mind to do their unfettered best next day.

Just occasionally, in a dream you are aware that you are dreaming. Usually you are close to waking when this happens. You are in some unusual place doing something odd and you say to yourself, "This is just a dream and I will wake soon." This sort of awareness is called "Lucid Dreaming". Some people think it is a gift that should be encouraged. They feel, just as many analysts feel, that dreams are a path into your unconscious store of memories. If you could train yourself to enter that store knowingly you would be able to browse around like you do at a library, picking up a memory here and there and using your cerebral store more effectively.

I do not think this is so.

Encouraging yourself to be able to reach a state where you are aware that you are dreaming so that you can influence what happens in that dream is counterproductive. Dreams tell you what your unconscious is struggling with. To change that, changes the message your dreaming brain is trying to give you. It defeats the purpose of the dream which is to point you to the problems that prevent your peace of mind. You are meant to remember the dream and act on it. Change the dream and you lose that message.

What you are likely to be doing in lucid dreaming is rising into a sort of mixture of REM and light non-REM sleep stages where you have partial control over your thoughts. This sort of dreaming can be used to nullify nightmares and is close to one of my techniques for doing so, although I do not think you need to enter REM sleep to find a pleasant finish to a nightmare. You know that a nightmare stems from overwhelming anxiety. Ameliorating its ending is beneficial. You can then avoid repetition of its horror. You are also well aware that you must disperse your anxiety during the day to prevent nightmare repetition.

Dreams become more simplistic with nightly interpretation. It is as if you get a dialogue going between your waking and dreaming brain. On one side a warning of problems glimpsed but not appreciated

in the day or days previous. On the other, acknow-
ledgement and desire to rectify these problems. I
believe that this is what dreams are there for and
how they should be used.